WELCOME

I think by far the most important bill in our whole code," Thomas Jefferson wrote in 1786 to George Wythe, his teacher and friend in Williamsburg, "is that for the diffusion of knowledge among the people. No other sure foundation can be devised for the preservation of freedom, and happiness."

The bill to which Jefferson referred (and which Jefferson had drafted in 1778) was based on the premise that the best hope for democracy was "to illuminate . . . the minds of the people at large, and more especially to give them knowledge of those facts, which history exhibiteth."

We at Colonial Williamsburg share Jefferson's conviction that democracy depends on its citizens' seeing the connections between past and present. Our Revolutionary City programs are designed to show the enduring relevance of our founding documents and principles—documents and principles that were in large part shaped right here in Williamsburg, Virginia.

Every day, in the Revolutionary City, our interpreters and our guests explore the challenges of men and women working to advance the cause of liberty. These people—rich and poor, free and enslaved—created America.

The American experiment in democracy did not end with the Revolution. It continued throughout our history, and it continues today. We celebrate the origins of the American republic and its continuing strength. But, perhaps, we should also consider this cautionary note: Jefferson's bill for the "diffusion of knowledge" never made it through the Virginia General Assembly. It was not until 1796 that the legislature passed an act to establish public schools, and many of Jefferson's proposals were never addressed. Today, too, amidst the press of other concerns, history and citizenship education is too often overlooked.

Colonial Williamsburg is proud to be a center for history and citizenship. When you visit the Revolutionary City, we invite you to join us in this ongoing experiment in democracy—and to have an enjoyable time doing so.

Your generous patronage is the single largest source of support for Colonial Williamsburg and essential for maintaining the Revolutionary City and for presenting our award-winning educational programs. All of us at Colonial Williamsburg deeply appreciate your support for our mission.

MITCHELL B. REISS, President and CEO
The Colonial Williamsburg Foundation

Colonial Williamsburg

THE OFFICIAL GUIDE

Colonial Williamsburg

The Colonial Williamsburg Foundation

Williamsburg, Virginia

colonialwilliamsburg.org

Contributors: Taylor Stoermer, Barbara Brown, Carl Lounsbury, Ronald L. Hurst, Paul Aron, Amy Watson

Photography: David M. Doody, Tom Green, Lael White, Barbara Lombardi

Book design: Shanin Glenn

Special thanks to David Arehart, Tom Austin, Edward Chappell, Brenda DePaula, Lisa Fischer, Jay Gaynor, Wesley Greene, James Horn, Peter Inker, Angelika Kuettner, Rose McAphee, Richard Nicoll, Emma L. Powers, Linda Rowe, Diane Schwarz, Kenneth Schwarz, Jenna Simpson, Tim Sutphin, Laura Viancour, Bill Weldon, William E. White, Katie Williams, Garland Wood, Buck Woodard

2025 24 23 22 21 20 19 18 17 16 15 14   1 2 3 4 5 6

Library of Congress Cataloging-in-Publication Data

Stoermer, Taylor, 1970-
   Colonial Williamsburg : the official guide / Taylor Stoermer, Barbara Rust Brown, and Carl R. Lounsbury.
      pages cm
   Includes index.
   ISBN 978-0-87935-265-3 (pbk. : alk. paper) 1. Colonial Williamsburg (Williamsburg, Va.)—Guidebooks. 2. Williamsburg (Va.)—Guidebooks. 3. Historic sites—Virginia—Williamsburg--Guidebooks. I. Brown, Barbara Rust. II. Lounsbury, Carl. III. Colonial Williamsburg Foundation. IV. Title.

   F234.W7S76 2014
   917.55'425204--dc23
                  2014027829

Published by
The Colonial Williamsburg Foundation
PO Box 1776
Williamsburg, VA 23187
colonialwilliamsburg.org

Printed in the United States of America

CONTENTS

THE REVOLUTIONARY COMMUNITY

IN THE MOMENT | *A Declaration of Independence*

THE REVOLUTIONARY COMMUNITY

THE TRADES

The REVOLUTI

What makes a Revolutionary City? People? Events? Ideas? Between 1775 and 1781, all these came together in one place unlike any other: Williamsburg, Virginia. All its inhabitants—free and enslaved, women and men, young and old—had to face the most important question of their lives: Should they join the effort to start a new nation based on principles never before tested or remain loyal to a government and way of life that had made many of them the most free and prosperous people on earth? To answer that question, the people of Williamsburg had to experience their own personal revolutions. Just like Patrick Henry, Thomas Jefferson, and George Washington, each member of the Revolutionary community had to choose between competing concepts of freedom and equality, and they had to do so amid the challenges of war. The consequences of those choices transformed this place—and the world—forever.

When you enter Colonial Williamsburg's Historic Area—the Revolutionary City—you do so as an inhabitant of those exciting and uncertain times. You won't just watch the action. You will meet the people, participate in the events, and discover the ideas that informed the Revolution. You become a part of the

ONARY CITY

story, from the collapse of the old order in and around the Governor's Palace to building a new nation at the Capitol to the debate over the many possible meanings of the Declaration of Independence. What role would you have played? Would you have chosen to remain loyal to the king—arguing that holding onto your British past was a more certain guarantee of liberty than promises made by Americans? Might you have been an enslaved servant wondering what the language of liberty meant for you? Would you have been a radical patriot fighting for a future in which your entire society would be transformed based on principles of freedom? The questions raised by the Revolution are as relevant today as they were then.

The Revolutionary City is not just a place, the streets and buildings of Williamsburg. It is also a community of people and their stories—a community that includes you. You will experience firsthand the excitement and peril of America's founding as it happened in Williamsburg, where ideas that flew around the globe turned into action that changed the world. You can find this experience everywhere you turn in the Historic Area, whether you are part of a group of townspersons storming the Governor's Palace, engaging with Enlightenment thought at the George Wythe House, exploring a spy mission critical to the outcome of the War for Independence as part of RevQuest: Save the Revolution!, interacting with our many costumed interpreters, eating at one of our taverns, or participating in one of Colonial Williamsburg's many other innovative programs.

The years between 1775 and 1781 mark the beginning of our collective historical memory. The men and women of the Revolutionary City, through their words and deeds, eloquently articulated the principles and sentiments that transformed loyal subjects of the British king first to resistance, then to rebellion, and finally to revolution. That story is not a simple one. It is contentious and conflicted, then and now, and was marked—and in some cases sparked—by tensions driven by ideology, religion, and race. Yet, regardless of such strains, the patriots of the Revolutionary City committed themselves to a common set of beliefs, invoking principles that many of them learned here, that, as Thomas Jefferson wrote in the Declaration of Independence, "all men are created equal, that they are endowed by their Creator with certain unalienable Rights, that among these are Life, Liberty and the pursuit of Happiness. That to secure these rights, Governments are instituted among Men, deriving their just powers from the consent of the governed." People today across the globe take those principles to be "self-evident" and the military victory in the War for Independence that secured them as almost inevitable, but, by participating in the stories told in the Revolutionary City, you will experience and perhaps rethink the meanings of Jefferson's words.

The moment you set foot in the Historic Area, you will join a living Revolutionary community, one full of tradespersons, politicians, shopkeepers, soldiers, planters, slaves, and others. You will witness (and participate in if you so choose) seminal Revolutionary events that occurred between 1775 and 1781.

Specific scenes and interactions vary from season to season. The day may begin just as it did on April 21, 1775, as militia and townspersons descended on the Palace and the royal governor to demand the return of gunpowder he seized. That gunpowder belongs to the public—to you. Other scenes and sites might insert you into the moments that followed, such as the midnight flight from the Palace of the governor and his family, in fear for their lives, and the fateful decision at the Capitol of Virginia's elected leaders to issue a Declaration of Rights that would provide a foundation on which a new nation might be built. At midday the Revolutionary community may gather for the first public reading of the Declaration of Independence, on July 25, 1776, at the Capitol, where you are invited to join with your neighbors in considering the ideas it contains. What does "all men are created equal" mean to an enslaved man or a free woman? Is the fight for independence about independence from Great Britain or about revolutionizing an entire society?

Afternoons demonstrate the challenges that building a nation creates. You may enter into important historical moments that reflect a community at war—with the British and with each other. On the streets, it could be May 14, 1779, at the Courthouse steps, when Governor Patrick Henry confirms what has only been rumored, that a British army has arrived in Virginia and is destroying everything in its path, which, for the first time since the conflict began, brings the stark reality of war to Williamsburg's doorstep. Or it might be April 20, 1781, when the community comes face-to-face with the American hero-turned-traitor Benedict Arnold, here with his enemy troops to occupy the city. In the George Wythe House,

the project of reforming Virginia's society based on Enlightenment principles is reflected in the reorganization of the College of William and Mary and the appointment of George Wythe as America's first professor of law. At the Public Armoury, blacksmiths toil to ensure that the troops have the weapons and supplies they need.

Your day may end on September 28, 1781, when you greet Virginia's own George Washington as he recruits members of the community to join his army in what might be the final battle in the War for Independence. The general then addresses the community, steeling you for the final push against the British troops at Yorktown, before he orders his combined French and American forces to ready themselves to march, maybe for the last time.

These scenes, and more, reflect the historical moments that shaped the new nation, and not just because legendary leaders—like Thomas Jefferson and George Washington—were part of them. It was because members of the Revolutionary community were also part of them. In the Revolutionary City, you have the chance to join them.

T
he Historic Area is quite large—a mile long and about a quarter mile wide. Over forty exhibition sites and museums, various places to shop and dine, and numerous programs offer a variety of ways to experience the Revolutionary War period.

Planning
YOUR VISIT

VISITOR CENTER

The best place to begin your visit is the Visitor Center. You can buy your tickets at several Colonial Williamsburg ticketing locations, but if you have not already done so, the Visitor Center staff can help you plan your visit, select the appropriate ticket options, and make reservations for dining, lodging, and special programs. Your admission ticket is your passport to the programs and sites in the Historic Area—the Revolutionary City—and to world-class museums. Various ticketing options are available; guest services agents can explain them and also help you select programs that most appeal to you. With your ticket you will receive a copy of the weekly program guide, which lists the programs being offered in the Revolutionary City and the museums. At the Visitor Center you can see *Williamsburg—The Story of a Patriot*. This dramatization of events in Williamsburg on the eve of the American Revolution plays throughout the day.

International guests can listen to the film *Williamsburg—The Story of a Patriot* in French, German, Italian, Japanese, Portuguese, Russian, or Spanish. Colonial Williamsburg brochures in several languages are also available.

As you leave the Visitor Center, you will find buses waiting to take you directly to the Historic Area. All guests of Colonial Williamsburg's hotels and all guests who have purchased admission tickets may ride the shuttle buses,

which circle the city and stop at numerous locations. Streets in the Historic Area are closed to motor vehicles, and there is limited parking in the immediate area. If you are staying at one of Colonial Williamsburg's hotels, leave your car at your hotel and walk or take the bus to the Historic Area. If you are staying somewhere else, leave your car at the Visitor Center and walk or take the bus from there. Parking is free at the Visitor Center.

If you choose to walk from the Visitor Center, the five-hundred-foot pedestrian Bridge to the Past connects the Visitor Center with a path to the Historic Area. Plaques embedded in the walkway help you make the transition to and from the past.

VISITING THE REVOLUTIONARY CITY

There is no right or wrong way to visit the Revolutionary City. You can follow the order of the sites in this guide and start at the Capitol, but whether you begin at the Capitol, the Governor's Palace, or the Shoemaker's Shop, you will find plenty to see and do. However, if your visit is limited to a day or two, you might want to consider in advance where and how you want to spend your time. At some sites (such as the trades) you can wander in and out at will; others (such as the Capitol) feature interpreter-led tours; still others (such as the Courthouse) feature scheduled programs as well as tours. And Revolutionary City programming occurs throughout the day. Not all sites are open every day, and opening times can vary. You can find the particulars in the weekly program guide that you receive with your admission ticket.

Consider starting your visit with an orientation tour, which is included in your admission ticket. When available, the thirty-minute orientation walks provide a quick overview of the town and the things you can see and do in the

a candlelit concert at the Governor's Palace. Decide the innocence or guilt of the "Virginia witch." Hear tales of the unexplained as you walk through the long shadows of Williamsburg after dark. Check your weekly program guide or online or call 1-855-368-3287 for the current schedule and tickets. You can also purchase tickets at the Visitor Center and the Lumber House ticket office.

Cameras and recording equipment are permitted for personal use unless they interfere with interpretations and programs. In such cases, you will be asked not to use them.

Revolutionary City. Sixty-minute special-interest walking tours, offered mid-March through December, explore topics such as the American Revolution, African American life in colonial Virginia, religion in the colony, and consumerism during the eighteenth century. Make reservations for walking tours at any ticket sales location on the day of the walk. Tickets for carriage and wagon rides can be purchased at any ticket sales location on the day of the ride. Rides sell out quickly during peak seasons, so buy your tickets early in the day.

Colonial Williamsburg offers plenty to do at night as well as during the day. Experience the life of the common soldier at the Magazine. Engage in festivities at the Raleigh Tavern, or laugh at the antics of a traveling troupe of entertainers at the Courthouse. Attend

Colonial Williamsburg's Historic Area is open every day of the year. Sites are generally open 9 a.m. to 5 p.m. with special programming in the evening. "This Week," the weekly program guide, will provide you with a daily listing of schedules and programs.

You can learn more about the Revolutionary City and make your vacation plans online at colonialwilliamsburg.com or by calling 1-855-368-3287. You can make lodging and dining reservations and purchase admission and special program tickets or book a full vacation package.

Colonial Williamsburg's Guide for Guests with Disabilities provides a detailed description of services and facilities available, including parking, restroom locations, wheelchair rentals, telephone assistance, transportation facilities, service animals, sign language interpreters, movie captioning, headsets, and other auxiliary aids. It is available at the Visitor Center.

For more information, contact:

The Visitor Center Administrative Office
Colonial Williamsburg Visitor Center
101A Visitor Center Drive
Williamsburg, Virginia 23185
(757) 220-7205

Getting to Williamsburg

By car: Williamsburg is located 150 miles south of Washington, D.C., midway between Richmond and Norfolk. Take Interstate 64 to exit 238. After exiting, follow Route 143 east for a half mile. Turn right onto Route 132. Go about a mile and a half. Turn left onto Route 132Y (Visitor Center Drive). Colonial Williamsburg's Visitor Center is on your left. The physical address is 101 Visitor Center Drive, Williamsburg, Virginia 23185.

By air: Newport News/Williamsburg International Airport is twenty minutes from Williamsburg; Richmond International Airport and Norfolk International Airport are each fifty minutes away in opposite directions. All have rental car and limousine services.

By train or bus: Amtrak and Greyhound serve the Williamsburg Transportation Center. The center is just blocks from the Historic Area and provides car rentals and a cab stand.

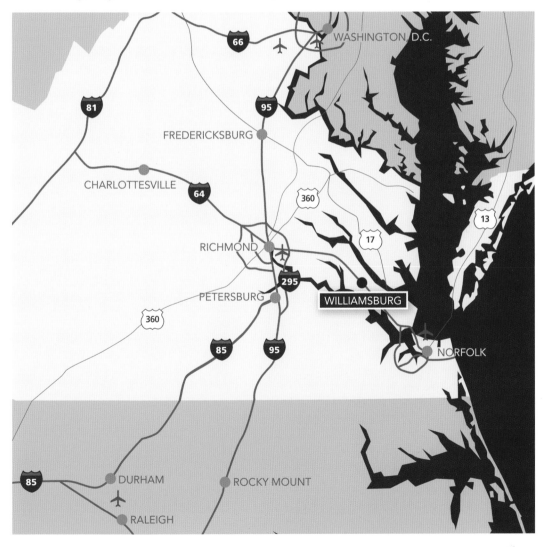

STORMING *the* PALACE!

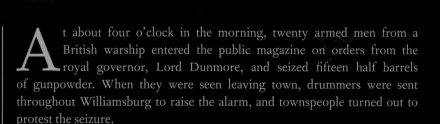

At about four o'clock in the morning, twenty armed men from a British warship entered the public magazine on orders from the royal governor, Lord Dunmore, and seized fifteen half barrels of gunpowder. When they were seen leaving town, drummers were sent throughout Williamsburg to raise the alarm, and townspeople turned out to protest the seizure.

By sunrise, Williamsburg's independent company of militia, under command of James Innes, assembled with their muskets and decided to march on the Governor's Palace to demand the gunpowder's return. In the meantime, the city's leaders met to draft an address condemning the seizure for undermining the ability of Virginians to defend themselves. They politely asked Dunmore for the same thing that the militia wanted to compel, the return of the gunpowder.

The stage was set for a clash in front of the Palace between those who sought to defend their rights with the force of arms and those who believed that the situation could be resolved with words, not weapons. Dunmore and his family looked on, believing, as the governor later wrote, "it was their resolution to seize upon, or massacre me, and every person found giving me assistance if I refused to deliver the Powder immediately into their custody." The militia, surrounded by townspeople, advanced toward the Palace but was stopped by Peyton Randolph and other city leaders. A heated debate followed. Would war begin here?

Randolph succeeded in convincing Innes and his men to stay where they were while he, the mayor, and the treasurer presented their address to Dunmore. The governor replied that he ordered the seizure of the gunpowder because of a rumored slave insurrection and would return it immediately if the people proved to be in need of it to defend themselves. Another heated discussion followed, during which Dunmore was informed of the "fury of the People." Randolph then returned to the militia and the townspeople, gave them Dunmore's answers, and persuaded them to return home, still on the edge of revolution.

Peyton and Betty RANDOLPH

Likely born in Williamsburg, Peyton Randolph (ca. 1722–1775) was the son of Sir John Randolph, a prominent lawyer and politician who was knighted by George II in 1732, and Susannah Beverley Randolph. His father died in 1737, leaving all his books to his son. Randolph also inherited slaves and land in and around Williamsburg, along with two small plantations farther away. Two years later, on October 13, 1739, he followed his father's wishes and was admitted to Middle Temple, one of the Inns of Court in London, where he studied law for much of the next five years.

Randolph's experience in the English political world that had for decades been defined by the person and practice of Sir Robert Walpole (whom he knew personally) permanently shaped his political and cultural perspectives. Under Walpole's influence, Randolph came to understand not only England's constitutional history but also Britain's relationships to modern geopolitical challenges as it battled France and other European powers. He was thrust into the middle of colonial politics as friends such as John Hanbury, perhaps the most influential of Chesapeake tobacco merchants at the time, successfully lobbied for Randolph's appointment in 1744 as Virginia's attorney general at the age of twenty-two and even before he had finished his legal studies.

On his return to Virginia, Randolph represented not only the colony but also clients such as George Washington and the new lieutenant governor, Francis Fauquier. He was elected to the House of Burgesses and to the vestry of Bruton Parish Church. By then he had married the formidable Elizabeth "Betty" Harrison (ca. 1723–1783), the sister of Benjamin Harrison, a signer of the Declaration of Independence, and a master of parlor politics in her own right.

In the 1750s, Randolph entered what was something of a family business: protecting the colony's political and economic interests, which often meant resolving disputes between the Virginia General Assembly and the resident royal governor. In 1765, political divisions between moderate and radical Virginians began to appear over the most effective way to register opposition to the Stamp Act. Randolph was strongly opposed to Patrick Henry's approach, believing that the strident language of Henry's Stamp Act resolves would do more harm than good to their common cause. On May 31, the radicals claimed victory when five of Henry's resolves narrowly passed the House of Burgesses, causing Randolph to exclaim (according to Thomas Jefferson), "By God, I would have given one hundred guineas for a single vote." On November 6, 1766, Randolph was elected Speaker of the House. His brother John succeeded him as attorney general.

For the rest of the colonial period, in every major assembly in which Randolph sat—from the House of Burgesses to informal associations to the Virginia Conventions to the Continental Congress—he would be elected to lead it. When the First Virginia Convention, of which he was appointed president, elected delegates to the First Continental Congress in August 1774, Randolph topped the list. When he arrived in Philadelphia in September, he was warmly greeted by delegates from other colonies and unanimously chosen by the Congress as its chairman. He continued as Speaker of the House of Burgesses and as moderator of each of the succeeding Virginia Conventions and returned to head the Continental Congress on May 10, 1775. He resigned the presidency of Congress later that month when Virginia's royal governor summoned the General Assembly to Williamsburg.

There can be little doubt that the constitutional crisis between Britain and the colonies was also a personal one for Randolph. Under orders to not do anything that could be interpreted as official recognition of the Continental Congress, British Commander in Chief Thomas Gage used an acquaintance with Randolph during the Seven Years' War to open a personal line of communication about reconciliation in September 1774. Jefferson later criticized Randolph's constitutional views as "stopped at the half-way house of John Dickinson who admitted that England had a right to regulate our commerce, and to lay duties on it for the purposes of regulation, but not of raising revenue." Edmund Randolph, Peyton's nephew, remembered him rather more kindly as, "in official rank and ostensible importance," he "stood foremost in the band of patriots" and "halted not for a moment" when it came to "the great American question."

Randolph did not have the opportunity to make a choice on "the great American question" because he died while at dinner outside of Philadelphia on October 22, 1775, more than seven months before the vote on American independence. His funeral in Philadelphia was widely reported as the largest that city had ever witnessed. His body remained in a vault at Christ Church until November 1776 when it was escorted to Williamsburg by Edmund and laid to rest next to Sir John Randolph in the crypt of the chapel of the College of William and Mary.

Betty stayed in Williamsburg throughout the Revolution as a respected figure. She endured the British occupations and then opened her home to the comte de Rochambeau for him to use as a headquarters while he and Washington planned the Yorktown campaign. Betty also watched as almost one-third of her enslaved men and women chose to seek their freedom with the British, perhaps because they had learned that her will stipulated that they were to be split up among several of her relations. Betty Randolph died in Williamsburg in January 1781 and was buried next to her husband.

▲ *Washington and His Generals at Yorktown.* The Colonial Williamsburg Foundation.

The Revolution in Williamsburg

Williamsburg became the capital of Virginia in 1699 when, after a series of fires and decades of political unrest, the government moved from Jamestown to the small village then called Middle Plantation. First settled in 1632, and pleasantly situated on high ground between two deep creeks that connected it to two of Virginia's great rivers, the York and the James, Middle Plantation drew to it a parish church, a tavern, several houses, and, in 1695, the College of William and Mary. Virginia's leaders, chief among them Francis Nicholson, the royal governor at the time, renamed the town Williamsburg, when it became the capital, after the reigning monarch, William III. Nicholson, a former soldier who had designed Maryland's new capital at Annapolis when he was governor of that colony, probably also assumed responsibility for the formal design of the town.

Today's Revolutionary City still reflects Nicholson's vision. Central to Nicholson's layout was the mile-long main street named for the young heir to the throne, the Duke of Gloucester. The street is anchored at one end by the college and at

The HISTORY

the other by the Capitol. It is flanked by two back streets, Francis and Nicholson, and crossed by several broad avenues and greens in the style of an orderly English village. Other streets remind us of Williamsburg's British heritage, with names such as Scotland, England, Queen, Nassau (the name of the royal Dutch house of William III), and Prince George (of Denmark, the husband of Queen Anne, William's successor). In the eighteenth century, the quieter part of town was the western end, between Bruton Parish Church and the college. The eastern end, near and around the Capitol, was a dynamic commercial neighborhood.

For the first fifteen years of Williamsburg's existence, the capital city grew slowly. During those years Britain was almost constantly at war with France and Spain, which retarded the economic and population growth of the colony.

➤ William, Duke of Gloucester. The Colonial Williamsburg Foundation.

Tobacco, the commercial lifeblood of Virginia throughout the colonial period, was expensive and hazardous to ship, and growing it depended increasingly on the labor of enslaved Africans. With transatlantic voyages almost constantly threatened by enemy warships and pirates, migration to Virginia between 1699 and 1714—both voluntary and forced—was a trickle, and the tobacco trade earned substantial profits for only the most fortunate and well-connected planters. That changed in 1714. The Peace of Utrecht ended decades of warfare in Europe, and the accession of King George I and the house of Hanover to the throne of Great Britain quieted concerns in London about the future of the Protestant monarchy. For much of the next fifty years, the British Atlantic world experienced an almost unprecedented level of stability. This stability enabled the mother country and her twenty-six American colonies, from Canada to the Caribbean, to flourish.

Virginia benefited especially, since it was more politically, socially, culturally, and economically tied to London than any other colony. By 1750 Virginia had become the largest and most prosperous colony in British North America. According to one writer of

the period, Virginia was "the most antient and loyal, the most plentiful and flourishing, the most extensive and beneficial colony belonging to the crown of Great Britain." New England might have been "a receptacle of dissenters," Pennsylvania "the nursery of Quakers," Maryland "the retirement of Roman Catholicks," North Carolina "the refuge of run-aways," and South Carolina "the delight of buccaneers and pyrates," but Virginia "may be justly esteemed the happy retreat of true Britons." A visitor to Williamsburg wrote in 1724 that *"The Habits, Life, Customs, Computations,* &c. of the *Virginians* are much the same as about *London,* which they esteem their *Home."*

Williamsburg grew, in stature, size, and wealth, as the colony grew. The spacious Capitol was finished by 1705, and an elegant Governor's Palace was completed in 1722. Taverns, trades shops, stores, other public buildings, and even a theater filled the city lots, along with more than one hundred private homes and outbuildings. By 1748 Williamsburg had more than 750 permanent residents, a number that swelled considerably during the sessions of the legislature and courts and during regular market days. A decade later it was reported that Williamsburg had

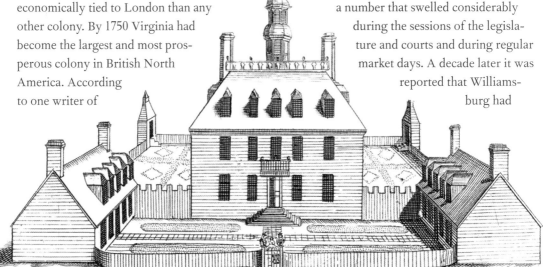

▲ Governor's Palace, detail from eighteenth-century plate found in Bodleian Library in Oxford. The Colonial Williamsburg Foundation.

about two hundred houses and "one thousand souls."

By then the character of the city was solidly established. About half of Williamsburg's souls were enslaved men and women of African descent while most of the rest of the population were the families of lawyers, doctors, merchants, and tradesmen, like carriage makers and tailors. Native Americans were often seen in Williamsburg, visiting the governor and delivering students to the College of William and Mary's Brafferton Indian school.

Williamsburg was robustly English. Its news and goods were dominated by imports from London, which was a mere six weeks away by ship. (Consider that, for most of the eighteenth century, it was faster for a Virginian to send a letter to Philadelphia by way of London first than it was to deliver it over land or along the coast.) Most of the inhabitants, including many slaves, were literate, as schools and tutors were available to all sorts of people.

The Church of England was firmly established in Virginia, in that colonial legislation required Virginians to support it financially, and parishes such as Bruton also had the pastoral responsibility to care for the poor and the needy. Faith was almost a matter separate from church, and relatively few people were penalized for not attending church services.

Politically, the spirit of moderation reigned. Most resident governors (appointed by the Privy Council in London in the name of the king), his councillors, and the elected legislators that governed colonial affairs followed their English brethren in believing, as one Speaker of the Virginia House of Burgesses put it, that "Heat or Intemperance in our Debates . . . are always unnecessary." One Williamsburg

politician later recalled it was then unwise "ever to push to extremity any theory which by practical relations may not be accommodated." And that was just fine with most inhabitants of the city. They were enthusiastically patriotic Britons who celebrated the birthdays of the royal family and condemned the rebels in England who attempted to overthrow them.

▲ Tobacco planter negotiating with ship captain. The Colonial Williamsburg Foundation.

Economically, everyone, regardless of social status or religious belief or political persuasion, depended in one way or another on the tobacco trade.

So by the middle of the eighteenth century, Britain defined—in thought, word, and deed—what it meant to be an inhabitant of Williamsburg. But between 1750 and 1775 something dramatic changed in the hearts and minds of many of those inhabitants. The stability they had known vanished into a sea of tension and uncertainty. In the first place, the number of hearts and minds in Virginia doubled, from 236,000 to almost 500,000 free and enslaved people. The largest increase was among free people, as Virginia became the target for waves of immigration from across Europe, but particularly for Scots and Ulster Scots (traditionally called *Scotch-Irish*). A large number of slaves imported directly from Africa and representing many different peoples, each with their own language and culture, added considerably to the social diversity of the colony.

Economically there was a major change, too. For most of Virginia's history, London had dominated the tobacco trade, mostly due to the fact that the majority of the population and the best, most profitable tobacco were concentrated in the Tidewater region, the center of which was Williamsburg. Tidewater planters cultivated a sweet-scented variety that smokers across the Atlantic, especially those in England, embraced and consigned it to merchants in London to sell on their behalf for a commission. To guarantee a steady supply to English consumers and discourage their purchase of tobacco from Spanish and French colonies, Parliament gave Virginia a virtual monopoly on growing sweet-scented tobacco. But the expanding population outside of the Tidewater could not grow sweet-scented tobacco. The soil in northern and western Virginia would not support it. So the planters of the Northern

▲ Tarpley, Thompson & Company broadside advertisement. The Colonial Williamsburg Foundation.

Neck and Piedmont, like George Washington and Thomas Jefferson, instead grew oronoco tobacco, a bitter variety best suited to be ground into a powder, mixed with flavors like vanilla, and marketed as snuff, which was voraciously consumed in Europe. The two kinds of tobacco created important divisions within Virginia. First, sweet-scented was worth five times the value of oronoco at market, creating economic disparities among Virginians. Second, while London dominated every aspect of the sweet-scented trade for English smokers, Glasgow became the heart of the oronoco trade and connected Virginia to France, the Netherlands, and other European consumers of snuff. The Scottish traders conducted business quite differently from the London merchants by establishing hundreds of stores across Virginia managed by factors. These stores supplied

◄ Seventeenth-century print of a tobacco plant. The Colonial Williamsburg Foundation.

smaller planters with ever more easily available goods, based on liberal credit terms, in direct exchange for their tobacco. The arrangement significantly increased the amount of debt owed British merchants.

Perhaps the most dramatic change resulted from the end to the decades of relative peace between Britain and France. The Seven Years' War, often known in America as the French and Indian War, began in 1754, when a twenty-two-year-old militia officer named George Washington led an expedition to warn French troops to get out of British territory in western Pennsylvania. The battle, which ended in Washington's surrender of Fort Necessity on July 4, ignited a global conflict. It also was the beginning of the end of British America, for the cost of victory transformed the relationship between Great Britain and her colonies.

By the time the war ended in 1763, the British national debt had doubled, to £132,600,000. Who was going to pay for it? And there was not just the cost of paying down the debt but also the expense of keeping British troops in North America to protect colonial borders against the French and their Native American allies. It was pretty clear to British ministers that English taxpayers were not going to foot the bill. They were already paying to maintain the empire through stamp taxes, sales taxes, and land taxes. The answer in the minds of many Englishmen was the American colonies had to pay more. The colonists paid little, if anything, in taxes, a fact virtually every British taxpayer knew and resented.

From that question—who would pay for the Seven Years' War and the troops necessary to keep the peace—arose the revenue acts and, ultimately, the American Revolution. The Sugar Act of 1764, the Stamp Act of 1765, the Townshend Acts of 1767, and the Tea Act of 1773, all were intended to make the Americans contribute to their own defense of their nation, even if in the case of the Tea Act this was largely symbolic.

▲ "No Stamp Act" teapot made in England for the American colonists to commemorate the repeal of the Stamp Act. The Colonial Williamsburg Foundation.

The disputes over tax bills led to the collapse of the British order in America because they led to another question: Who had the authority to say who was going to pay taxes? It was an accepted principle of the British constitution that taxes could not be levied on the people without their own consent, which was expressed through their elected representatives. As patriot leaders meeting in Williamsburg at the Capitol put it in 1764, in a protest to Parliament over the proposal for a stamp tax, it was "a fundamental Principle of the *British* Constitution, without which Freedom can no Where exist, that the people are not subject to any Taxes but such as are laid on them by their own Consent, or by those who are legally appointed to represent them."

In the 1760s and 1770s, plenty of people on both sides of the Atlantic still believed that all British subjects were represented in Parliament. Members of the House of Commons did not represent particular people or the districts that elected them but the common interests of all British peoples, wherever they happened to reside—or at least so the theory went. But by the 1760s a growing number of Britons, especially in America, did not agree that Parliament represented the interests of all British subjects. Leaders such as Williamsburg's Richard Bland started to express a different view—that Parliament had no authority over the colonies at all. The true representatives of Virginians, and therefore the only people who could tax them, were those for whom they could vote directly. These were the burgesses who regularly sat in session in the Capitol at the east end of Duke of Gloucester Street. This point of view was echoed in Boston and Pennsylvania and came to be accepted by a rising generation of colonials, such as Thomas Jefferson.

Teachers such as George Wythe encouraged his pupils, including Jefferson, to investigate the histories of the Greek democracies and Roman republics and the philosophical notions of natural law and rights that were springing out of the Enlightenment. As Enlightenment thinking circulated in America, it further increased the beliefs of some on this side of the Atlantic that America might require a different—and different kind of—government.

Still, almost ten years of debate over representation had little direct impact on the vast majority of free and enslaved Virginians. Even the Boston Tea Party, on December 16, 1773, appears to have merely reinforced the idea held by many people in Williamsburg that New England bred troublemakers. George Washington, for example, condemned dumping the tea into Boston Harbor as a criminal act and offered to help pay for the lost tea. But the Coercive Acts, which included an act to close

Boston Harbor until the tea was paid for, were passed in 1774. Parliament's efforts to punish Massachusetts for the Tea Party began to bring matters to a head.

News of the Boston Port Act reached Williamsburg at the beginning of May. The community was already in a state of unprecedented fear and tension for reasons that had little to do with taxes and representation. Two years earlier, in 1772, James Somerset, a slave owned by an erstwhile Virginia trader with close ties to Williamsburg, attempted to take his freedom in London. An English court let him have it in an opinion that rocked the Atlantic world. Slaves in Virginia began to run away from their owners in presumed attempts to get to England. On the commercial front, in 1773, a credit crisis shattered Britain's economy. This crisis caused merchant houses in Scotland and London to fall like dominoes, British creditors to demand payment from Virginia debtors with ever greater urgency, and interest rates to rise on existing debt. Many Virginia planters were still reeling from the Great Fresh of 1771—a major flood that killed hundreds of people and destroyed warehouses full of tobacco on the main Virginia rivers—and a short tobacco crop the next year that left them with very little money to pay the increased demands of their creditors.

This, then, was the period during which Williamsburg became a Revolutionary city. Once news of Parliament's closure of Boston Harbor reached Williamsburg, many inhabitants came to believe that they simply could no longer trust the British government.

In May, the House of Burgesses passed a resolution to express support for Boston by holding a "Day of Fasting, Humiliation, and Prayer" for its members "to implore the Divine

Interposition for averting the heavy Calamity which threatens Destruction to our civil Rights, and the Evils of civil War." Virginia's last royal governor, John Murray, the Earl of Dunmore, then dissolved the House of Burgesses. Dunmore informed his superiors in London that he had no choice, that the resolution would likely lead to others that might "inflame the whole country, and instigate the people to acts that might rouse the indignation of the mother country against them." Far from intimidated, the former burgesses met at the Raleigh Tavern, drafted a call for a general congress to meet to represent all the colonies, and adopted an association against the importation of tea and other goods "in Support of the constitutional Liberties of AMERICA, against the late oppressive Act of the British Parliament respecting the Town of Boston, which, in the End, must affect all the other Colonies."

Other colonies joined Virginia in organizing a continental congress to be held in Philadelphia in September. Meetings were held across Virginia in advance of a convention held at the Capitol in August to elect delegates to the congress. For the consideration of that convention, Thomas Jefferson wrote *A Summary View of the Rights of British America*, which was printed in Williamsburg. This pamphlet, in the form of a letter to the king, became one of the most famous statements of the American mind of the Revolutionary period. Jefferson followed Richard Bland in arguing that Virginia had only been connected to Britain through the monarchy, therefore Parliament had no authority whatsoever to pass laws for the colony. John Randolph, the attorney general of Virginia and brother of Peyton Randolph, the Speaker of the House of Burgesses, countered with a staunch loyalist pamphlet, *Considerations on the Present State of Virginia*.

⌃ Patrick Henry. The Colonial Williamsburg Foundation.

When the First Continental Congress met, Peyton Randolph was selected as its president. Patrick Henry declared (according to John Adams's notes), "The distinctions between Virginians, Pennsylvanians, New Yorkers, and New Englanders, are no more. I am not a Virginian, but an American." The Congress established the Continental Association, expanding Virginia's association into an intercolonial nonimportation and nonexportation agreement that required the creation of committees of inspection in every locality in America. Virginians quickly created local committees and adopted resolutions that pledged their opposition to Parliament. Nearly five hundred merchants, tradespersons, and others staged a public signing of the Continental Association in Williamsburg in November.

At the end of 1774, Lord Dunmore, after refusing to call a new session of the Virginia General Assembly, organized a war in the west to protect the colony's land claims against the Shawnee Indians. He won a resounding victory and returned to Williamsburg as a hero. A ball was held at the Governor's Palace to acknowledge the event. Dunmore's former troops, however, still stationed on the frontier at Fort Gower, were not in a celebrating mood. They made clear their loyalties by resolving to "exert every Power within us for the Defense of American Liberty, and for the Support of her just Rights and Privileges."

The next eighteen months set the course for Revolution. Between January 1775 and July 1776, Virginia was transformed from the oldest and most loyal British colony into an independent American commonwealth. In Williamsburg, the Reverend Samuel Henley, a professor at the college, reported to an English correspondent that here "the people are hurrying themselves into perdition by their violence. The least tyranical of the patriots here are greater tyrants than the most absolute princes in Europe, over all those who will not embrace their measures." Another Virginian worried that "the train of miseries consequential of the intemperate warmth displayed by the people here, are too apparent."

George Washington explained to an acquaintance in February that "the minds of men are exceedingly disturbed at the measures of the British government." He closed his letter, "A little time must now unfold the mystery, as matters are drawing to a point." The future of the once stable British world—the old order—that most people in Williamsburg took for granted was in serious doubt. For more than a few people here, that was a dangerous notion. For them, the British Empire and its constitution, the legacies of representative government and the rule of law, were to be celebrated not cast off.

Given Dunmore's reluctance to allow the burgesses to meet again, another convention was held in March 1775, this time in Richmond. The main item for consideration was whether to take the next fateful step: to place Virginia in a state of military readiness to defend itself against Great Britain. Henry took center stage. Although the precise language of the speech was not recorded until decades later, no one who heard it that day ever forgot his exhortation that peace was at an end and war had already begun and that, while others might take a different course, "give me liberty, or give me death!" The convention adopted the proposal, and counties throughout Virginia began to raise companies of infantry and cavalry independent of the existing militia.

Dunmore tested the resolve of those who might choose liberty over death in the early hours of April 21, 1775. He arranged for twenty British sailors to seize fifteen half barrels of the colony's gunpowder from the public magazine. The town's response was immediate and intense. The local independent company assembled, and hundreds of the town's inhabitants gathered in front of the Palace in a high state of anxiety, prepared to compel the return of the gunpowder. Williamsburg's leaders, under the influence of Peyton Randolph, quickly gathered and protested directly to the governor at the Palace and then convinced the crowd to disperse. They narrowly averted violence, but tensions remained high. Dunmore was heard to declare that, if anyone threatened him or his officers, "he would declare Freedom to the Slaves, and reduce the City of *Williamsburg* to Ashes."

At almost precisely the same time, Williamsburg was deluged with news—some true, much false. Reports arrived of the battle fought between militia and British regulars at Lexington and Concord in Massachusetts. The *Virginia Gazette* printed a rumor that a "black list" of patriots to be arrested and executed by the government had been discovered in London— and it included the name of Peyton Randolph. On top of all that, the *Gazette* reported that a death sentence was passed on two Norfolk slaves accused of conspiring to raise an insurrection there. Williamsburg printer Alexander Purdie wrote, "The *sword is now drawn*, and God knows when it will be sheathed."

In May Henry led Virginia militiamen to within a day's march of Williamsburg to challenge Dunmore over the gunpowder, and in June three Williamsburg youths were wounded by a gun rigged to go off if anyone entered the magazine. The newspapers charged Lord Dunmore with attempted murder while Lord Dunmore's wife believed it was part of an assassination plot against her husband. Several days later, Dunmore and his family departed the Governor's Palace for the safety of a British warship in the York River. Neither the governor nor his family would ever return. The Revolutionary War had begun.

Williamsburg was in a state of confusion for the next several months. Militia companies poured into town, sleeping in every available building and training on the greens and squares. Leaders such as George Wythe and Peyton Randolph returned to Philadelphia for the meeting of the Second Continental Congress. Randolph's loyalist brother, John, and his family left Williamsburg for London, in the hope of negotiating some sort of resolution

▲ Reconstructed plate with Dunmore family coat of arms, excavated from Governor's Palace site. The Colonial Williamsburg Foundation.

to the growing conflict. Word arrived that the king had proclaimed the colonies in a state of rebellion, and Dunmore gathered loyalist and some regular troops about him in Norfolk (after sending his family back to England). These troops included former slaves Dunmore freed by a proclamation, issued in November, granting them their liberty should they choose to take up arms against their rebel masters. Dunmore's proclamation may have pushed some moderates into the Revolutionary camp.

A temporary government was created in Williamsburg to fill the vacuum of authority created by Dunmore's departure. An eleven-member "Committee of Safety" was established to manage the colony's affairs between meetings of the conventions. For most of the next year, the committee acted as the executive branch of Virginia's government while the convention served as its legislature.

In Philadelphia, the Continental Congress was creating an army, which then surrounded British-occupied Boston, and appointed George Washington to lead it. In Williamsburg, the committee was desperately trying to put together something that looked like an army and to maintain a government. They attempted to address issues with Virginia's economy, no easy task, given that the transatlantic trade with Great Britain was no more. They worked to build military and naval forces from scratch, without any way to manufacture on a large scale guns or ammunition or even make the powder to fire them. Virginia also needed salt to feed cattle and preserve meat and fish; before the war it had been imported primarily from Britain or the West Indies. Troops required clothing, but almost all cloth had come from Britain and India.

Fortunately for the inhabitants of Williamsburg, very little of the fighting touched Virginia at first. A battle at Great Bridge, near Norfolk, Virginia, on December 9, 1775, forced Lord Dunmore's troops to take refuge on an island off the coast. Even other fronts were largely quiet. The Continental army, which had almost no troops from Virginia, was then besieging Boston, where the single bloodiest battle of the entire Revolutionary War had already been fought on two heights north of the city—Breed's Hill and Bunker Hill.

In Williamsburg, the members of the Revolutionary community were considering the purpose of the conflict. Was it a fight to guarantee their rights as British subjects, or was it something more? At the beginning of 1776, George Wythe, Thomas Jefferson, Richard Henry Lee, and other patriots argued this was more than an effort to reconcile with Britain on favorable terms. They were convinced that it was an opportunity to break with the British past and create a new, independent nation, founded on principles of equality and freedom. Jefferson himself had recently written, in the *Declaration*

of the Causes and Necessity of Taking Up Arms, that Americans were "resolved to die Freemen rather than to live Slaves."

Early in 1776, the Continental Congress called on each colony to draft a written constitution that established a new government. At the same time, Thomas Paine was inspired to write *Common Sense*, which made the case for independence in passionate, even religious, language that almost any American could understand. Paine's work began to be published in the *Virginia Gazette* on February 2, despite the opinions of some Virginians that Paine advanced "*nonsense* instead of *Common Sense*." Another Virginia Convention was called to meet in Williamsburg in the spring of 1776 to act on Congress's suggestion.

The Fifth Virginia Convention began its session in the Capitol on May 6, 1776. It took its members less than two weeks to adopt a resolution directing its delegates in Congress to move for independence from Great Britain, after which "the british flag was immediately struck on the Capitol, and a continental hoisted in its room." A few weeks later, on June 12, they adopted the Virginia Declaration of Rights, largely drafted by George Mason, which stated that "all men are by nature equally free and independent." The twenty-five-year-old James Madison won an important political battle— the first of his career—ensuring that the Declaration also enshrined the principle that "all men are equally entitled to the free exercise of religion."

It took the convention another few weeks to agree on a new republican-style government and pass a constitution, on June 29. The constitution created Virginia as a commonwealth with a weak executive and most power vested in the elected House of Delegates. The delegates then chose Henry to be the commonwealth's first governor.

The first rumors that Congress had declared American independence reached Williamsburg on July 12. The news was confirmed a week later when the newspapers printed the entire text of the Declaration of Independence. The *Virginia Gazette* reported that on July 25 "the DECLARATION of INDEPENDENCE was solemnly proclaimed at the Capitol, the Courthouse, and the Palace, amidst the acclamations of the people, accompanied by firing of cannon and musketry, the several regiments of continental troops having been paraded on that solemnity."

Neither women nor enslaved men were considered citizens of the new republic, which bestowed rights and responsibilities on white, male property owners. For those excluded in 1776, the road to liberty was going to be filled with obstacles. But in the summer of 1776, about 2.5 million people, comprising a loose, weak confederation of individual and strikingly diverse colonies, became a nation.

Declaring independence was one thing, winning it something else. While the people of Williamsburg were debating the nature and application of Enlightenment ideals, the British government was planning to put down the rebellion with massive force. From a base in Nova Scotia, the British army, under the command of Sir William Howe, intended to separate troublesome New England from the ostensibly more reasonable and moderate colonies to the south. The plan was to take New York City and move up the Hudson River Valley from there. Calls went out to Williamsburg for troops for the Continental army. Several

regiments were sent, including one in which the young James Monroe was an officer. Howe hit New York in August, and Virginia forces got their first taste of fighting against British and Hessian regulars. Washington's untrained army was no match for Howe's. By November, the British had captured thousands of Continental troops and controlled the lower Hudson River Valley. Washington and his rapidly dwindling army were then chased through New Jersey by British troops under Charles Cornwallis. They barely made it across the Delaware River into Pennsylvania on the night of December 7, 1776.

While Washington was attempting to keep his troops from going home, the first session of the House of Delegates met in Williamsburg to begin the work of reshaping Virginia society. Jefferson returned from the Continental Congress specifically to be part of that project, living with his family in George Wythe's house. The delegates moved quickly to create a republic that treated citizens more fairly. They abolished the ancient practice of entail, a legal maneuver that barred landowners from selling or otherwise dividing inherited property. They exempted Protestant dissenters from the legal requirement to contribute to the support of the Episcopal Church. And, believing that they were strengthening the commonwealth by purging it of its supposed enemies, they expelled from Virginia all British merchants who had not demonstrated a clear attachment to the American cause.

Not going so smoothly was the effort to raise and keep troops for the Continental army. In Williamsburg in the fall of 1776, desertion and illness robbed many units of their strength. Edmund Randolph, John's son and Peyton's nephew, reported to Washington that Williamsburg, "which has hitherto been proverbial for general Health, is now notorious for the Contrary." Randolph despaired that new recruits in Williamsburg or elsewhere could not be obtained. Nor were there clothes or weapons for new soldiers even if they did sign on. Only a few months after the celebration of independence, it seemed that patriotic spirit was waning.

When Washington crossed into Pennsylvania in early December, his army numbered no more than two thousand men—and their enlistments would expire at the end of the year. It was at this point that Thomas Paine once again put pen to paper. The result was *The American Crisis,* a pamphlet in which Paine acknowledged that "these are the times that try men's souls" but reminded his countrymen that "tyranny, like hell, is not easily conquered; yet we have this consolation with us, that the harder the conflict, the more glorious the triumph." Washington had copies printed and distributed throughout his army. Perhaps as a result, enough of his soldiers remained— mainly Pennsylvanians and Virginians—for him to launch a surprise attack on a Hessian force at Trenton, New Jersey. The result was a morale-boosting rout that cost only four killed and four wounded, including James Monroe, who would carry the bullet he received in the neck for the rest of his life.

In wartime Williamsburg, new barracks were built, and prisoners of war, loyalists, counterfeiters, and deserters filled the public jail over its capacity. Prisoners escaped with such frequency that the jail keeper, Peter Pelham, was investigated by the House of Delegates. The question of loyalty was on the minds of many. Landon Carter, a planter who had been

a leading member of the old House of Burgesses during the disputes over the Stamp Act, recorded in his diary that anyone who opposed the position of the "multitude" of patriots was "an enimy to his Country."

THE ALTERNATIVE OF WILLIAMS·BURG.

▲ Signing a loyalty pledge protesting the Coercive Acts. The "alternative" is suggested by the barrel of tar and bag of feathers suspended from the gallows. The Colonial Williamsburg Foundation.

In May, about forty Cherokee Indians, including several chiefs, arrived in Williamsburg to build a relationship based on friendship between the two nations. The Cherokees met with Governor Henry and his council at the Palace to ratify a peace treaty, after which they celebrated. Despite such diversions, the community felt the pinch of being at war against a nation with the mightiest navy on earth.

In September, news reached Williamsburg that the British had embarked on their next campaign—to take Philadelphia. Virginia

▲ Cherokees in London. At their request, three Cherokees were escorted to London in 1762 to meet the king. The Colonial Williamsburg Foundation.

suffered dearly in the battles that eventually resulted in the loss of the capital and the flight of the Continental Congress. But there was good news from a different front. On October 30, news reached Williamsburg of the surrender of a large British army under John Burgoyne at Saratoga, New York, due largely to the heroic exploits of Benedict Arnold. The inhabitants of Williamsburg paraded through town and marked the occasion with "13 discharges of cannon, 3 vollies from the infantry, together with 3 huzzas from all present" and the "ringing of bells, illuminations, &c" and, two weeks later, a ball at the Capitol. Burgoyne's surrender provided the first clear evidence to members of the community that Americans could beat the British.

In the absence of volunteers, the Virginia General Assembly in December turned to drafting unmarried men, and the increased scarcity of supplies made it necessary to pass a law allowing the military to seize necessary goods. Governor Henry called on every Virginia county to supply one pair of shoes, stockings, gloves, or mittens for each of the county's soldiers then serving in the Continental

army, which was in winter quarters at Valley Forge. As the winter wore on, affairs assumed an even more somber aspect. In contrast to the congeniality that surrounded the visit of the Cherokees, the Virginia government called on George Rogers Clark to launch a western campaign against Indians loyal to the British and "punish the Aggressors by carrying the War into their own Country." And in Northern Virginia there were riots against the draft that went on for two days.

The prospects for the American cause improved considerably when the French agreed to an alliance with the United States. Word reached Williamsburg in the spring and was printed in the *Virginia Gazette* on May 8. A Williamsburg cabinetmaker, Edmund Dickinson, serving in the Continental army, expressed the optimism engendered by the treaty. He wrote to his sister in Williamsburg of "the Joy circulating through our Camp at the Glorious news from France" and his firm belief that "it will cause a Peace before the leaves (which now are just buding out here) falls from their tender Sprigs."

The British abandoned Philadelphia a few weeks later to consolidate their forces in New York. Washington's army caught them at Monmouth Courthouse, New Jersey. It was one of the bloodiest battles of the war, and Virginia troops were heavily engaged. When it was all over, Edmund Dickinson, the young tradesman turned soldier who had been full of hope for the future only weeks before, lay dead on the field. The battle at Monmouth would prove to be the last major engagement of the Revolutionary War in the north.

In Williamsburg, a sort of quiet settled over the town for the rest of 1778, and minds could once again consider the foundations of a society based on freedom. The House of Delegates passed a law banning the slave trade and further suspended the payment of public salaries to the Anglican clergy. Inhabitants began to make postwar plans, think about boundary disputes with the other new states, and discuss the potential of the vast western lands that would be theirs once the Indians were dealt with.

In 1779 the harsh realities of the conflict hit Williamsburg. In January, the economy began to collapse as prices rose and speculation in supplies became rife. Thomas Nelson Jr., a major Yorktown merchant, returned to Williamsburg in February from having served in the Continental Congress in Philadelphia. He described the situation of the city and the nation as the most critical since the beginning of the war. The General Assembly continued to rely on drafts as the main means of supplying soldiers to the Continental army; every other means repeatedly failed. In February, George Rogers Clark virtually ended the war in the west by capturing Vincennes and Fort Sackville. The commander of the British and Indian forces in that region, Henry Hamilton, was brought to Williamsburg in chains and thrown into the already crowded jail. Thomas Jefferson, then only thirty-five years old, was elected governor in June. Virginia's paper currency was in the midst of a seemingly unstoppable and rapid depreciation; by the middle of the year, goods cost twenty times what they had cost the previous December.

And in May, the real war arrived in Virginia in the form of a major British invasion that took Portsmouth, only fifty miles and two days' march from Williamsburg, at the mouth of the James River. The British burned the supply depot at nearby Suffolk. They captured or

▲ Thomas Jefferson. The Colonial Williamsburg Foundation.

destroyed more than 130 ships, three thousand hogsheads of tobacco, and two million pounds' worth of supplies. They withdrew on May 24 with barely a shot fired against them.

The invasion was a shock to the community. It revealed the almost complete inability of the state to defend itself. The government issued a proclamation announcing "horrid ravages and depredations" committed by the British, "such as plundering and burning houses, killing and carrying away stock of all sorts, and exercising other abominable cruelties and barbarities." The consequences would change Williamsburg forever as the House of Delegates voted to move the capital to Richmond, effective April 1780.

The rest of the year was a flurry of activity, the sort of which Williamsburg had not witnessed in years. Jefferson and George Wythe introduced in the House of Delegates their report on revising Virginia's laws to make them more consistent with a republican society. It included proposals for coeducational public education, more equitable penalties for crimes, securing religious freedom, and abolishing slavery. The legislature set aside that project (and did not bring it up again until after the war) but did approve the confiscation and sale of loyalist property, including slaves, as a means of raising money for the state.

In July, a group of townsmen met to attempt to arrest the continuing collapse of the economy. Nothing they did worked, and by December the currency's value had shrunk so much that what had cost a single shilling at the beginning of 1779 cost forty shillings at the end of the year. The government cut back on spending in almost every category, including the military and naval forces. Heated disputes arose about fulfilling Virginia's commitments to supply troops and weapons to the Continental army as an increasing number of people began to think both were needed more at home.

Then word arrived that further unsettled Williamsburg society: The British army had issued the Phillipsburg Proclamation, which granted immediate freedom to any slave of a patriot who made it behind their lines. The news flew through communities of enslaved men and women across the Tidewater, giving them a new incentive to escape to the enemy.

As 1780 dawned, the government prepared to move to Richmond. The currency was by then virtually worthless, and Virginians relied more on bartering tobacco or other commodities for goods they needed. Another British army landed in an attempt to establish a permanent base of operations, to conduct raids up the rivers, energize loyalists, and thereby paralyze Virginia, but they were soon recalled and sent south to join a British army under Charles Cornwallis. Cornwallis's army was moving,

⋀ Enslaved girl. Depictions of enslaved African Americans are rare, particularly images that lack the distortions of caricature and stereotyping. The Colonial Williamsburg Foundation.

after capturing Savannah, northwards into South Carolina.

On April 7, 1780, eighty-one years of history came to an end in Williamsburg as the city ceased to be Virginia's capital. Taverns closed, the newspapers moved, and many inhabitants, especially tradesmen, shifted west. Another dose of reality hit the town a month later when word arrived that the British had taken Charleston, South Carolina, forcing the surrender of a large American army that included almost every Virginian still in Continental service.

In October the British renewed raids of the Virginia coastline. In November, the House of Delegates began to consider a proposal to increase enlistments by providing a slave to every recruit. James Madison was horrified when he learned of the measure. He suggested that it would be more effective to give freedom to slaves who were willing to fight for freedom. "It wd. certainly be more consonant to the principles of liberty," he wrote to a friend, "which ought never to be lost sight of in a contest for liberty." The measure eventually passed, although circumstances precluded it from being put into effect.

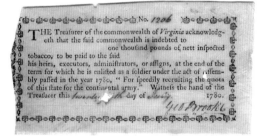

▲ Tobacco note from the Commonwealth of Virginia for one thousand pounds of tobacco. The Colonial Williamsburg Foundation.

Scarcities of all sorts challenged the commitment of the people of Williamsburg to the American cause. Lead for ammunition was so scarce that some militiamen stripped the covering off the cupola of the old Capitol. Governor Jefferson was empowered by the legislature to obtain clothing and blankets for troops by seizing them from merchants, even permitting procurement officers to "break open, in the day time" any place where goods are supposed to be kept. One Virginian, who used the pen name of Timothy Standfast, observed, "Difficulties at length grew upon us, and we have learned to forget our duty." He then issued a plea: "For God's sake, my countrymen, rouse from your lethargy, look into consequences, and return to your pristine vigor." It was a timely call to action because, on the same day it was printed, December 30, a large army made up of 1,600 British regulars and loyalists, including many Virginians, landed on Virginia's shore. They

were under the command of the former American hero Benedict Arnold.

Arnold moved quickly up the James River. More than any before, this year was one of crisis in Williamsburg. One visitor observed that "on my arrival there, I found the Town in confusion, and the inhabitants alarmed by the expectation of an immediate engagement." The traitor to the patriot cause, and one of the best field commanders the Americans had had, dealt easily with the slight militia opposition he encountered. Arnold took Richmond on January 5, forcing the government to flee.

As Arnold destroyed supplies and warehouses up and down the river, hundreds of loyalists and slaves in search of their freedom flocked to his army. The Virginia militia was in such a sorry state that one observer reported in January that "they had much better be dismissed altogether; they are not able to do any thing in the field." James Innes, attempting to rally troops in Williamsburg, informed Jefferson a few weeks later that the militia in Williamsburg "are lousy dirty and ragged, and from those Circumstances becoming every day more sickly." He feared mutiny if their concerns were not soon addressed. The Reverend James Madison retained hope that "Virginia still contains Citizens who are willing to risque all in the Cause."

The situation went from bad to worse. Arnold remained unopposed. A French fleet sent to block his reinforcement by sea was defeated by a British naval squadron in the Battle of Cape Henry on March 16, which kept the Chesapeake Bay firmly under the enemy's control. Washington, in command of the Continental army outside New York City, understood the seriousness of the situation and dispatched the marquis de Lafayette with 1,200 Continental soldiers to try to trap Arnold. He arrived in Williamsburg at the end of March only to learn that thousands more British troops had landed under Major General William Phillips, who took over command from Arnold. The British continued to make devastating raids from their Portsmouth base, which Lafayette could do little to prevent. Washington lamented to a friend that "we are at the end of our tether, and that now or never our deliverance must come."

There would be no immediate deliverance for Williamsburg. On April 20, 1781, the British flag flew once again as Phillips and Arnold occupied the city for several days. Arnold's time in Williamsburg provided an opportunity for some, such as former printer William Hunter Jr. Hunter began to spy for the enemy and probably informed Arnold of the location of the Chickahominy navy yard, Virginia's primary naval base, situated just a few miles from Williamsburg. Arnold promptly destroyed the base.

Phillips and Arnold left the city after a few days, but news was hard on their heels that Cornwallis, with one of the largest British armies in America, was on his way to recover all of Virginia for the king. Jefferson and other Virginians became ever more nervous about the tenuous commitment of their countrymen, so the governor ordered Innes to arrest suspected loyalists in and around Williamsburg. On May 2, Jefferson wrote, "It is indispensably necessary to punish [loyalists] for their Crimes by way of Example to others, or to disable from doing Mischief."

Just a few weeks later, on May 20, Cornwallis arrived and joined Arnold's forces at Petersburg, near Richmond (Phillips had died

> Charles, 1st Marquis Cornwallis. The Colonial Williamsburg Foundation.

from an illness a short time before). Cornwallis had about seven thousand men, a number that grew every day with Virginia loyalists who joined him. Washington tried to help Lafayette by sending another eight hundred Continentals under "Mad Anthony" Wayne, but Lafayette knew that his small numbers could do very little against Cornwallis. And Washington had no intention of sending more troops to Virginia because what he wanted was a combined French and American attack on the main British army in New York. Cornwallis kept up targeted raids, such as one on June 4 that forced Governor Jefferson and most of the Virginia General Assembly to flee Charlottesville, where the government had been meeting, to avoid being captured by British and loyalist cavalry. Lafayette complained that "government in this state has no energy, and laws have no force." Some Virginians drafted petitions that lamented the Revolution and asked for reconciliation with Great Britain.

Cornwallis was intent on carrying out operations in the interior of Virginia but then changed his mind and began to chase Lafayette's much smaller force around the area between Richmond and Williamsburg. Lafayette stayed just out of his reach, causing Cornwallis to deplete his supplies. Cornwallis also became bogged down with more than a thousand loyalist refugees and former slaves, including a dozen or so who had belonged to Jefferson. Cornwallis's superior, Sir Henry Clinton in New York, ordered Cornwallis to stop following Lafayette, return to the coast, establish a base, and send part of his force to New York, where Clinton was waiting for Washington's attack.

Cornwallis retreated down the Virginia Peninsula, arriving in Williamsburg on June 25. He had hoped to find supplies here for his troops and refugees, but what he found instead were more people who were willing to join him. Cornwallis's army remained in Williamsburg until July 4. When he departed, his army left behind smallpox and, according to one witness, St. George Tucker, a plague of flies: "It is impossible to eat, drink Sleep write, sit still, or even walk about in peace from their confounded Stings." Cornwallis took with him many loyalists and even more former slaves, including perhaps a third of those who had once belonged to Peyton Randolph. The town was in a desolate state. When James Innes arrived with militia a few weeks later, he reported it was a "miserable place—where there is not one necessary supply to be procured."

▲ St. George Tucker. The Colonial Williamsburg Foundation.

After a sharp fight at Green Spring, near Jamestown at the crossing of the James River, Cornwallis marched his troops to Portsmouth but then chose to move his base to Yorktown, less than a day's march from Williamsburg. Cornwallis thought Yorktown was more defensible. He arrived on August 2. Lafayette and Wayne took up a position just outside of Williamsburg to make sure that the British remained at their new Yorktown base.

Lafayette, sensing an opportunity that might never come again, pressed Washington to act in Virginia rather than New York: "The sooner we disturb him, the better," wrote the marquis to his friend and commander. Washington remained intent on attacking Clinton in New York, but the French commander, the comte de Rochambeau, was not keen on that plan, having a very low opinion of the American forces. In the end it was not Washington, Rochambeau, Clinton, Cornwallis, or Lafayette who decided what would come next. It was Admiral François de Grasse, who commanded a major French fleet in the West Indies. He informed Washington and Rochambeau that he would come to their aid, but he was not interested in helping them attack New York. Instead, he intended to go to Virginia, and, moreover, he would stay in America only until October 15. Washington had exactly two months to win the war in Virginia or else his French allies would be gone.

What happened next was improbable at best. Washington orchestrated the rapid movement of thousands of his troops almost four hundred miles from New York to Williamsburg. He had to keep the operation secret from Clinton long enough to prevent him from sending reinforcements to Cornwallis, determine how the French

▲ George Washington. The Colonial Williamsburg Foundation.

and Americans would actually work together on the field of battle, and develop an effective plan for forcing Cornwallis to surrender. And he had to do it all in eight weeks.

Again, the decisive role was played by the French navy. A squadron in Newport, Rhode Island, set out to join de Grasse, who arrived in the Chesapeake on August 30. Three thousand French troops, according to Lafayette, "landed with amazing celerity" and were immediately embraced by the people in Williamsburg both for their manners and their money. De Grasse's fleet of twenty-four ships then disappeared. No one in Williamsburg knew where they had gone. But de Grasse had departed to engage a British fleet, sent to sweep the French out of the bay. The result was the Battle of the Capes, fought on September 5, which de Grasse won. His win secured control of the sea and sealed off Virginia from any British reinforcement or any possibility of escape for Cornwallis.

On September 14, at about four o'clock in the afternoon, Washington himself arrived in Williamsburg. St. George Tucker reported that "Men Women & Children seem'd to vie with each other in demonstrations of Joy, and eagerness to see their beloved Countryman." The combined French and American forces moved out from Williamsburg on September 28, forcing Cornwallis to abandon his forward positions. Washington knew that Cornwallis was in a bad situation because he had intercepted a letter from Cornwallis to Clinton in which Cornwallis admitted to having only a few weeks' worth of supplies left after killing all of his horses and turning out all "useless mouths," which included hundreds of former slaves (although many more remained with Cornwallis).

▲ Washington and Lafayette at the Battle of Yorktown. The Colonial Williamsburg Foundation.

By October 9, when French heavy artillery opened up on Cornwallis, from fairly close range, Clinton had realized what was happening and took action. He rushed to get to Virginia with more troops and a bigger fleet. But a failed attempt by Cornwallis to escape over the York River to Gloucester so that he could march northward, away from Washington's forces, destroyed the last of Cornwallis's resolve. On October 17, the very day that Clinton set sail from New York, Cornwallis entered into surrender negotiations. Two days later, on October 19, it was all over. Cornwallis laid down his arms,

▲ The surrender of Cornwallis at Yorktown. The Colonial Williamsburg Foundation.

and the people of the Revolutionary community turned out to witness the event. One eyewitness reported that "the concourse of spectators from the country was prodigious, in point of numbers was probably equal to the military, but universal silence and order prevailed." The marquis de Lafayette informed the French government that "the play is over . . . the fifth act has just ended."

As far as active campaigning was concerned, that was the end of the Revolutionary War, although the British remained in possession of New York until 1783, when they evacuated with more than eight hundred former Virginia slaves. In London in February 1782, Parliament called for a halt to all offensive operations in America and voted to open peace talks with American representatives.

In the months after the surrender, the French further endeared themselves to the inhabitants of Williamsburg, throwing parties and holding parades that must have made it seem a bit like the Williamsburg of old. But, with the departure of the French on July 1, 1782, the town became part of an ever-receding past. The collapse of the tobacco economy, with the end of British protection of the trade and a dedicated market of consumers, put a full stop to its former wealth. With a small population, a few taverns, and the college, it seemed to many subsequent visitors a quaint place, with only traces of its former vigor and importance.

THE RESTORATION

After the capital moved to Richmond, Williamsburg did not die as Jamestown had. It continued to be a county seat, and it continued to house the College of William and Mary and the Public Hospital for individuals with mental disorders. Eighteenth-century buildings were repaired, renovated, and continued in use into the twentieth century.

In the early years of the twentieth century, the Reverend W. A. R. Goodwin, rector of Bruton Parish Church, envisioned restoring Virginia's colonial and Revolutionary capital to its former glory. "It has been said that the best way to look at history is through windows," Goodwin said. "There are windows here, and [there] were others which might be restored, through which unparalleled vistas open into the storied history of the nation's past."

Goodwin's efforts to enlist support for his vision initially met with little success. Then, in 1926, he persuaded John D. Rockefeller Jr., heir to the Standard Oil fortune, to tour Williamsburg. Rockefeller agreed to fund the project on one condition—that it would encompass the

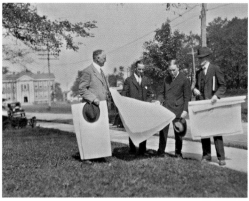

▲ Examining plans on the front lawn of the George Wythe House are (left to right) W. A. R. Goodwin, engineer Robert Trimble, John D. Rockefeller Jr., and Arthur Shurcliff, Colonial Williamsburg's first landscape architect.

entire town. The renaissance of the colonial capital began with the purchase of the Ludwell-Paradise House in 1926. The Raleigh Tavern opened as the first exhibition building in September 1932.

Rockefeller and Goodwin planned more than the mere preservation of historic buildings and

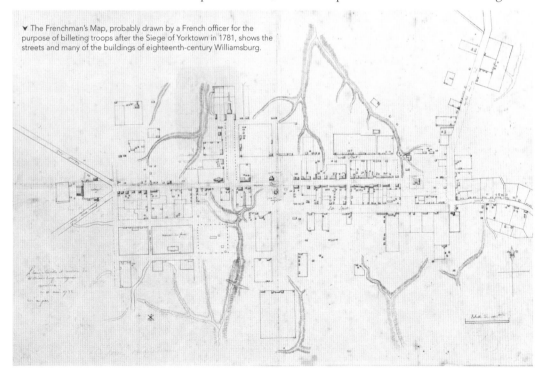

▼ The Frenchman's Map, probably drawn by a French officer for the purpose of billeting troops after the Siege of Yorktown in 1781, shows the streets and many of the buildings of eighteenth-century Williamsburg.

settings. They intended to re-create and interpret life in the capital.

Research focused on period maps, deeds, inventories, plans, contemporary drawings, and accounts of the capital. Early photographs documenting the exterior appearances of many of the historic buildings enhanced the restoration efforts.

Perhaps the most important find was an engraved copperplate discovered in 1929 in the Bodleian Library at Oxford University. It was the only known eighteenth-century image of the colonial capital's principal buildings, and it became the basis for the restoration of what is today known as the Wren Building and the reconstruction of the Governor's Palace and the Capitol. Without the Bodleian Plate, said Rockefeller, "we would have been acting in the dark; with it, we have gone forward

▲ The top row of the Bodleian Plate shows the three original buildings of the College of William and Mary. The middle row has renderings of the Capitol and the Governor's Palace. The bottom row (not shown) depicts images of flora, fauna, and Native Americans.

with absolute certainty and conviction." The engraved copperplate is on display in the Bassett Hall reception building.

Archaeological research was also crucial. Exploratory cross trenching unearthed the remains of the Governor's Palace in 1930, including foundation walls, steps, doorways, and stone pavings in the cellar. Additional artifacts discovered there offered guidance for faithfully reconstructing paneling, the hall's

▼ Duke of Gloucester Street around 1928.

marble floor, and other features. Archaeologists also recovered fragments of brick, stone steps, fireplace tiles, hinges, shutter fasteners, locks, and keys. These discoveries and the Bodleian Plate guided the reconstruction of the Governor's Palace on its original eighteenth-century foundations.

⌃ Excavation of the Governor's Palace basement and foundations.

Research revealed not only the painstaking craftsmanship of colonial designers and builders but also a new uniquely American adaptation of classical architectural traditions. Research also brought into focus the vibrant cultures, lifestyles, and thoughts of the residents of Williamsburg, which reflected the Age of Enlightenment as well as the Revolutionary concepts of self-expression, self-determination, and individualism that led to the birth of a new nation with a character all its own.

The Rockefellers' interests were not limited to American history. Their concern for African American education led them to contribute also to the building of Bruton Heights School, which opened just outside Williamsburg's Historic Area in 1940 and which served as not only a school but also a community center. By the mid-1950s, Bruton Heights School had about

⌃ Bruton Heights School graduates outside the school in the 1950s.

one thousand students. More than a decade after the Supreme Court's decision in *Brown v. Board of Education*, the school was integrated. In the late 1980s, it was marked for demolition, but a restoration project saved the building. It reopened in 1997 as part of Colonial Williamsburg's Bruton Heights School Education Center. The former school now houses offices and studios for, among others, Colonial Williamsburg's educational outreach initiatives. Across the courtyard are the Foundation's library and state-of-the art facilities for its curators and conservators.

The restoration of Williamsburg is an ongoing process with changes to many builings and entirely new reconstructions continuing into the twenty-first century. The building that once housed Charlton's Coffeehouse and that stood until about 1889 was reconstructed in 2009. The reconstruction of the Public Armoury, based on extensive archaeological and architectural research, was completed in 2013. The most recent reconstruction is of the Market House.

It is fitting that the restoration continues because so, too, does the experiment in democracy that began here. This was—and is—the Revolutionary City.

The Young FOUNDERS

Without the benefit of photography, it is difficult for us to see many of America's founders as they saw each other: as young men unaccustomed to leadership but inspired by Enlightenment ideas. George Washington, who is often portrayed with his familiar powdered white hair, seems, in historical perspective, much older than forty-three—his age when he assumed command of the Continental army in 1775. Thomas Jefferson was thirty-two when he wrote the Declaration of Independence, and Patrick Henry had just turned forty when he became the first governor of an independent Virginia. But they were elder statesmen compared to the men who drove much of the Revolution in Williamsburg. Chief among them were James Innes, James Madison, James Monroe, and Edmund Randolph, all of whom were in their twenties when they played pivotal roles.

JAMES INNES (1754–1798) was twenty-one years old in 1775 when he incited his militia company and townspeople to storm the Governor's Palace and demand the return of the gunpowder Dunmore had seized. Innes was the son of an Episcopal minister and grew up on a small, isolated farm several days' ride north of Williamsburg. In 1770, he entered the College of William and Mary. After graduating in 1773, he remained there as the head usher of the grammar school and likely began to study law, perhaps under George Wythe. In the spring of 1775, he became a leader of the Williamsburg volunteer company, a militia unit made up partly of students from the college. He also helped raise and train a company of artillery and was appointed a major in a Virginia regiment. As the war progressed, Innes joined the Continental army as a lieutenant colonel in time to serve under Washington in the Battle of Trenton and subsequent campaigns in New Jersey and Pennsylvania, where he saw some of the most brutal combat of the war, including the Battle of Brandywine. Innes was back in Williamsburg on recruiting duty in January 1778, having just left Valley Forge, but he never returned to the army. He resigned in June and married Elizabeth Cocke of Williamsburg. Later that year he was appointed Virginia's commissioner of the navy. In 1779 he gave up the navy post to take a seat in the House of Delegates. That summer he was appointed to the Board of War and worked to devise measures to halt the collapse of the economy. Throughout 1781, from the arrival of Benedict Arnold to the surrender of Cornwallis, Innes was tireless in his command of militia units to defend Virginia. After the war, he moved to Richmond, where he practiced law and was a member of the Virginia Convention of 1788 that met to ratify the U.S. Constitution, which he supported with his customary eloquence and passion. He succeeded his friend Edmund Randolph as attorney general of Virginia and might have followed Randolph as attorney general of the United States had not poor health led him to decline Washington's offer.

JAMES MADISON (1751–1836), fresh from  graduating from the College of New Jersey (now Princeton University), had just turned twenty-five when he entered the business of Revolutionary politics, which would become his life's work. Born on his mother's family's plantation in the Northern Neck of Virginia, his own family lived on a smaller farm in Orange County, far to the west of Williamsburg. As a college student under the renowned Reverend John Witherspoon, Madison gained an intense appreciation for religious diversity. He appreciated it even more as a witness to the persecution of Baptists near his home. As a member of the Fifth Virginia Convention in 1776, he won the inclusion of religious freedom in the Virginia Declaration of Rights and helped write the first Virginia Constitution. He was later a member of the House of Delegates before he rose to a seat on the executive council in 1779, after which he was appointed to the Continental Congress. That ended his association with Williamsburg. After the war, Madison returned to the House of Delegates, by then in Richmond, where he worked to pass many reforms introduced by his dear friend Thomas Jefferson, including the Virginia Statute for Religious Freedom. He wrote much of the U.S. Constitution and many of the Federalist Papers, which helped ensure the Constitution's acceptance by the key states. He personally took charge of combating Patrick Henry in the Virginia ratifying convention of 1788 to secure the Constitution's success. Under the new government, Madison narrowly defeated James Monroe for a seat in the first federal Congress, where he wrote and worked for the adoption of the Bill of Rights, the first ten amendments to the Constitution. Jefferson appointed him secretary of state in 1801, and he was elected president of the United States in 1808. He served two terms, aided by his popular wife, Dolley, and led the United States during the War of 1812. He then retired to his home, Montpelier, in Orange County, where he died on June 28, 1836.

JAMES MONROE (1758–1831) was the youngest of the founders, only a  teenager when the Revolution began. Born into a small-to-middling planter family in Westmoreland County, Virginia, Monroe arrived in Williamsburg in 1774 as a student at the College of William and Mary. Monroe was caught up in the Revolutionary fervor that gripped the community as a member of his friend James Innes's militia company. He joined with other young men to seize more than 230 guns and 300 swords that Dunmore left behind in the Palace in the summer of 1776. Monroe remained in Williamsburg training as an officer in the Third Virginia Regiment until it left to join the Continental army in August 1776. One of only two American officers wounded at the Battle of Trenton, he continued to serve through the bloody campaigns in Pennsylvania and New Jersey as a staff officer but resigned his Continental commission in 1779 to return to Williamsburg. The legislature made him a lieutenant colonel of Virginia forces and gave him temporary command of the troops in the capital city, but for any permanent command he had to raise the troops on his own. He cajoled almost any male of age who crossed his path in Williamsburg and the surrounding area, but he found it an impossible task. Consequently, Monroe tried to serve his country in Williamsburg as part of the State Garrison Regiment. In 1780, he began to study law under Thomas Jefferson and might have attended several of George Wythe's first lectures. In 1781, when the war came to Virginia in earnest, Monroe volunteered to serve on the staff of the marquis de Lafayette, who used him to carry dispatches. Like his fellow young patriots, Monroe turned to politics after the war, serving in the House of Delegates, the executive council, and the Continental Congress while practicing law in Fredericksburg, Virginia. Stung somewhat by his defeat at the hands of Madison for a seat in the first Congress, Monroe made up for that by being appointed to the U.S. Senate from Virginia and then, near the end of Washington's administration, U.S. minister to France. A major difference of opinion with Washington over a new treaty with Great Britain led to Monroe's recall, but he was shortly thereafter elected governor of Virginia. A string of appointments followed, making Monroe a truly unusual figure in American political history for their sheer number and scope: minister to negotiate the Louisiana Purchase, U.S. ambassador to Great Britain, secretary of state and then secretary of war under President Madison. He succeeded Madison as president in 1816. He served two terms and became known as the "last cocked hat" for his insistence on wearing the same style of clothing that had been popular in Williamsburg during the Revolution. He died in New York City on July 4, 1831.

EDMUND RANDOLPH (1753–1813) was, of

the young founders in Williamsburg, the one with the closest ties to the city. Born and raised in Williamsburg, the son of Virginia's most famous loyalist, the nephew of one of its most prominent patriots, and a graduate of the College of William and Mary, Randolph was indeed the "child of the revolution" he would later proclaim himself to be. Randolph's father begged him to reconsider in the summer of 1775 when he went off to join George Washington's staff: "For Gods Sake," John Randolph wrote, "return to your Family & indeed to yourself." But Randolph followed his heart to Washington's headquarters in Massachusetts just as his family left for London never to return. He was not there long. His uncle Peyton's death soon required him to return to Williamsburg to assist his aunt Betty and attend to the estate. He was appointed Virginia's first attorney general at the creation of the new government in the summer of 1776 and then married Elizabeth Nicholas. He also served as mayor of Williamsburg in 1777, clerk of the House of Delegates in 1778, and a member of the Continental Congress in 1779 and 1781. George Washington appointed him the first attorney general of the United States.

Lydia BROADNAX

An enslaved and later free woman in the household of George Wythe, Lydia Broadnax (?–ca. 1827) may first have appeared in the documentary record on January 24, 1778, when Martha Jefferson noted that she "Gave Mrs. Wythe's cook" eighteen shillings. Broadnax's name appeared again on the personal property tax lists of 1783, 1784, and 1786.

Like other enslaved people, Broadnax had opportunities to take her freedom during the Revolution, especially during the British occupations in 1781. She chose to remain with the Wythes. Others took a different path; almost a third of the enslaved men and women at the Randolph house, for example, were listed in 1782 as "gone to the enemy." Many who joined the British died of smallpox while others were returned to the owners.

After the war, Wythe freed Broadnax. The 1787 deed of emancipation noted she was over forty-five at the time. Broadnax remained in his household, probably one of two free blacks living at the Wythe property between 1789 and 1791. She moved to Richmond with Wythe in 1791.

By 1791, she owned fifty dollars' worth of property. By 1799, she was taking in boarders and had adopted the surname Broadnax, a name associated with one of the Williamsburg area's prominent seventeenth- and eighteenth-century families.

Wythe died in 1806. He may have been murdered by his nephew George Wythe Sweeney, but Broadnax was unable to testify at Sweeney's trial because she was a woman of color.

Also in 1806, Broadnax received a letter from Thomas Jefferson. He wanted to borrow a portrait of Wythe to make a copy. Broadnax offered the original to Jefferson in return for a copy. She also asked Jefferson for financial help because of "my distressed situation": her eyesight was failing, perhaps, she thought, an effect of the same poison that killed Wythe. Jefferson sent her fifty dollars to pay for glasses.

In 1810 the U.S. census listed Lydia Broadnax as the head of a household of six free and two enslaved persons. Ten years later, the census reported she was the head of a household with three free women. She earned money by taking in boarders.

The SITES

CAPITOL

On the eastern end of Duke of Gloucester Street stands the Capitol, which dominates a collection of government buildings that includes the Secretary's Office and the Public Gaol. For most of the eighteenth century, the Capitol was the center of political life in Virginia. As the home of elected assemblies and appointed councils, it witnessed some of the most important and dramatic moments in American history. The colonial House of Burgesses had met regularly at the site since at least 1705, earning a reputation as staunchly loyal and firmly moderate. The events of the American Revolution changed all that. In May 1765, the Capitol's walls rang with the sound of Patrick Henry's voice. He declared the Stamp Act an attempt to "destroy British as well as American Freedom." Some labeled him a traitor to king and country. Nine years later, the House of Burgesses adopted a resolution calling on its members to observe a day of fasting, humiliation, and prayer in support of Boston, the port of which had just been closed by the British Parliament as punishment for the Boston Tea Party. Two days later, Virginia's royal governor, the Earl of Dunmore, dissolved the House of Burgesses to stop it from passing any other measure that "could tend only to inflame the whole country." Dunmore's decision brought Virginia's government to a near halt until the spring of 1776 when an elected convention, many of whose members had once been burgesses, met to form a new, independent government and define the principles on which it should be based.

When you enter the Capitol, you might find yourself in the midst of a seminal historical moment. One occurred on June 12, 1776, only a few weeks after the convention adopted a resolution for independence from Great Britain. On that day, they considered the final vote on a document unlike any before written—a declaration of rights that clearly articulated "the basis and foundation of government." Written by George Mason, and debated by the likes of Patrick Henry and James Madison, this was a truly revolutionary document. It pronounced that "all men are by nature equally free and independent" and that the best government is that which is capable of producing the greatest degree of happiness and safety for its people. Yet even in that pursuit of such high ideals, the members of the convention argued over the scope of human liberty and who should enjoy the privileges given to mankind by nature. In one of the most vigorous disputes over the declaration, the twenty-five-year-old James Madison, who would later take on the fight for the Constitution and the Bill of Rights, succeeded in replacing religious toleration with a broader freedom of religion. In the end, the Virginia Declaration of Rights was adopted that day. It influenced the Declaration of Independence, which was written soon after, and in 1789 the Bill of Rights and the French Declaration of the Rights of Man.

Another moment you might encounter happened almost exactly three years later, on June 18, 1779, when the Virginia state legislature was presented with the results of one of the

most extraordinary projects in the history of the American Enlightenment. That morning a committee led by Thomas Jefferson and George Wythe introduced a comprehensive set of 126 new laws designed to transform the Declaration of Rights' ideals into reality. It included proposals to ensure religious freedom, establish public education, create a fair criminal justice system, and abolish slavery. Many delegates were not interested in changing their society either so quickly or so dramatically and opposed the measures. It was the toughest possible test of the commitment of patriots to their Revolutionary principles. However, the imperatives of war intervened. A recent British invasion highlighted Virginia's unpreparedness to meet an enemy threat, so the project was set aside. Of all the proposed republican measures, only a revised Statute for Religious Freedom made it into law, and not until 1786.

▲ Virtual model of Williamsburg's second Capitol, which, while similar in layout to the first Capitol, was visually distinct from its predecessor because of the portico on the west end and the squaring off of the rounded sides of the building.

The building itself has an H-shaped plan, a design that reflects the composition of Virginia's colonial government. The Council and the House of Burgesses sat on opposite sides of the building, with a committee room on the second floor bridging the two halves. The structure you see today represents the first Capitol built in Williamsburg, between 1701 and 1705, and reconstructed during the 1930s. This first Capitol was destroyed by fire in 1747. The second Capitol constructed on the site, completed in the early 1750s, had essentially the same shape. The current building is furnished to reflect the last days of the colonial period and includes the original chair of the Speaker of the House of Burgesses (which became the House of Delegates). It also includes symbols of royal authority and portraits of British monarchs, several of which, such as the portrait of Queen Anne that hangs in the General Court chamber, remained in place throughout the Revolution. The most prominent absence is a large statue of the Baron

de Botetourt, a popular royal governor. You can see a replica of it today standing in front of the College of William and Mary; the original is in the Botetourt Gallery of the college's Swem Library. During the Revolution, the statue dominated the center of the piazza.

PUBLIC GAOL AND SECRETARY'S OFFICE

Next to the Capitol are two buildings that reflect much different aspects of official life in eighteenth-century Virginia—the Public Gaol (the eighteenth-century spelling of "jail") and the Secretary's Office (previously known as the Public Records Office). Closest to the Capitol, the Secretary's Office, looking much as it did during the Revolution, is located in an area known during the colonial period as "the Exchange" because merchants regularly gathered here to share news and negotiate the exchange rate between the British pound sterling and Virginia currency. One of Colonial Williamsburg's original buildings, it was built in 1748 to protect the colony's official papers after fire destroyed the Capitol. Concerned about the safety of the papers in the wake of this disaster, Virginia's Secretary Thomas Nelson proposed a structure for the preservation of the public records. Before that time, the records of the colony did not have an official home;

they were stored in the Capitol and at the Secretary's house. The fiery destruction of the Capitol gave impetus to a push for a separate, secure building to house the colony's important documents. (This concept of a fireproof storage facility for important documents was ahead of its time; similar archives would not come into fashion elsewhere until the end of the eighteenth century.)

Just down the hill from the Capitol and Secretary's Office is the Public Gaol, which is connected to the home of its keeper. Before the Revolution, the gaol was used primarily to house criminal defendants awaiting trial, but it occasionally held debtors (in a separate building) and, until the Public Hospital was constructed in 1773, those considered mentally ill. Perhaps its most infamous prisoners were several pirates who had served under Blackbeard and were captured with him in 1718. It was uncommon for any gaol in the eighteenth-century British world to hold prisoners for long periods of time. The prevailing theory of criminal justice focused on swift punishment after sentencing, which rarely consisted of extended confinement (convicted felons were frequently executed by hanging at the gallows on Capitol Landing Road, one mile north of Williamsburg).

In the Gaol you will encounter the ways in which the American Revolution fundamentally changed the role of the gaol and its keeper, Peter Pelham. From almost the beginning of the conflict in 1775 until the capital moved in 1780, the gaol's cells were almost constantly filled with men and women from a variety of backgrounds, from criminals to spies. They waited months, even more than a year, for some determination of their fate. For instance, on January 17, 1776, the gaol housed eighty-five prisoners, almost entirely prisoners of war, suspected loyalists, and runaway slaves, a number of whom were still there in November awaiting trial. However, for some, the gaol also proved surprisingly easy to escape. In 1777, Pelham, who was also the organist at Bruton Parish Church, was investigated by the Virginia Assembly for negligence and possible treason, despite the fact that three of Pelham's

sons served in the Continental army. The investigation stemmed from the seeming ease with which prisoners departed from his custody. Pelham was a popular man in the community; one neighbor testified that "he never saw him disguised with liquor in his own house, though sometimes, as other men, cheerful when abroad and in company." He was cleared of any wrongdoing.

A number of prisoners noted Pelham's kindness towards them. Among these was Williamsburg's infamous Revolutionary War prisoner Henry Hamilton, the British lieutenant governor at Detroit. Hamilton was known as the "Hair-Buyer General" because it was alleged that he offered cash rewards to Indian tribes in the west in return for patriot scalps. Captured in early 1779 by George Rogers Clark, acting under orders from the Virginia government, Hamilton arrived at the gaol in June and was soon placed in irons for, as Governor Thomas Jefferson wrote, inciting Indians to the "indiscriminate murther of men, Women and children." The harsh treatment generated a debate over the treatment of prisoners of war, which resulted in his being released from chains in September at the urging of George Washington. Hamilton remained incarcerated until October 1780 and later recollected the ways in which Pelham eased the experience, despite the cramped and uncomfortable conditions.

Although many bricks were removed by Union soldiers during the Civil War, what was left remained in use as a jail until 1910.

CHARLTON'S COFFEEHOUSE

Charlton's Coffeehouse is located strategically near the Capitol, in the busiest part of the Revolutionary City. Conspicuous for its signpost of a hand holding a coffeepot, the Coffeehouse represents one of the most significant institutions of the eighteenth century. As central places for exchanging the latest political, economic, and social information, coffeehouses connected the inhabitants of Williamsburg to cities around the Atlantic world, from London and Paris to Boston and Philadelphia. A coffeehouse was usually the first stop of visitors to Williamsburg. Here they would pick up mail, often delivered by transatlantic ships, and get the most recent news and gossip.

Eighteenth-century Williamsburg does not seem ever to have been without at least one coffeehouse, almost always found close to the Capitol. The first evidence we have of a coffeehouse in town was 1709, only a decade after Williamsburg was established. It appears to have frequently shifted locations. By 1751, it was called the English Coffee House and situated at what is now Shields Tavern. Richard Charlton opened a coffeehouse across the street, on the current site, in the 1760s.

On October 30, 1765, Charlton's was the scene of a passionate—and dangerous—protest against the Stamp Act. Dozens of inhabitants threatened the life of a fellow Virginian, George Mercer, who had been selected to act as an agent to distribute the stamps for the colony. It took the personal intervention of the popular lieutenant governor Francis Fauquier (who had been seated on the porch of the coffeehouse) to avoid violence. By 1767, however, Charlton had turned his business into a tavern, and the coffeehouse likely moved next door to Edinburgh Castle, where it remained through much of the Revolution.

To enter Charlton's is to enter the historical moment of the coffeehouse, which played

a critical role in circulating revolutionary Enlightenment ideas and generating discussion about them. You will meet the people who frequented the coffeehouse, learn about the business transacted there, and perhaps enter into your own revolutionary debate. What's more, you will have the chance to sample authentic eighteenth-century coffee, chocolate, or tea.

RALEIGH TAVERN

In the heart of the commercial district of the Revolutionary City, conveniently near the Capitol, is the Raleigh Tavern, the scene of several of the most important moments in American history. A meeting place for both travelers and townspeople since about 1717, the Raleigh was a favorite spot of dining and merriment for the likes of George Washington and Thomas Jefferson. The Apollo Room—one of the largest indoor spaces in Williamsburg—and the smaller Daphne Room were frequent sites of concerts, meetings, and subscription balls. Here took place a celebration in 1751 of the visit of a large delegation of Cherokee Indians and, on a more personal level, a dance in 1760 during which the future Rebecca Ambler spurned the marriage proposal of a young Jefferson. On its grand front porch, with the head of Sir Walter Raleigh looking down from on top of the main entrance, were held less sanguine events, such as the frequent auctions of enslaved men and women. One visitor recalled that, at the Raleigh, "more Business has been transacted than on the Exchange of London."

^ Recent research uncovered evidence of the Raleigh Tavern's original front porch, depicted in this virtual rendering but not present on the reconstructed building today.

As political tensions grew in the 1760s and 1770s, politics overtook entertainment as the central preoccupation of those who entered the Raleigh. The Raleigh earned a reputation as an unofficial headquarters for the radical sort of Virginians who were driving the movement for independence. Patriots led by men such as Jefferson and Patrick Henry regularly met at the Raleigh to decide how to respond to offenses committed by the British government against American rights. Here, in 1773, men conceived the first plan to properly unite the American colonies through committees of correspondence. Here, a year later, patriot leaders adopted a nonimportation agreement against British goods and called for a continental congress. During the Revolution, the Raleigh's owner, James Southall, occasionally rented out his rooms to the state of Virginia as a barrack for officers.

The Raleigh was the backdrop for other memorable scenes of life in wartime Williamsburg.

In 1776, officers who had served under Patrick Henry saluted him at a dinner to lament his resignation from command of the First Virginia Regiment. Later that year, students of the College of William and Mary met here to establish the Phi Beta Kappa honor society. In 1779, it was the scene of one of the first public celebrations anywhere of George Washington's birthday. Several enthusiastic Continental army veterans, led by James Innes, attempted to mark the occasion by firing cannons down the length of Duke of Gloucester Street. Four years later, on May 1, 1783, the Raleigh marked the end of the Revolutionary War by hosting a massive celebration of the peace treaty that granted American independence.

Southall owned the Raleigh from 1771 until his death in 1801. The building continued to be a center for Williamsburg culture well into the nineteenth century. In 1824, a banquet was held in the Apollo Room for the marquis de Lafayette during his tour of America. Besides Lafayette, Chief Justice John Marshall and Secretary of War John C. Calhoun were present. Benson Lossing, in his attempt to capture what remained in America of the Revolutionary era in the 1840s for his *Pictorial Field-Book of the Revolution*, made it a point to sketch the Apollo Room and wrote that it was "hallowed by so

^ Apollo Room, possibly original sketch for Benson Lossing's *Pictorial Field-Book of the Revolution*, ca. 1835. The Colonial Williamsburg Foundation.

many associations connected with our war for independence."

Still in use in 1859, the Raleigh burned to the ground shortly after the last recorded event held there: a banquet for alumni of the College of William and Mary that included John Tyler, former president of the United States.

WETHERBURN'S TAVERN

Wetherburn's Tavern is one of Williamsburg's original buildings, carefully restored thanks in part to a detailed inventory of Henry Wetherburn's personal property, dated just a month after his death in 1760. This document and extensive archaeological research were used to refurnish his tavern with appropriate period objects.

JAMES ANDERSON'S BLACKSMITH SHOP AND PUBLIC ARMOURY

On this site during the Revolutionary War, blacksmith James Anderson operated a public armory for the Commonwealth of Virginia. By 1765 Anderson was one of Williamsburg's most successful blacksmiths and was appointed armorer to the magazine at the age of twenty-five. He served the colony of Virginia in that capacity until 1775 when the Committee of Safety and later the Commonwealth of Virginia contracted him to serve as an armorer maintaining weapons owned by the state. He was public armorer for Virginia until the war ended in 1783.

Anderson owned the southern half of the neighboring lot to the east (now called the Dr. Barraud property), lived in the house on the corner of Francis and Botetourt Streets, and worked in his blacksmith shop behind that house. In 1770 he purchased the James Anderson House property and rented the house and kitchen to Christiana Campbell, who operated a tavern on the site. In 1775, as the Revolutionary War began and demand for an armorer's work increased, Anderson evicted the tenants and expanded his operations onto this lot. By 1780 when the capital moved to Richmond, the armory complex had grown into the largest and most diverse industrial site in Williamsburg.

The armory consisted of blacksmith and gunsmith shops, a tin shop, facilities for restocking muskets and casting lead bullets, and a kitchen with a paid cook who prepared food for the workmen. Specialized workmen repaired muskets, manufactured nails, and shod

horses. They made bits, spurs, and stirrups for cavalry; files to polish and finish metalwork; and hardware to mount artillery on carriages and to build ships, wagons, barracks for soldiers, and hospitals for the sick and wounded. The house may have served as living quarters for the workmen or as additional work space for cleaning weapons. Between 1775 and 1780, Anderson's workforce expanded from six to over forty workmen plying their trades in several shops within the complex. He employed paid journeymen, indentured apprentices, American soldiers, skilled slaves, Scottish prisoners of war, and French technical experts here under a contract with Congress to assist the United States in establishing weapon manufactories. Men and boys of diverse backgrounds worked together to supply metalware necessary to keep an army in the field. The importance of industrial development during the war was summed up by Richard Henry Lee in a letter to Thomas Jefferson: "Let us have Cannon, Small Arms, gun powder, and industry; we shall be secure—But it is in vain to have good systems of Government and good Laws, if we are exposed to the ravage of the Sword, without means of resisting."

In 1780 Anderson followed the government to Richmond when the capital moved to a more defensible spot. When the British under Benedict Arnold attacked Richmond, Anderson relocated farther west to a new armory in Fluvanna County. In the summer of 1781, the British attacked and destroyed the armory, captured Anderson briefly, and granted him a parole. Once freed from British hands, he was assigned administrative duties until war's end.

Following the war, Anderson operated a private shop in Richmond, returning in 1795 to Williamsburg and his old shop. He operated a business here until his death in 1798.

MAGAZINE

At the center of town, across Duke of Gloucester Street from the Courthouse on Market Square, stands one of the Historic Area's most distinctive original structures: the octagonal Magazine. Built in 1715, it housed the colony's and local merchants' weapons, gunpowder, and ammunition under the watchful eye of a keeper appointed by the House of Burgesses. In it today, and in the neighboring Guardhouse, you will find examples of the armaments it contained and learn about its role in the War for Independence. Described by a visitor during the Revolution as "a small, circular, Brick Building . . . at present surrounded with Chevaux de Frize [a defensive work made up of large wooden spikes]," the magazine was the central storehouse and inspection point for the weapons and other military supplies that Virginia's army and navy desperately needed.

In April 1775, one of the sparks that lit the Revolutionary torch in Williamsburg was struck here. British sailors, under orders of the royal governor, easily broke into the magazine and seized fifteen half barrels of gunpowder that belonged to the militia. After that debacle, Gabriel Maupin, the owner of the tavern next door, was appointed the keeper of the magazine. Between the fall of 1775 and the summer of 1776, Maupin saw more than five thousand muskets and rifles—as well as many other sorts of weapons—go through its doors as the new Virginia government tried to ready the people of Williamsburg to defend themselves against Great Britain. The task of obtaining, organizing, and maintaining weapons became increasingly difficult after British forces began raiding Virginia in 1779. The British destroyed much-needed supplies and hundreds of thousands

of pounds of tobacco that the state needed to use as currency to purchase more armaments and gunpowder in Europe. Even with James Anderson's public armory in full operation, local troops faced critical shortages of guns and almost everything else they needed, from rum to shoes. In addition, the Continental Congress heavily pressed Virginia's leaders to supply George Washington's army with more guns and men. The magazine was therefore a place where people considered an important question: where do your responsibilities as a citizen lie, with Virginia or with America? Should scarce weapons and ammunition remain here to protect Williamsburg or be sent north to defend New England, Pennsylvania, or New York? Those questions were asked with increasing frequency as British attacks on Virginia became more frequent, leading up to the

1781 invasion when the entire theater of war focused on the Williamsburg region.

After independence, the building served a wide variety of purposes. Imagine it as a market house, a Baptist church, a dancing school, and a stable—all of which it became at one point or another in its long history. During the Civil War, it was briefly returned to service as an arsenal for the Confederate army, and it came to be known as the "Powder Horn." After the Civil War, it became seriously dilapidated.

COURTHOUSE

In the middle of the Historic Area, you will find the Courthouse. The location is appropriate since local courthouses were, in many ways, at the core of life in British Virginia. In them, all of the king's subjects—free and enslaved,

men and women—expected to receive the degree of justice guaranteed to them by English law. The system was built on centuries of custom and precedent, and it touched almost every aspect of people's existence. You will encounter within these walls the principles and institutions that were turned upside down during the struggle for independence.

The courthouse was built in 1771 to house the city government and the James City County Court. An original structure, the Courthouse today appears almost exactly as it appeared to our Revolutionary predecessors. The front pediment and cupola were probably inspired by those on the second Capitol building.

The collapse of the old British order began here, and in other local courthouses. In 1774, after the House of Burgesses adopted a day of fasting, humiliation, and prayer in support of

Boston, the royal governor dissolved the legislature. He did so before the burgesses could pass a bill setting the fees that people would pay for judicial services. The failure to pass a bill effectively brought to a halt all civil court cases and other proceedings such as debt collection. And when the royal government completely collapsed in the spring of 1775, the colonial-era county court system came to an end, too. In its place, local committees, elected by freeholders (eligible voters), were established in cities and counties across Virginia. These committees enforced directives from the Continental Congress in Philadelphia and the eleven-man Committee of Safety, which replaced the royal governor and his Council as the executive arm of Virginia's government from July 1775 to June 1776. An important role of the local committees—sometimes called *committees of observation*—was to investigate whether members of the Revolutionary community were receiving goods banned by nonimportation agreements or were speaking out against the actions of the patriot movement. With the adoption of the

Virginia Constitution in June 1776, the county courts returned. Williamsburg's courthouse reopened its doors with even more responsibility in some areas than it had under the old colonial government. It now had greater authority over welfare for the poor, which it had previously shared with the local parish of the Church of England. In other ways, Virginia's county courts had less responsibility for judicial affairs because the constitution established a larger, more comprehensive system of courts, under which different courts dealt with particular kinds of law.

When you stand on this building's steps, you'll be on the spot where occurred some of the most significant events in the history of Williamsburg. On July 25, 1776, the inhabitants of Williamsburg gathered around the courthouse to hear Benjamin Waller, the city's mayor, read aloud the Declaration of Independence for the first time (it was also read that day at the Capitol and the Palace). Almost exactly three years later, "Inhabitants of this

City," including James Madison, "roused by the extortions of the times" met here in a memorable attempt to stop the Virginia economy from collapsing. They then adopted a committee of inspection to ensure that local merchants were not charging exorbitant prices or hoarding needed goods.

Unlike almost every other public building in town, the removal of the capital to Richmond did not measurably impact the role of the courthouse in local affairs. Its steps continued to provide a forum for political debate and

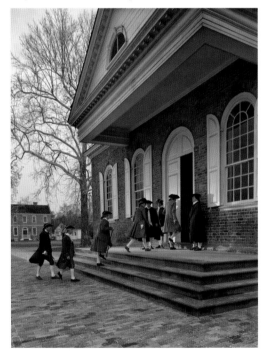

community announcements. Except for a brief period during the Civil War, when it was a hospital for Confederate wounded after the Battle of Williamsburg, and in 1911, when the interior was destroyed by a fire, the building remained in operation as a courthouse. Its 160 years of judicial service came to an end in 1931 when Colonial Williamsburg acquired the building and surrounding green.

MARKET HOUSE

At the center of town, on Duke of Gloucester Street near the Magazine and across from the Courthouse, is the Market House, one of the most dynamic places in colonial Williamsburg and the latest building to be reconstructed in the Historic Area. Although market houses were common in England, there were only a handful in eighteenth-century Virginia's cities. In a large colony, with a population spread over a great distance and relatively few towns, only political and economic centers like Williamsburg could support a building constructed primarily to promote local commerce. Colonial leaders began calling for a market house to be constructed in Williamsburg in the early 1700s, but not until April 26, 1757, did a committee meet at Wetherburn's tavern to make arrangements with a carpenter. Vendors at the Williamsburg market house sold butchered livestock, seafood, cheese, eggs, vegetables, fruit, and baked goods. The customers of typical eighteenth-century market houses—housewives, servants, slaves, and visitors—purchased weekly supplies of essential foodstuffs in addition to firewood, hay, baskets, and other goods supplied by countrypeople. As a result, the market house was the site of the mixing of more sorts of people on a regular basis than at any other place in Williamsburg. It

⌃ Modern sketch of the marketplace illustrating the bustle of market day with the market house, scale house, and freestanding stalls.

is not known how long the market house stood, although it probably remained through the Revolution since a 1781 map of the city clearly lists it as a feature in the center of town.

James Geddy House

When you arrive at the corner of Palace Green and Duke of Gloucester Street, you are greeted by the L-shaped James Geddy House. James Geddy Jr. was primarily a goldsmith and silversmith, but he and his older brothers, William and David, engaged in a variety of related trades, including gunsmith work at the shop behind the house, and rented out adjoining shops to merchants such as milliner Mary Dickinson. James Geddy was also a public servant, having been elected to Williamsburg's Common Hall, the city's governing body. By 1772, William Waddill, Geddy's brother-in-law, had joined his shop as an engraver, which gave Geddy a substantial boost in the competitive Williamsburg business environment. He nevertheless felt compelled the next year to assure potential customers that his prices were so reasonable that he hoped it would "remove that Objection of his Shop's being too high up Town" from the more convenient commercial neighborhood near the Capitol.

Geddy embraced opposition to Great Britain. He enthusiastically joined the association to protest parliamentary taxation even though it forced him to halt the imports of gold and silver from Britain that made up the core of his business. He appealed to "those Ladies and Gentlemen who are friends to the association" to consider purchasing his "neat assortment" of jewelry and other pieces made in Virginia. His brother William, the gunsmith, also supported the patriot cause by "casting ball" (making ammunition) and repairing firearms; he even sold his own musket to aid the effort. But the War for Independence transformed their lives and fortunes. In 1777, no longer able to make a living at his trade, Geddy moved his wife and five children away from Williamsburg and advertised his home for sale (William had already left the city). A merchant, Robert Jackson, bought the property in 1779 and lived there until his death in 1781.

Bruton Parish Church

Bruton Parish Church has occupied the same space on the northwest corner of Duke of Gloucester Street and Palace Green since 1683. The present building was completed in 1715. It was the most prominent local symbol of the Church of England and the Protestant faith that dominated Virginia culture and thus played a crucial role in community life. It was also a tangible symbol of the connection between politics and religion in the eighteenth-century British world. When you enter its grounds, you will share space once occupied by royal governors such as Edward Nott and Francis Fauquier, who are buried in and near the church; famous early American ministers such as George Whitefield, who preached from its pulpit; and patriots and loyalists alike, such as Thomas Jefferson, George Washington, and John Randolph, who worshipped in its pews. The church was also a place for social engagement and entertainment. In August 1769 a young Williamsburg lady reported that there is "scarce an Evening . . . but we are entertain'd with the performances of Felton's, Handel's, Vi-vally's" issuing from the church's organ.

One of the most important moments in the history of Williamsburg took place within these walls. On June 1, 1774, members of the House of Burgesses gathered here to observe a day of fasting, humiliation, and prayer to support the people of Boston, whose port had been closed that day by the first of Parliament's inflammatory Coercive Acts, passed to punish the Boston Tea Party. The burgesses' political action, although couched in the language of religion, compelled Virginia's royal governor, Lord Dunmore, to dissolve the colonial legislature, which never again met in a full session.

During the chaos of the Revolutionary War, the church's popular rector (an Episcopal minister in charge of a parish), the Reverend John Bracken, struggled to maintain its relevance in Virginia society. Some patriots such as James Madison sought to break all connection between the church and the new commonwealth through measures to establish religious freedom. They targeted especially those ties that ensured public financial support of the church and its responsibilities, such as caring for the poor. Many Episcopal churches disappeared in the decades after the war. Bracken succeeded in preserving the church and its shrinking congregation from collapse. He remained the church's rector until 1818.

The church was used as a Confederate hospital for the Battle of Williamsburg in 1862. Union officials suspended services for a brief period in 1863 while the Union army occupied the city because the church's rector attempted to replace prayers for the president of the United States with those for the governor of Virginia.

The graveyard surrounding the church is the final resting place of prominent Williamsburg residents such as Martha Washington's first husband, Daniel Parke Custis, and two of their children; patriot printer Alexander Purdie; public armorer James Anderson; signer of the Constitution and justice of the first U.S. Supreme Court John Blair; Letitia Tyler Semple, daughter of President John Tyler; and Confederate general George Taliaferro Ward. Other Confederate soldiers killed at the Battle of Williamsburg in 1862 are also interred on the grounds.

▲ W. A. R. Goodwin and John D. Rockefeller Jr.

In many ways, Bruton Parish Church also marks the beginnings of Colonial Williamsburg as we know it today. The Reverend W. A. R. Goodwin's passion for restoration took root when he was appointed rector in 1903. His first project was to return the interior of the church to its colonial appearance. His broader vision was well on the way to fruition thirty years later when, again serving as rector after a hiatus, Goodwin saw to the complete restoration of the church as part of the effort to restore the town.

AFRICAN AMERICAN RELIGION EXHIBIT

Near the intersection of Nassau and Francis Streets, you encounter one of the hidden stories of the Revolutionary City, that of African American religion. In a city in which half of the population was African or of African descent, the faith of that population was an important issue. From Williamsburg's earliest days, the African American inhabitants were expected to share in the Anglican faith of their owners. Many were baptized at Bruton Parish Church and regularly attended services. However, as other Protestant denominations gained strength across Virginia, African Americans were influenced by them. An especially strong influence was the Baptists, which, before and during the American Revolution, placed people of different races on a relatively equal footing when it came to worship.

African Americans appear in eighteenth-century records as Baptist preachers, such as Moses, who often preached in Williamsburg and is credited with establishing the first African American Baptist church in Virginia as early as 1776. Gowan Pamphlet, an enslaved member of the household of Jane Vobe, the keeper of the King's Arms Tavern, was inspired by Moses. According to some sources, Pamphlet took over leadership of the Williamsburg congregation before the end of the Revolution. He was later freed and in the 1790s oversaw the acceptance of his Williamsburg church into the general Baptist association. That church met in a wooden carriage house on the northwest corner of the Nassau and Francis Streets intersection, where there is now a marker that explains the historical importance of the site.

The congregation itself still exists as the First Baptist Church, located a few blocks away on Scotland Street. Just across Nassau Street, in the Taliaferro-Cole Stable, is the African American Religion Exhibit, which details the religious experience of African Americans in the eighteenth century.

GOVERNOR'S PALACE

Eighteenth-century visitors to Williamsburg reacted to the Governor's Palace, prominently situated at the north end of Palace Green, much like today's guests: they recognized it as one of the most elegant and imposing structures in the entire city. One resident observed in 1724 that the Palace is "a magnificent structure . . . finished and beautified with . . . walks, a fine canal, orchards, etc. with a great number of the best arms nicely posited." As fine a building as it is, however, it became known as a "palace" by accident rather than by design. The sheer cost of its construction and architectural embellishments inside and out quickly exceeded the appropriations of the House of Burgesses, who complained to the British government about the public money that the royal governor at the time, Alexander Spotswood, was "lavish[ing] away" on the building. It thus became rather derisively known as the Palace, even though the rancor was eventually forgotten and the name remained. It was finally finished in 1722, when it was furnished and its grounds were developed with gardens, fish ponds, a number of outbuildings, and even a canal (which Spotswood had to pay for himself). Guests then as now admired the lavish interior appointments of a marble floor from England in the entrance hall and beautiful marble fireplace mantles in other rooms. The private weapons of the governor (in contrast to the public arms kept in the magazine) were displayed throughout the building in a way similar to that of contemporary British manor houses and lodges.

The Palace served as a home, office, and arsenal for the governors of Virginia for the next fifty-eight years, until the capital moved to Richmond. The last royal governor to reside in the Palace was John Murray, fourth Earl of Dunmore. Lord Dunmore previously had been governor of New York and strenuously opposed the decision to move him to Virginia in 1772 to replace Norborne Berkeley, Baron de Botetourt, who had died in the Palace in 1770. The irascible Dunmore could not have provided

a more striking contrast to the affable Botetourt. Where Botetourt's congeniality and conciliatory nature had made Virginians comfortable in the belief that he was on their side in the growing disputes with Parliament, Dunmore had a habit of saying and doing precisely the wrong things at exactly the wrong times. Nevertheless, Dunmore did have a major ally that Botetourt did not have: a charming wife with good political sense, Lady Charlotte Stewart Murray, the daughter of the sixth Earl of Galloway. One visitor to Williamsburg described her as "a most agreable pretty Woman," and her arrival with six of their children in early 1774 had an almost immediate positive effect on relations between Dunmore and his political opponents. Relations warmed further on December 3, 1774, when Lady Dunmore gave birth to a daughter, whom they named Virginia, shortly after her husband returned from winning a popular war against the Shawnee Indians. But, given the pace of Revolutionary events and Lord Dunmore's unhelpful temperament, the warmth could not last. Political conditions in Williamsburg deteriorated so quickly that only six months later the family fled the Palace in the middle of the night. A local newspaper noted that "this amiable lady's departure seems to give the utmost concern to every Virginian." The newspaper did not lament her husband's absence.

This is the historical moment into which you step when you enter the Palace. It is a time of tension and uncertainty in the place that, more than any other in Virginia, represented the old royal order and the social, political, and cultural ties that had bound colonial Americans to Great Britain since 1607. You might arrive on January 18, 1775, and participate in one of the last spectacles of the British colonial world: a ball given in honor of the queen of Great Britain's birth night, the birth of Lord and Lady Dunmore's new daughter, and the successful completion of Lord Dunmore's campaign to defeat the Shawnee in western Virginia. That night, Virginia's British heritage was on full display, complete with charm, politeness, and fashion. However, whispered beneath the traditional forms and ancient symbols and slipped between the country dances and minuets, you can hear talk of revolution. It is already dividing guardians of the old order from the builders of a new nation.

Or perhaps you arrive several months later, at the very moment that the British world came crashing down around Dunmore and his family. On June 8, 1775, rampant rumors of violence drove them from the Palace in the dead of night. After two months of conflict between Dunmore and patriot leaders, during which the governor had seized gunpowder from the magazine and threatened to arm slaves and set fire to the town, the family left their home, leaving behind most of their belongings. The result was confusion within and without the Palace walls. The future of the British world that had shaped life in Virginia for generations now seemed to be in question. Without the governor, there could be no government, and, without government, how could the rights of the people be protected? Did this mean that Virginia's connection with Britain was also at an end? And what might replace it? The departure of Lord and Lady Dunmore left the fate of the people at the Palace—and of all inhabitants of Williamsburg—hanging in the balance.

Lord Dunmore did not return. Instead, he gathered loyalist and regular British forces around him (including hundreds of former slaves he freed by making them part of his Ethiopian Regiment) and opposed the Virginia patriots in battle. Almost exactly a year after the family left the Palace, on June 25, 1776, the new independent Commonwealth of Virginia sold at an auction all of their belongings, from clothes and furniture to servants and slaves, all of whom faced a very uncertain future. All the proceeds from the sale, including from the slaves, went to support a state engaged in a fight for freedom.

The Palace did not stay empty for long. For a few months in the spring of 1776, the American general Charles Lee, always accompanied by a pack of hounds, made it his headquarters before he assumed command of the Continental army in the south. In June 1776, the Palace returned to service on the election of Patrick Henry as the first governor of the commonwealth. He served three terms as governor, until 1779, and lived in the Palace for much of that time. During that time another daughter was born to a governor in the building with the arrival of Dorothea Spotswood Henry on October 20, 1778. In 1779, a much different kind of family moved into the Palace when Thomas Jefferson was elected governor. He brought to Williamsburg his wife, Martha; their daughters; and the Hemings family of enslaved men and women. They lived in the building until the capital moved to Richmond in the spring of 1780.

The Palace remained empty for several months, cared for by a gardener, John Farquharson, in exchange for his being able to live in one of the buildings. But that didn't stop a small group of young men and women in the town, including future Chief Justice John Marshall, then a student at the college, from using it as a site of merriment. In June 1780 the group had a party in the Palace that "was like most of the entertainments of the present time, simple and

frugal . . . but for the brilliancy of the company too much cannot be said." The Palace assumed a much graver aspect not long after when it was pressed into use as a hospital. During and after the Yorktown campaign in 1781, there were wounded and sick soldiers in every room; 156 soldiers were buried in one of the Palace gardens. The end of the Revolution marked the end of the building itself. It burned to the ground on the night of December 22, 1781, in a blaze of such magnitude that it threatened other buildings nearby, including the George Wythe House. It took only three hours to destroy what had stood since 1722.

The reconstruction of the Palace complex was aided by archaeology, the Bodleian Plate, and Thomas Jefferson. During his tenure as governor, Jefferson envisioned alterations to the building. He sketched, in characteristic detail, measured drawings of the interior, including a floor plan, room dimensions,

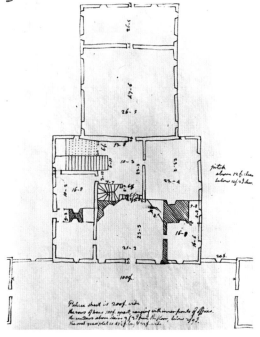

▲ Jefferson's plan for the Governor's Palace.

ceiling heights, wall thicknesses, window placements, and chimneys. Jefferson even noted the location of trees on Palace Green.

GEORGE WYTHE HOUSE

On the west side of Palace Green is the imposing brick home of the most influential, though by no means best-known, member of the Revolutionary community: George Wythe. Richard Taliaferro, an accomplished Virginia architect, built this original house in the mid-1750s and gave it to his daughter, Elizabeth, who married Wythe. For almost forty years, the Wythes, who had no children of their own, and their slaves occupied the house. This home became the epicenter of Enlightenment thought in Williamsburg. Although Wythe had no formal education, his mother encouraged him to learn Greek and Roman history and literature. Later, after a rather rudimentary introduction to the practice of law, he embraced the philosophies of John Locke, Isaac Newton, Jean-Jacques Rousseau, and the baron de Montesquieu with a fervor that could hardly go unnoticed. During the decades before the Revolution, Wythe drew to him students, such as Thomas Jefferson, who looked to him for instruction about the proper foundation of politics and law in a society based on equality and liberty. When the war began, Wythe was a prominent lawyer and clerk of the House of Burgesses. He was selected as a delegate to the Second Continental Congress, and his name appears first among the Virginia signers of the Declaration of Independence—a document that owed its genesis to ideas that circulated through the rooms in his house. In Philadelphia, just as he did in his own house, Wythe preached a religion of reason and experience that identified inherent truths and combined them with an understanding of natural law and philosophy, producing a Revolutionary optimism among all his adherents. They believed that they not only could make their world a better place but they also had the responsibility to try and make it so. John Adams wrote to Wythe in 1776, "You and I, my dear Friend, have been sent into life, at a time when the greatest law-givers of antiquity would have wished to have lived."

Not just a mere classroom for appreciating classical history and eighteenth-century philosophy, the Wythe House is once again a laboratory for revolutionary thought and how to apply it. When you enter the house, you might consider the responsibility that a citizen of a free republic has to improve his or her world. It could be August 1776 as Wythe prepares to depart for Philadelphia to sign the Declaration of Independence. Or the setting could be December 1779 when the College of William and Mary was completely reorganized to reflect the basic premise of Enlightenment thought

applied to a republican society: The people must be educated to be proper citizens. The result was Wythe's appointment as the first professor of law in American history. The broader context remains the same: the Revolutionary Enlightenment that created perhaps the most powerful force for progress in human history. The gardens, grounds, and outbuildings—the layout of which stresses balance and usefulness—assiduously reflect that perspective.

After his work with the Continental Congress was over, Wythe remained in Williamsburg to assist Jefferson, who had become his closest friend (and who, with his family, lived in the Wythe House briefly at the end of 1776), in transforming Virginia society from a hierarchical system into a republican order. In the House of Delegates, he and Jefferson drove the project to create a more rational system of laws for Virginia. He was elected Speaker of the House before his appointment as a judge to one of the state's highest courts while he continued teaching students. Among his students was future Chief Justice of the Supreme Court John Marshall, who gained his only formal legal education during the six weeks he spent with Wythe in 1780.

When war came to Virginia in 1781, closing the college and courts, it also came to George Wythe's house. George Washington used it as his headquarters while he planned for the Yorktown campaign. After Cornwallis's surrender, the French commander, the comte de Rochambeau, resided in the house. Once the war was over, the college and courts reopened, and Wythe returned to what he did best: teaching. In 1787, however, Wythe left the house once again to go back to Philadelphia, this time as a delegate to the Constitutional Convention. While there he was described by a colleague as "confessedly one of the most learned legal Characters of the present age." He left the convention before he could sign the document because he received word that his wife was ill. She died not long after he returned to Williamsburg. Several days later he freed one of his slaves, Lydia, and transferred ownership of many others to his brother-in-law. He moved to Richmond in 1791, with Lydia and Ben, another slave he had freed, maintaining his position as one of Virginia's most important judges and teachers of law. Henry Clay, one of the major figures of nineteenth-century American politics, was among his last students. Wythe lived in the new capital until 1806 when he died under mysterious circumstances; his nephew was tried for his murder but acquitted. Wythe is buried in the graveyard of St. John's Church in Richmond.

THOMAS EVERARD HOUSE

The Thomas Everard House is noted for its fine staircase with its elaborately turned balusters, sweeping handrails, and richly ornamented carvings. Its rooms have been carefully furnished with antiques that reflect the Virginia-made furniture and goods imported from other parts of the British Empire that filled the house during the occupation of Thomas Everard, one-time mayor of Williamsburg.

PEYTON RANDOLPH HOUSE

Few original buildings in the Historic Area carry the weight of as much history as the Peyton Randolph House, situated at the corner of Nicholson and North England Streets. In 1724, John Randolph, a young lawyer in Williamsburg, purchased the corner lot along with a two-story house built around a central chimney and moved into it with his growing family. Later in 1724 he bought the adjoining lot on Nicholson Street. Randolph quickly grew in prominence, becoming attorney general for the colony in 1726 and Speaker of the House of Burgesses in 1734. He was frequently tasked with traveling to London to settle disputes between Virginia and English interests, and he was knighted by King George II in 1733. Nevertheless, you might consider it a modest, even crowded, home for him, his wife, their four children, and a number of slaves and something of a relic from the architectural period before Georgian proportions came to dominate building tastes. The large property also includes a number of outbuildings, including a kitchen

and a smokehouse. A tireless advocate for religious toleration and political moderation, as well as a keen gardener, Sir John Randolph did not live long enough to build on his achievements or further improve his property: he died in 1737, at the age of about forty-three, and received the singular honor of burial in the crypt of the chapel at his alma mater, the College of William and Mary. He left his wife, Lady Susannah, with life rights to the property.

Although Lady Susannah lived well into the 1750s, their son Peyton took over the house, his father's love of the law, and the responsibility of resolving Virginia's disputes in London. Married in 1746 to the formidable Elizabeth ("Betty") Harrison—whose brother Benjamin would sign the Declaration of Independence and whose nephew William Henry would become president of the United States—they lived in the house as he built his career. He became attorney general himself in 1744, arguing a case against unfair taxation in London in 1754, and he was elected Speaker of the House of Burgesses in 1766. It was about the time of his return from London in the mid-1750s, after which he was voted a £2,500 award by the House of Burgesses, that the property assumed the form you see today.

Throughout that period, Peyton gained a reputation on both sides of the Atlantic as a staunch supporter of liberty and the British constitution. On September 4, 1774, John Adams wrote that a delegate to the First Continental Congress in Philadelphia rose from his chair and successfully moved that Peyton, a "Gent[leman] present who had presided, with great Dignity over a very respectable Society, greatly to the Advantage of America," be elected the first president of the Congress. On his return to Williamsburg, a troop of militia delivered an address to him that proclaimed Peyton "the Father of Your Country." We will never know whether he would have signed the Declaration of Independence since he died in Philadelphia just over a year later, attending the Second Continental Congress.

Although Peyton and Betty had no children of their own, they frequently opened their home to younger relations, such as Betty's many nieces and nephews and Peyton's nephew Edmund. Peyton's brother John, who succeeded Peyton as attorney general, lived in the most impressive private house in town, which stood on what is now South England Street, near the current Williamsburg Lodge, oriented so that its front door faced Peyton's. The young Edmund's patriotic opinions created a rift with his loyalist father, who left Williamsburg with Edmund's mother and two sisters in the fall of 1775, not long before Peyton's death, never to return. Edmund would go on to become the first attorney general of the United States and the second secretary of state.

In addition to the free members of the household, nearly thirty men and women, the largest group of slaves in Williamsburg, were bound for life to attend to every need of the Randolphs and their property. When you enter the house, expect to confront the challenges that faced the free and enslaved members of the household as they struggled over choices about the rights they could claim for themselves and the responsibilities they might owe to one another. You might encounter the story of Johnny, Peyton's personal servant, who accompanied his master throughout his Revolutionary travels. What must he have thought when, one evening in August 1774, *A Summary View of the Rights of British America*, a pamphlet written by Peyton's cousin Thomas Jefferson, was read aloud for the first time in the elegant dining room. That night these words echoed throughout the house: "The God who gave us life gave us liberty at the same time; the hand of force may destroy, but cannot disjoin them."

For people like Johnny, that language must have raised questions about the nature of liberty. Two years after Peyton's death, Johnny—an educated mulatto who could have easily passed for white—left the Randolphs, taking his own freedom. Of the twenty-seven members of the enslaved community at the Randolph house in 1775, nine of them, including Johnny and eight who were later noted on a house inventory as "gone to the enemy," left during the war. Eve and her son George, it appears, chose to join the British army in July 1781 when it occupied Williamsburg and extended to all slaves an official offer of freedom. Eve was behind the British lines at Yorktown when the British surrendered that autumn. What was going through her mind when she thought about what the future might hold for her and her son? What might your own choice have been?

In 1781 the house was used as a residence by the commander of the French forces in America, the comte de Rochambeau, while the Yorktown campaign was planned. Betty continued to live in the house until her death in the early 1780s. There being no direct heirs, the house and property were sold at public auction on February 19, 1783. It went through a succession of owners and was even employed as a boardinghouse in the 1800s when the marquis de Lafayette used it as a headquarters of sorts during his triumphal visit to Williamsburg in 1824. Lafayette accepted formal greetings from visitors on the house's front porch. By 1938, when Colonial Williamsburg acquired the property, the main house remained surprisingly intact, but all of the outbuildings and the small house attached to the east end of the structure in the 1750s had been demolished. In 1997, Colonial Williamsburg tradespeople reconstructed the "urban plantation" of the free and enslaved Randolphs, rebuilding the storehouse, dairy, smokehouse, and kitchen with its covered walkway.

MILITARY ENCAMPMENT

At the corner of Botetourt and Nicholson Streets is one of the most important military sites in the Revolutionary City: the Military Encampment. On March 23, 1775, Patrick Henry urged his fellow delegates at the Third Virginia Convention, meeting in Richmond, to prepare to defend themselves against the forces of Great Britain. He is said to have proclaimed,

"Give me liberty, or give me death!" to help convince his colleagues to issue a call for independent militia companies to be raised across the colony.

Before 1775, each county and town had a militia company, formed under the authority of the Crown, but they were more famous for the amount of alcohol they consumed than for the keenness of their training. With the threat of armed conflict looming, the call for new companies that reported to local patriot committees and to the Virginia Convention was answered with enthusiasm, and Williamsburg became an active hub for troops to organize, train, and be equipped for war. After the battles at Lexington and Concord in Massachusetts, and

the subsequent creation of a Continental army under the command of George Washington, the demand for trained soldiers increased. In addition to the volunteer militia companies, Virginians also organized battalions of soldiers and "minutemen," who were to be ready for duty at a moment's notice. Virginia patriots such as James Monroe, who left the College of William and Mary to fight the British, spent much of 1776 drilling in fields just like the Encampment and then marched to New York. Virginia still needed troops at home, however, so the General Assembly, in May 1778, established "a battalion of infantry," part of which was stationed in Williamsburg, "to be raised for garrison duty at the ports & harbours of this State." The Virginia State Garrison Regiment spent much of the next two years preparing to defend the state against British invasion. As the war raged on, there were never enough recruits to meet the increasing demand. Consequently, the General Assembly offered generous bounties, including slaves, to boost enlistments and even instituted a draft, which caused tension among the raw troops and led to threats of mutiny.

It is this historical moment—when patriots accepted the responsibility to defend liberty on the battlefield—that you encounter at the Military Encampment. Here you will learn about the lives of Revolutionary soldiers, their hardships, and their sacrifices. They came from across Virginia, from the Chesapeake to the Shenandoah Valley, to fight for freedom. Here you will hear their stories and decide for yourself whether to enter the ranks, drill, and learn what it meant to prepare to defend liberty.

The site of the Encampment, known as Ravenscroft, went through many owners and uses before the Revolution. During the war, it was owned by William Royle, the infant son of a former newspaper printer, but leased to several tenants. The State Garrison Regiment was housed in nearby barracks, one of which was located just north of the modern Visitor Center and another a short distance east of the city. The regiment frequently marched along Duke of Gloucester Street and drilled and paraded on the market green.

BENJAMIN POWELL HOUSE

At the eastern end of the Historic Area, situated on Waller Street behind the Capitol, is the large home of Benjamin Powell. Here you can experience family life during the American Revolution in Williamsburg and engage in a wide range of eighteenth-century activities, both indoors and outdoors.

Powell played an important role in building the city of Williamsburg, both literally and figuratively. As a carpenter and a joiner, he repaired the gaol, built the steeple of Bruton Parish Church, renovated the woodwork at the Governor's Palace, and constructed the Public Hospital. When the war came, he was charged with building a barracks and a hospital for soldiers. He also held public office, including justice of the peace for York County from 1778 to 1783 and marshal of the court of admiralty, a position in which he oversaw the seizure of enemy naval vessels and their cargoes. Powell was also a husband and the father of several daughters who were just beginning to think of leading their own lives when the conflict began. The family, along with the enslaved members of the household, had to face the challenge of maintaining their daily existence in a city at war. As much as things changed during the Revolution, the Powells struggled to keep them the same within the walls of their home.

PRESBYTERIAN MEETINGHOUSE

Across from Christiana Campbell's Tavern, on Waller Street, is housed the Presbyterian Meetinghouse. On the outside, the whitewashed building looks like an ordinary outbuilding owned by any prosperous member of the community. And that's precisely what it was—a stable on the lot of George Davenport, a Williamsburg attorney whose large family

featured prominently in Williamsburg affairs. But pass through its doors and you enter the world of eighteenth-century dissenters from the Church of England and the fight for religious freedom in America. You can sit on its benches or stand in its pulpit and hear the story of that struggle.

Since the Act of Toleration of 1689, part of the British constitution, any Protestants who dissented from the relevant articles that defined the Anglican faith could worship as they pleased so long as their ministers were licensed and meetings were registered (Catholics and other non-Protestants were expressly excluded). A 1705 law clarified that the act applied to Virginia, reinforced in a 1725 legal opinion by Virginia's attorney general, Sir John Randolph. By the middle of the eighteenth century, the growing number of Presbyterians in Williamsburg—often Scottish tradesmen—needed a place to meet whenever a licensed minister, such as the famous Reverend Samuel Davies, came to town. It appears that George Davenport, whose large house has been reconstructed at the corner of Waller and Francis Streets, offered a building on his lot as a proper place for the Presbyterians to gather. On June 17, 1765, a group of Williamsburg Presbyterians registered by informing the York County Court that they intended to use a building on George Davenport's property

as a meetinghouse "for occasional Worship when we have opportunity to hear any legally qualified Minister." It was the first legally recognized religious establishment outside the Church of England in Williamsburg, but it would not represent the only dissenting voices heard here. Baptists, New Light Presbyterians, Quakers, and others preached occasionally in town. In 1777, a Methodist minister preached in the Capitol; one observer recorded that "he appears to be an honest man, but does not shine as a Preacher."

The revolutionary ideals of the Enlightenment steadily turned the tide of opinion from Protestant toleration to complete religious freedom, a point reached in 1776 when James Madison succeeded in enshrining in the Virginia Declaration of Rights the principle that "all men are equally entitled to the free exercise of religion." Madison's language was strengthened in 1779 when Thomas Jefferson's Statute for Religious Freedom was introduced in Virginia's House of Delegates. The measure passed into law in 1786.

Bassett Hall

Bassett Hall is an eighteenth-century frame house located on 585 acres of gardens and rolling woodlands. The house looks much as it did

in the 1930s and 1940s when John D. Rockefeller Jr. and Abby Aldrich Rockefeller made it their home during the restoration of Williamsburg, which they financed. Bassett Hall is located near the Capitol, off of Francis Street.

GREAT HOPES PLANTATION

With very few towns the size of Williamsburg, a majority of the almost five hundred thousand free and enslaved Virginians in the 1770s and 1780s lived on small plantations. At Great Hopes Plantation, re-created on the edge of the Historic Area along the pathway from the Visitor Center, you enter into that world. This site is based on a farm that existed not far from the capital. Great Hopes represents the broader experience of life in the Tidewater where plantations were often owned by "middling" or "small" planters who might not have had more than one hundred acres to cultivate and whose few slaves comprised the greatest part of their wealth. On plantations such as Great Hopes, farmers and slaves—and occasionally Indians—blended together European, African, and Native cultures to form a distinctly "American" way of life.

When you arrive at Great Hopes, you encounter those people, trying to scratch an existence from the soil. Here you might find the middling planter and members of his family wondering about what a war that threatens the way of life built on slavery and tobacco might mean for them. Or you could find enslaved African Americans working to carve out lives and a culture of their own, toiling with the crops, and considering whether the promises of liberty made by patriots and their British enemies could make it easier for them to gain their freedom.

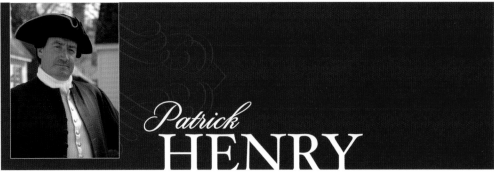

Patrick HENRY

The name of Patrick Henry (1736–1799) became known to all of Virginia, and then to all of America, mostly because of what he did in Williamsburg. Henry's first recorded visit to Williamsburg was in 1760 when, after failing as a planter, a merchant, and a tavern keeper, he came to the city to obtain a license to practice law, after studying the subject on his own for a very short time. To get the three signatures required, he approached George Wythe, John Randolph, Peyton Randolph, and Edmund Pendleton—four of the most prominent lawyers in Virginia. Wythe and Pendleton, after examining him, declined to sign Henry's license, but both Randolph brothers did. After Henry promised he would study more, Pendleton then provided the final signature, which allowed Henry to practice in county courts. Three years later he gained notoriety across the colony as a brilliant speaker and political leader in a case that became known as "the Parson's Cause."

It was his return to Williamsburg in 1765 as a new member of the House of Burgesses that made him a figure of national stature. At a tavern outside of Williamsburg, Henry penned several resolutions in opposition to the Stamp Act. The fifth, and most strident, declared that any attempt by a body other than the Virginia legislature to lay taxes on the colony "has a manifest Tendency to destroy British as well as American Freedom." Henry accompanied his resolves with a speech that few who heard it could forget. A French eyewitness recalled that Henry rose in the House chamber in the Capitol on May 30 to state that "Julius [Caesar] had their Brutus, Charles had his Cromwell, and he Did not Doubt but some good american would stand up, in favour of his Country." According to the eyewitness, the Speaker of the House stopped Henry at that point and said that he "had spoke traison, and [the Speaker] was sorey to see that not one of the members of the house was loyal Enough to stop him, before he had gone so far." Henry explained that "what he had said must be atributed to the Interest of his Countrys Dying liberty which he had at heart." The Caesar-Brutus speech had its intended effect, and Henry's resolves, including the fifth, were passed. News of them spread throughout the colonies, where they were published in newspapers and adopted by several legislatures. The royal governor of Massachusetts wrote that they sounded "an Alarm bell to the disaffected." Henry's reputation as a radical opponent to unconstitutional British actions was made that day in Williamsburg.

Thomas Jefferson later described the debates over the Stamp Act as "the dawn of the revolution." The influence of "all the old members . . . in the house had, till then, been unbroken," Jefferson recalled, "but torrents of sublime eloquence from mr Henry . . . prevailed." Williamsburg's Edmund Randolph wrote that Henry bound "a band of patriots together to hurl defiance at the tyranny of so formidable a nation as Great Britain."

The death in early 1775 of his first wife, Sarah, as the result of profound mental illness must have weighed heavily on his mind. But Henry threw himself into political activity. In March, during a meeting at St. John's Church in Richmond, Henry added to his stature with a call for liberty or death.

Back in Williamsburg, the collapse of the royal government pushed Henry again to the front of Revolutionary affairs. Lord Dunmore, Virginia's royal governor, confiscated much of the colony's gunpowder, creating a public uproar. While moderate leaders, such as Peyton Randolph, were able to calm uprisings in other parts of Virginia, Henry took command of hundreds of militiamen and marched on the capital city intending to compel Dunmore to return the gunpowder. Dunmore moved cannons to the front of the Palace and proclaimed that, should the patriots advance near Williamsburg, he would fire on the town. He also ordered marines from a nearby warship to join him as a defensive force. Riders galloped between Henry's camp and the Palace trying to negotiate a peaceful resolution to the standoff between the temperamental governor and the implacable radical. After several days, Carter Braxton and Thomas Nelson Jr.—both of whom would later sign the Declaration of Independence—paid for the missing gunpowder. That was enough for Henry, who disbanded his forces, but Dunmore made Henry into the Crown's top enemy in America.

In the summer of 1775, the Virginia Convention put into action Henry's plan for defense, creating two state infantry regiments, and named Henry commander in chief of all Virginia forces. Henry relished the appointment and his new rank of colonel. Not everyone was as pleased. George Washington, in a letter to a friend, wrote, "I think my countrymen made a capital mistake, when they took Henry out of the senate to place him in the field; and pity it is, that he does not see this, and remove every difficulty by a voluntary resignation." Others echoed Washington's misgivings and refused to give Henry the authority to exercise his command, so Henry resigned his commission in February 1776.

Although Henry's brief military career ended in Williamsburg, his standing as a Revolutionary leader only grew when, just a few months later, during the Fifth Virginia Convention, he helped draft a resolution for independence and assisted young James Madison in adding the protection of religious freedom to the Virginia Declaration of Rights. He also helped draft Virginia's new constitution, which was adopted on June 29, 1776.

Henry was elected the first governor of the Commonwealth of Virginia, a position he held for three years. Although the position was relatively weak, the force of Henry's personality exerted considerable influence, and he guided the state through the first years of the war, overseeing the creation of not only a government but also the transformation of a society. Henry raised troops, organized their supplies, and directed campaigns against the British and Indian allies in the western part of the state. While governor, he remarried, in 1777, to Dorothea Dandridge, the granddaughter of the first governor to live in the Governor's Palace, Alexander Spotswood. Henry and his family then moved into the Palace, where his wife attempted to restore the building to some of its prewar splendor.

British blockades and increasing disaffection within the state brought Virginia's economy to near collapse, enemy troops began to regularly raid the state's coastline, and the structure of the new government proved woefully inadequate to meet the many challenges facing it. Henry imposed an embargo on the export of goods and instituted a draft to fill Virginia's commitment to the Continental army. He stopped short, despite the urging of his council, of using enslaved men as currency to purchase supplies. (Henry was opposed to the institution of slavery but insisted that he was "drawn along by the general Inconvenience of living without them.") He retired as governor in the summer of 1779 and declined election to the Continental Congress, but he served in the House of Delegates through the rest of the war and was reelected governor in 1784.

Henry came to oppose many of the social reforms that Jefferson, Wythe, and Madison wanted to enact. Among these was Jefferson's Statute for Religious Freedom. His experience as governor during the war convinced him that the people did not possess the public virtue necessary for a republic to work. Such a moral foundation could come only from religion, which therefore should be supported by the state. The bill nevertheless passed. Henry also failed in perhaps the last great political fight of his life—to defeat ratification of the U.S. Constitution because it did not contain a bill of rights to protect the liberties of the people (though of course a bill of rights was soon added).

Henry spent the last ten years of life engaged in his law practice but removed from public affairs. Horrified by the French Revolution and what he saw as a lack of moral virtue in republican leaders on both sides of the Atlantic, Henry became increasingly dissatisfied with Jefferson, Madison, and their followers. In 1799, at the urging of George Washington, he ran again for the House of Delegates, but as a Federalist opponent to his old Revolutionary allies. He won but died at Red Hill, his plantation, before he could take his seat.

A DECLARATION
of INDEPENDENCE

At four o'clock in the afternoon, the Declaration of Independence was proclaimed at the courthouse, the Capitol, and the Governor's Palace, "amidst the acclamations of the people, accompanied by firing of cannon and musketry, the several regiments of continental troops having been paraded on that solemnity."

News of the passage of the Declaration had been circulating around town for almost a week. The full text of the Revolutionary document had been published in the *Virginia Gazette* on July 20, though only a select few knew the author's identity. Those few days gave the inhabitants of Williamsburg, free and enslaved, time to think on its words and the ideas it contains, especially the "self-evident" truth that "all men are created equal."

It soon became clear that Virginians were not of one mind about the document, and different people took away from it strikingly different things. For some, it was nothing more than a statement of the reasons why a political separation from Great Britain was necessary. For others, it was the defining document of the American mind, promising the benefits of liberty to everyone. And for still others, it was a radical expression of an unrealistic dream, one that could undermine the very foundations of society. By July 25, the people of Williamsburg were familiar enough with the Declaration to begin a debate over its language and, therefore, over the meaning of the American Revolution—a debate that continues to this day.

Thomas JEFFERSON

Thomas Jefferson's mother, Jane Randolph, was born in a poor maritime neighborhood near the Tower of London to a ship's captain, but she was still a Randolph, which made her part of the most prominent family in Virginia. That gave her son a family network into which he easily fit when he first came to the capital. When Jefferson (1743–1826) entered the College of William and Mary as a sixteen-year-old student in the spring of 1760, there was a dispute over his preparation, which took two weeks to be resolved. During that time, he could call on more than a dozen cousins who lived in Williamsburg. They included leaders such as Peyton Randolph, the Speaker of the House of Burgesses, and his brother John, Virginia's attorney general, both of whom took a liking to the young man and invited him into their homes.

For the next two years, Jefferson shuttled between his home, Shadwell, near the colony's western frontier, and Williamsburg, where he studied under William Small. A Scotsman from north of Aberdeen, barely ten years older than Jefferson, Small was part of a growing movement in the Enlightenment of thinkers who wanted to change the very nature of education, from the subjects students pursued to the ways they were taught. Small and his compatriots hoped to sweep away the cobwebs of dead languages and learning by memorization in favor of teaching students, through examination and discussion, how to think and reason. In 1762, Jefferson left William and Mary to begin the study of law under one of Small's best friends and a fellow traveler down the path

of Enlightenment, George Wythe. Jefferson and Wythe, to whom Jefferson referred as his second father, would remain the dearest of friends for the rest of their lives. Wythe passed on to Jefferson a hefty dose of Enlightenment optimism—an understanding that the world comes with an obligation to improve it, which will ensure a future better than the past.

Jefferson studied law under Wythe for the next three years, also enjoying the social life of the town. He attended balls and parties and fell in love with Rebecca Burwell, who lived in Yorktown. Jefferson had hoped to attend law school in England and then return to marry "Belinda." This was not to be. Rebecca married her longtime neighbor Jacquelin Ambler, and Jefferson's inheritance, which he gained when he reached legal adulthood in 1764, was not enough to allow him to travel much outside the colony, much less over an ocean. Consequently, he focused on the practice of law and building a home on a mountain near Shadwell that he would call Monticello. He occasionally visited Williamsburg to appear in court. In 1768, he was elected to the House of Burgesses, which further required his presence in the capital city. By 1771, he was courting Martha Wayles, a widow who owned property that stretched from the outskirts of Williamsburg to the far side of Richmond. When the two were married on January 1, 1772, she added more than 135 enslaved men and women and eleven thousand acres to their holdings, three times as much property as Jefferson had inherited from his father. Together they became one of the wealthiest couples in Virginia, with farms in six counties.

While Martha and Thomas Jefferson split their time among Williamsburg, her father's home in Charles City County, and Monticello—which was still being built—another family entered their lives, in 1774, after the death of her father: the Hemingses. Expressly left to Martha in her father's will, the large Hemings family, which included half brothers and half sisters of Martha, took over all responsibility for running the household at Monticello. One in particular would have a major impact on Jefferson's life in Williamsburg: Martin Hemings, who replaced an enslaved man named Jupiter who had grown up with Jefferson. Hemings assumed responsibility for many household finances and accompanied Jefferson to Williamsburg, taking care of much of the Jeffersons' personal business.

Jefferson's business became increasingly political as the constitutional crisis worsened in the 1770s. Jefferson was in the Capitol in 1765 to witness Patrick Henry's speech against the Stamp Act.

Jefferson gradually emerged as a radical leader, supporting increasingly vehement measures to oppose the principle that the British Parliament, which did not contain a single representative of America, could levy taxes on the colonies. By 1773, after almost a decade of attempts by Parliament to do just that, Jefferson began to see independence

from Great Britain as the only way to protect liberty. In March, he met with Henry and others at the Raleigh Tavern to create the first American union of like-minded leaders from all the colonies through the committees of correspondence. The next year, after Parliament closed the port of Boston, Jefferson found in the Council's library in the Capitol an English civil war precedent for popular action through a "Day of Fasting, Humiliation, and Prayer" to show support for Massachusetts. Later in 1774, he wrote a set of instructions for Virginia's delegation to the First Continental Congress in the form of a letter to King George III. Shutting himself in his rooms at Monticello for several months over the summer, Jefferson poured over books on philosophy and history. The result was *A Summary View of the Rights of British America*, a pamphlet in which Jefferson articulated better than anyone before him the patriots' view of the proper relationship between Britain and the colonies: Parliament had no authority over them; they were connected only through the person of the king. He also reflected on the nature of freedom, writing, "The God who gave us life gave us liberty at the same time; the hand of force may destroy, but cannot disjoin them." Less than two years later a committee of the Second Continental Congress would choose Jefferson to draft the Declaration of Independence.

In 1776, after Jefferson's election to the new House of Delegates, he, Martha, and Martin were required to spend more time in the capital. They first lived with George Wythe and then rented rooms nearby. Their connection to the city only increased when Jefferson was elected governor in the summer of 1779, and the family, including their daughters, moved into the Governor's Palace. They lived there for the better part of the next year until the capital moved to Richmond.

The last year of the War for Independence would not be kind to Jefferson. The enemy invasion of 1781 made him first flee Richmond and then abandon Monticello. A number of his slaves joined the British, though Martin Hemings did not. The physical and emotional strain that came with having and then losing several children along with the war took a serious toll on Martha Jefferson. She died at Monticello on September 6, 1782. Hemings remained with Jefferson until 1792 when a dispute between them, rumored to be over Martin's half sister Sally Hemings, caused Martin to demand that Jefferson sell him. The last records of Martin Hemings note him as living in 1795 with Jefferson's son-in-law Thomas Mann Randolph near Monticello.

Jefferson, of course, would go on from Williamsburg to become America's first secretary of state and third president. He died on July 4, 1826.

▲ Monument marking Jefferson's grave at Monticello.

The tradespeople of Historic Trades play critical roles as members of the Revolutionary community. They show artisans at work and provide insights into the impact of the Revolution—of changing attitudes, economic challenges, and political and military events in the late eighteenth century—on the Williamsburg business community.

When you enter some trades shops, you might encounter the story of opportunities created by a state that heavily invested in building and maintaining the technological infrastructure necessary to support the war effort and a wartime

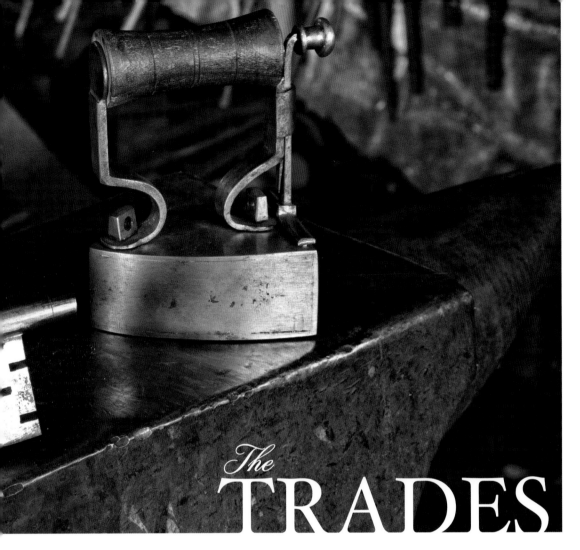

The TRADES

civilian community. You might find in other shops, such as those that produce luxury goods, artisans who lament the business challenges they face in a time of economic uncertainty and increasing commercial caution. Such stories rarely find their way into history books, yet they were crucial to a country waging a conflict for which it was not fully prepared and, at the same time, looking to a postwar future. The ways in which you will engage with these historical moments in the individual shops can vary as much as the trades themselves. In all of them, however, you will find men and women, masters and apprentices, who are employing successful technologies, attracting customers, adapting to shifting market demands for goods

and services, and earning a living. What they achieved was ultimately as important to the Revolution as winning battles.

It took time for the American Revolution to directly impact Williamsburg's trades. The local economy remained sound for several years as private demand and the new government boosted many businesses with orders for goods and supplies. When the economy began to weaken, some tradespeople pondered whether to continue to cast their lot with the patriots or go elsewhere before economic conditions worsened. That choice became starker by 1779 when the trades community began to face unprecedented challenges in building a new nation without raw materials, with little private demand for their goods, with rampant inflation, and with a government that could not properly pay them for what they ordered. On top of that, the prospect of a British army marching down Duke of Gloucester Street became a very real threat to many—and a serious business opportunity for others.

CARPENTER AND JOINER

Near the Capitol, in the Ayscough House, is the joiner's shop. In 1776, Williamsburg's joiners and house carpenters, such as Robey Coke and Francis Jaram, began to enjoy a measure of increased prosperity as something of a building boom hit the town: soldiers and a new government required buildings of all sorts, from barracks to hospitals to an armory. Advertisements for journeymen and apprentice joiners filled the town's newspapers. Throughout the war, they continued to build and repair structures across town, as well as make things for the army and navy, including tent poles, muskets, ammunition and medicine chests, canteens, wooden cartridge boxes, and coffins. By the end of the war, a family of joiners and carpenters, the Jarams, reconsidered their early support for the patriots and switched their allegiance back to the British.

APOTHECARY

Dr. William Pasteur and Dr. John Minson Galt had a partnership at the Pasteur & Galt Apothecary Shop from 1775 to 1778. Pasteur and Galt provided a wide variety of services to free and enslaved men and women. They practiced "Physic and Surgery to their fullest Extent" and kept "full and complete Assortments of Drugs and Medicines," and Galt paid "particular Attention to Surgery." Galt also practiced as a "man-midwife," the eighteenth-century term for a male who delivered babies. Their patients included both free and enslaved men, women, and children, including a few dignitaries such as Patrick Henry. Both doctors were patriots. Pasteur was elected mayor of the town for 1776. In the same year, he was paid for supplying the army with medicines and services. Galt was surgeon to the continental hospital in town and on the board of directors of the Public Hospital. During the war, both doctors dealt with public health issues such as smallpox and whooping cough and the problems of obtaining imported medical supplies. In the shop, you will enter the world of eighteenth-century science and medicine and learn about the theories and treatments used in ministering to the men and women of Williamsburg.

SILVERSMITH

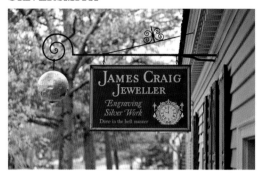

At the onset of the American Revolution, Williamsburg boasted several silversmiths, such as the former Londoner James Craig "at the Golden Ball." Craig worked in Williamsburg from at least 1746, importing and making a variety of jewelry and flatware and repairing clocks and watches. Though some smiths left the city during the war, Craig remained through the economic collapse of 1779–1780 and the British army occupations. The silversmiths in the shop today continue to make and sell hollowware, flatware, and jewelry.

MILLINER AND TAILOR

After 1771, milliner Margaret Hunter rented and later owned the brick shop across from Wetherburn's tavern. Her trade involved the making of fashionable accessories, which were called *ornaments* or *millinery*. These articles, made for everyone in the family, included shirts, shifts, cloaks, neck handkerchiefs, aprons, caps, and bonnets. In addition, Hunter advertised that she practiced the "Business in all its Branches," among which were making baby clothes, making and mending fans, embroidery, and doing fine laundry. As a shop milliner, she filled her shelves with boxes that contained imported goods that complemented what she made. A customer might buy shoes, toys, jewelry, fabrics, and tea while finding out the newest fashions from London. Hunter's millinery was one of five such shops in the city in 1774–1775. By 1780, she was the only milliner still open for business. She still had imported goods on the shelves, and it seems that, even with a war going on, people needed fashionable accessories for their wardrobes. Today, milliners also practice the trade of mantua making (dressmaking), which could be learned in the eighteenth century as part of a double apprenticeship.

On the eve of the Revolution, a dozen or more tailor shops were scattered about Williamsburg. Today, tailors practice and preserve all of the clothing trades in Margaret Hunter's

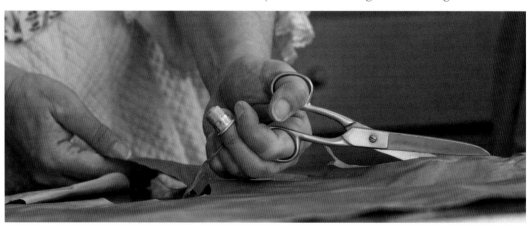

millinery shop. Williamsburg tailors cut to measure and constructed clothing for citizens of every station; the gentleman's fine suit, the lady's practical riding habit, the slave's utilitarian jacket and trousers were all made bespoke. The customer traditionally brought the fabric to the tailor, having bought it from a merchant in town. The onset of the war changed these arrangements. The increasing scarcity of goods following the nonimportation agreements decreased the number of civilian customers while the new demands to supply Virginia's army with uniforms and tents overwhelmed tailors, working under government contract, with work. Shops like that of James Slate, once directly across the street from Margaret Hunter's, prospered and hired new hands to accommodate the needs of the war.

WIGMAKER

Also in the city's commercial district, in the King's Arms Barber Shop, is the wigmaker. Williamsburg may have had as many as fifteen "perukemakers" working in the town by 1775. Edward Charlton, an Englishman, had been in the city since at least 1752, but he had competitors such as Walter Lenox at the Red Lion and George Lafong, a Frenchman who carried on his business *"TOUT A LA MODE."* The American Revolution had a major impact on some fashions, as a republican sense of simplicity began to change what people wore and how they wanted to be seen. Wigs began to go out of style, especially among the younger generation of Virginians, but many continued to wear them and brought them in for redressing as styles changed. Charlton and his professional colleagues did much more than make wigs. They were also "hairdressers" and barbers for men and women, and some made money with side ventures. Some were also merchants or ran a boardinghouse, as Lenox did. Such skills enabled them to weather the storms of the war, and ten were still in Williamsburg at the end of the conflict.

Blacksmith

In the heart of the city, surrounded by a mix of businesses and homes, James Anderson operated a blacksmith shop and public armory. For more than ten years, Anderson operated a very successful blacksmith shop behind his residence at the corner of Botetourt and Francis Streets. At the peak of its operation, during the war, the complex employed about forty workmen in about six buildings. The reconstructed armory is the most tangible example of the industrial infrastructure Virginia needed to keep an army supplied in the field. Valued for its strength, durability, and low cost, iron was used by everyone within the city as hardware for construction, furnishings for households and workshops, farm implements, vehicle hardware, and in wartime weapons maintenance. Today the work progresses much as it did in the eighteenth century. Iron and steel are heated in a coal-fired forge that is fanned with a bellows. The softened iron is worked with a hammer on an anvil to produce ironwork needed throughout the community.

Tin Man

Included within the eighteenth-century armory complex was a tin shop, opened in 1778 within a repurposed tenement house. Tinware was valued by soldiers for its durability, low cost, and light weight. The armory daybook records on June 25, 1779, that, among the workmen in the shop, "Mr. Nathaniel Nuthall Came to work . . . as Tin Man." The shop's production consisted of tinplate items necessary to the logistics and support of Virginia's military, namely camp kettles, cups, plates, saucepans, teakettles, artillery canisters, lanterns, measures, funnels, coffeepots, and speaking trumpets, which were used to project voices over long distances.

"Tin" actually refers to *tin-plate*—thin sheets of iron coated with tin. The tin coating protects the iron from corrosion, extending its life. Tin is thin and flexible enough to be worked cold. Today, you can see tin-plate workers cut, piece, and solder utilitarian tinware for use in the Revolutionary City.

POST OFFICE, PRINTER, BOOKBINDER

On the north side of Duke of Gloucester Street, between Colonial and Botetourt Streets across from the Public Armoury, are two buildings that reflect three separate but linked businesses—the Post Office, the Printer, and the Bookbinder. At the street level is the Post Office. By the middle of 1739, the postal service in the colonies extended from Boston through principal towns in New York, Pennsylvania, Maryland, Virginia, and North Carolina to Charleston, S.C. For many years, Williamsburg's post office was the responsibility of William Hunter Sr., a friend of Benjamin Franklin. They were both deputy postmasters general for America, Franklin for the northern colonies and Hunter for the southern, until Hunter's death in 1761. The post office of the eighteenth century functioned just as it does today, as the place where members of the community could pick up and send mail. In addition, such shops frequently sold books, ink, prints, pamphlets, playing cards, and many imported items. Again, today, you can purchase such items and post mail there.

Down the steps next to the Post Office to the lower level of the building, you will find the printer's pressmen and typesetters and, in a separate building, the bookbinder. In 1775, Williamsburg boasted three newspapers, all of which were called the *Virginia Gazette* and printed every week. William Hunter Jr. and

John Dixon operated the oldest of Williamsburg's newspapers on this site; John Pinkney and Alexander Purdie published theirs elsewhere in town. Hunter Jr. also inherited the management of the post office from his father. They all frequently needed the services of bookbinders, such as Thomas Brend, who bound imported books and pamphlets that often arrived in unfolded sheets. The American Revolution radically transformed the lives of these men and their businesses: Hunter remained loyal to Great Britain, giving up the newspaper and eventually joining the British army under Lord Cornwallis and fighting at Yorktown; Purdie died in 1779, just a year before his patriot soldier son died as a prisoner of war; and John Pinkney left for North Carolina in 1777 to become the state printer. By the end of 1780, not a single newspaper was left in the city.

COOPER

One of the most important trades in Revolutionary Williamsburg was that of the coopers, makers of casks of many sizes and sorts to carry everything that came into or went out of Virginia, from tobacco to wine. Simply put, commerce in the colonial world depended on the efforts of coopers, frequently trained slaves, who were in almost constant demand by planters, merchants, and anyone else who wanted to safely move goods. Cooperage, practiced in the Ludwell-Paradise Stable today, requires a keen understanding of the properties of different kinds of wood and the ability to effectively shape it into tight-fitting staves and to ensure a tight seal, all of which depends on what a barrel, a pipe, or a hogshead is intended to contain. Coopers also make buckets and pails. During the American Revolution, demand for their products exploded as gunpowder, flour, and other important materials had to be shipped to troops throughout the new nation.

CABINETMAKER

At Hay's Cabinetmaking Shop, fine furniture was made between 1751 and 1776 and is again today. When the war commenced, Williamsburg's cabinetmakers were engaged in a variety of activities, such as making furniture for the Governor's Palace, strong boxes, coffins, and stocks for guns. The war forced them to make choices. Edmund Dickinson, who leased the shop from Anthony Hay's widow in 1771, became an officer in George Washington's army and was killed at the Battle of Monmouth in 1778. Benjamin Bucktrout, a Londoner who had worked in Hay's shop, was later accused of being a loyalist. Most of the

other cabinetmakers in town, like Richard Harrocks and John Crump, focused on their craft, making and repairing "household and kitchen furniture." The Hay shop itself closed down during the war and was rented out by the state for James Anderson to use in fulfilling his responsibilities as public armorer.

MASONRY TRADES

The Brickyard provides the Historic Area with the tens of thousands of bricks it needs to construct and maintain its many structures. The masonry tradespeople also make lime and mortar and do plastering. They are just as busy today as they were during the American Revolution when men such as Samuel Spurr and Humphrey Harwood were engaged in a number of construction projects around town.

Spurr, the bricklayer who had constructed the wall around the Bruton Parish churchyard in 1752, also laid the brickwork for the Public Hospital in 1771. In 1779, as Virginia currency fell in value, he offered "about 15 or 20,000 bricks" in exchange for corn. By far the most active builder in Williamsburg during the war years was Humphrey Harwood, whose brickyard was east of the Capitol. There Harwood, his journeymen, apprentices, and slaves burned bricks and transformed oyster shells into lime to make the mortar to build and repair both public and private buildings, from exterior walls to kitchen ovens. Harwood was elected an officer in the local militia and served on numerous local committees during the war. In 1779 alone he was employed by enough projects to require the production of at least twenty-five thousand bricks as the capital city grew to meet the demands of the new government. At the Brickyard in the Historic Area, brickmakers use the same techniques that Harwood and his workers used, molding Virginia clay into bricks and then constructing and firing the brick kiln. In fact, you might be called on to lend a hand, if you don't mind getting your feet dirty.

MILITARY ARTIFICER

Soldiers needed all sorts of military materials to carry on the business of war. Military artificers, enlisted or contracted by the government, produced and maintained many of these items. During the eighteenth century, a typical artificer company consisted of a variety of artisans: Blacksmiths, carpenters, saddlers, tailors, shoemakers, and wheelwrights were common. In February 1778, Lawrence Howse was commissioned captain of the company of artificers in the State Artillery Regiment. Captain

Howse's company maintained a detachment in Williamsburg to support the garrison there until the capital moved to Richmond in 1780. Colonial Williamsburg's military artificers represent members of this company and specialize in the production of leather, textile, and fiber items that include cartridge pouches, belting, knapsacks and luggage, buckskin breeches, and felt hats and caps. The artificers also support other trade shops with leatherwork such as bellows, belts for lathes, upholstery, and machine fittings.

SHOEMAKER

The shoemakers of Williamsburg saw an immediate boost in demand for their wares

at the start of the war. Some of them tried to turn from making and selling satin and calfskin shoes and pumps to producing strong shoes and boots for the troops. Other entrepreneurs organized yet additional shoemakers, becoming opportunistic private military shoe contractors. However, such work could last only as long as master shoemakers such as Robert Gilbert had the leather and other materials they needed to make the footwear, which they had formerly imported solely from Great Britain. It was an expensive and inefficient system rife with corruption, so the state created its own shoe manufactory in Williamsburg, which failed. Shoemakers struggled as the economy collapsed and the survival of their businesses came to depend almost entirely on their ability to obtain leather. In today's shop, you can see all aspects of the eighteenth-century process for making men's shoes, including stitching by hand with eighteenth-century tools.

GUNSMITH AND FOUNDRY

Located behind the James Geddy House, founders cast and finish buckles, knobs, bells, spoons, and other objects in bronze, brass, pewter, and silver, and gunsmiths demonstrate the skills required to create and maintain eighteenth-century firearms and other weapons. Williamsburg's gunsmiths such as William Geddy, who likely worked on this site from at least 1751, were in great demand at the beginning of the Revolution. Geddy once advertised that he could provide "Gun Work, such as Guns and Pistols Stocks, plain or neatly varnished, Locks and Mountings, Barrels blued, bored, and rifled," among other kinds of metalwork. In 1775 and 1776, the new government desperately needed such skills as it purchased thousands of muskets and rifles from Virginians, all of which had to be inspected, cleaned, and repaired before being issued to soldiers. In that period, Geddy was paid by the Committee of Safety for both repairing arms and for casting ammunition. Gunsmiths became even more valuable as the demand for serviceable arms increased over the course of the war and were needed not just for armies in far-off places but also for troops to defend Virginia. However, that business was not enough to keep William Geddy in Williamsburg. He moved to nearby James City County at nearly the same time his brother James left the city and sold their family home, in 1777.

HISTORIC GARDENER

Professional, English-trained gardeners were employed at the Governor's Palace and the College of William and Mary throughout the colonial period. The last gardener employed at the Palace, John Farquharson, tended the gardens for the last two royal governors and then, in 1776, was appointed public gardener under Governor Patrick Henry. Farquharson managed the Palace grounds while the Palace served as a residence for the governors of the commonwealth and as a hospital. James, a slave of Nathaniel Burwell at nearby Carter's Grove and one of several enslaved gardeners who rose to prominence through their skills, was contracted to work at the Palace. At the Colonial Garden on Duke of Gloucester Street, historic gardeners use eighteenth-century tools and techniques to grow a wide range of period plants.

WEAVER

The weavers are located in the Taliaferro-Cole Shop on Duke of Gloucester Street, near Bruton Parish Church. Much of the building dates from the eighteenth century while the weavers within authentically represent centuries-old skills of textile production. Until the American Revolution, Williamsburg had very little call for weavers. Almost all of the cloth needed by merchants and families in Virginia was imported: Linen came from Ireland; brightly colored calicos were transported from India; and wool, cotton, and other materials were sent directly from the growing textile industry in England. As political tensions strained such trade networks in the 1760s and 1770s, patriots explored ways for the colony to become less dependent on Britain for cloth.

Virginia "homespun" cotton even became fashionable for a brief period. When the war began, fashion turned to necessity as all imports came to a halt. While networks of home-based weavers were employed by the new state to create uniforms for soldiers, enterprising members of the community saw the greater need to establish a weaving industry. In 1777, the newly established Williamsburg Society of Manufacturers established a manufactory nearby. It employed a number of weavers, spinners, and wool combers and created apprenticeships for poor boys and girls to learn trades. It remained in operation until 1784. All the skills required to produce eighteenth-century cloth, including making dyes and applying them to various textiles and of course spinning fibers, are represented at the weaver's shop today.

BASKETMAKER

Turn any corner in the Historic Area or walk down Duke of Gloucester Street, and you may encounter a basketmaker. Weaving strips of wood (preferably white oak) into baskets was most often done at home in the eighteenth century, but the job can be done anywhere an adult or, quite often, a child can sit and nimbly work the wood into durable containers. Throughout Williamsburg, every household and business required baskets for many practical purposes. They were prized for their strength rather than for any decorative purpose.

WHEELWRIGHT

The Elkanah Deane Shop was the site of carriage making two hundred years ago and is again today. Deane, who learned his trade in Dublin, established a carriage-making business after following Lord Dunmore (for whom he had made "a coach, phaeton, and chaise") to Williamsburg from New York in 1772. He advertised a wide range of related services, included making and repairing "all sorts of coaches, landaus, chariots, postchaises, phaetons, curricles, chaises, and chairs with harness of every sort" as well as painting and gilding "in the best manner, and on the lowest terms." Consequently, he employed a large number of workmen, many of whom were also Irish, perhaps the most important of whom were the wheelwrights. A carriage maker's entire reputation could rise or fall on whether the wheels of his coaches and wagons could withstand the rough colonial roads in all sorts of weather. Today, the Historic Area's wheelwrights employ the same skills, which demand precision, to fashion wood, such as elm, into a hub and then attach spokes and fellies, the wooden pieces that, when connected to each other, form the rim. The final task is to fit an iron hoop to the rim. Every step in the process requires the closest possible attention to detail or the entire assembly could fail. Deane's shop, one of several in Williamsburg, was in operation until Deane's death in 1775, although the business continued under several other managers well into the war years.

FOODWAYS

On any given day at the Public Armoury or the kitchen of the Governor's Palace, you have the chance to experience the sights, sounds, and smells of one of the central aspects of life in the Revolutionary City, courtesy of artisans who practice eighteenth-century foodways. In the early 1770s, a professor at the College of William and Mary observed the differences between meals in England and Williamsburg, concluding that "Eating seems to be the predominant passion of a Virginian." For those in Williamsburg who could afford it, and generally employed servants or enslaved cooks, "tables at dinner are crowded with a profusion of meat," "rivers afford them fish in great Abundance," and "Swamps and forests furnish them ducks teale blue-wing, hares, Squirrells, partridges and a great variety of other kinds of fowl." The farther one descended on the social scale, the more simple and meager the dishes, such as hoecakes and porridge. Today, the Historic Foodways chefs engage in a number of activities that demonstrate the many different tastes of the eighteenth century, including making chocolate and brewing beer. At the Public Armoury, you might see and smell the baking of bread, which was the staple food for the workers there during the Revolutionary War. Historic Foodways also works closely with chefs at Colonial Williamsburg's restaurants to create dishes for you that closely connect your dining experience to that of centuries ago.

HISTORIC FARMER

Historic farmers grow tobacco, corn, and wheat using eighteenth-century techniques, tools, and power sources (oxen and horses) at Great Hopes Plantation, located on the path between the Historic Area and the Visitor's Center. America's founding depended on agriculture, and the work of these tradespeople opens a window into the life of most Virginians. Most of the crops and livestock are heirloom varieties or rare breeds not found in agriculture today.

William HUNTER Jr.

Although Thomas Jefferson remarked that "a Tory has been properly defined to be a traitor in thought, but not in deed," there were plenty of men and women in Williamsburg who, as loyalists (a more accurate term for them), opposed independence in thought *and* deed. Much has been made of John Randolph, Peyton's brother, who left for England with his wife and daughters in 1775 in the vain hope that he could help breach the rift between the colonies and Great Britain. There were also Catherine Rathell, a milliner who tried to return to England but her ship was lost on the way, and the loud linen draper, Bernard Carey, who had to be saved from the noose by his fellow inhabitants simply because he would not keep his political opinions to himself (he later fled from the city).

But there were also loyalists who remained in Williamsburg and attempted to live their lives even when their community changed around them. One of the most prominent was the printer William Hunter Jr. (ca. 1754–after 1801). The illegitimate son of William Hunter and Elizabeth Reynolds, he was born in Williamsburg in a house near the present print shop. William Hunter Sr. had been Virginia's public printer and one of America's two deputy postmasters general (the other was his friend Benjamin Franklin). William Hunter Jr., known to his friends as Billy, moved to Philadelphia when he was ten to live with Franklin and learn the printing trade. Hunter spent the next four years in Philadelphia and was there when Franklin's home was attacked by a large mob because of his support for the Stamp Act. It was also during this time that Hunter developed a close relationship with Franklin's son William, the royal governor of New Jersey. Hunter returned to Williamsburg in 1767 and continued his education before assuming control of his father's business and property in 1774

(in town he owned the entire half of a block on which the print shop, his mother's reconstructed house, and the Sign of the Rhinoceros now sit).

As the war progressed, Hunter's politics made it increasingly difficult to operate a printing business in the patriot capital. While his competitors, Alexander Purdie and John Pinkney, printed excerpts of Thomas Paine's *Common Sense* in order to help convince Virginians of the necessity for independence from Great Britain, Hunter published full-length rebuttals of Paine's argument. By 1777, Hunter felt he had no choice but to give up the newspaper business that his father had built, leaving the running of it to his partner, John Dixon. Hunter later explained that "he declined his Business in 1777 as he found he could not continue according to his Prin[cip]les." He also tried to sell his properties, but he was unsuccessful. But life continued for him in Williamsburg. Between 1777 and 1780, he and his new wife, Elizabeth Davenport Hunter, had two children while he tried to keep a low profile managing his other businesses and properties.

All that changed in 1781 when Hunter became a spy for the British. In April, during Benedict Arnold's occupation of Williamsburg, he provided the enemy with the location of the Virginia navy yard on the Chickahominy River, which led to its destruction and the end of Virginia's fleet. Throughout 1781 he continued to supply the British with information until the beginning of the Yorktown campaign. Then Hunter left his children with his father-in-law and joined Cornwallis's army, taking up arms against his neighbors in a company of volunteers. After the surrender, he left with Cornwallis, eventually ending up in London. In 1784 Hunter, "late of the Colony of Virginia, Printer, Bookseller, and Stationer," claimed compensation from the British government for his losses. Among the supporters of his claim were Cornwallis and Governor William Franklin. Cornwallis wrote that Hunter had "rendered essential Service by procuring Intelligence of the Enemy, and by every other Means in his Power; and that he afterwards bore Arms at the Siege of York Town in a Company of Volunteers. He has sacraficed his Fortune to his Loyalty." Franklin strongly recommended Hunter's case stating that he was "well acquainted with Mr. William Hunter, late of Williamsburg in Virginia, that he is a Gentleman of good Character, was in good Business, and possessed a valuable Property in that Country at the time of the Commencement of the late Rebellion in America, which Property he has lost on Account of his having joined the King's Forces, and taken an active Part in support of his Majesty and the British Government." Hunter himself declared that he was "firmly attached to the British Constitution, and ever averse to the proceedings of the Americans." The British government allowed him a pension of thirty pounds a year for life. He did not return to Williamsburg, and there is no evidence that he ever saw his children again. In 1801, twenty years after Yorktown, Hunter was still in London, working in a print shop. The date of his death is unknown.

Hunter was one of the many inhabitants of Williamsburg who had misgivings about what Patrick Henry and Thomas Jefferson were doing in separating Virginia from Great Britain. As Williamsburg's Edmund Randolph, the son of John, recalled, history wrongly labeled them as traitors simply for remaining true to their own principles. He disagreed with his friend Jefferson's view of the subject, writing that "multitudes could now be cited, who, confounded by the new order of things suddenly flashing upon their minds and still entangled by the habits of many years, were branded as Tories, though spotless as to treason even in thought."

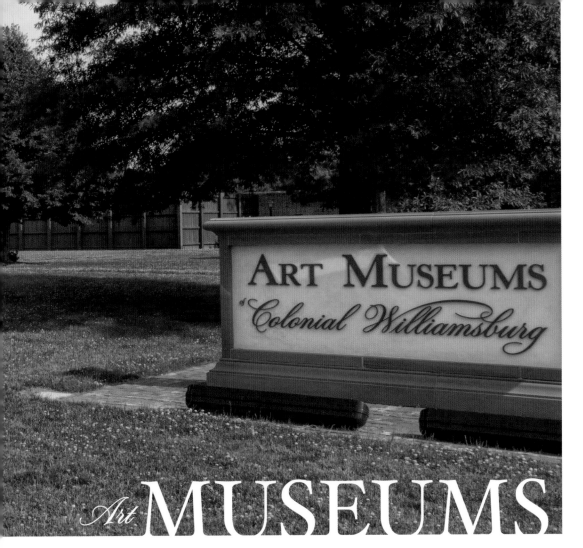

Art MUSEUMS

Colonial Williamsburg's collections include nearly seventy thousand examples of American and British fine, decorative, and mechanical art; five thousand pieces of American folk art; more than twenty million archaeological artifacts; and fifteen thousand architectural fragments. Many objects in the collections furnish more than two hundred rooms in the Historic Area. Others, including many of the most remarkable, are displayed in the Art Museums of Colonial Williamsburg, where both long-term and changing exhibitions illuminate life in Virginia and America before, during, and after the Revolution.

The DeWitt Wallace Decorative Arts Museum displays an extensive collection of American and British antiques, including furniture, metals, ceramics, glass, paintings, prints, firearms, and textiles from the seventeenth, eighteenth, and nineteenth centuries.

The Abby Aldrich Rockefeller Folk Art Museum exhibits the work of artists and craftspeople working outside the mainstream of academic art to record aspects of everyday life, making novel and effective use of materials at hand. Bold colors, simplified shapes, and imaginative surface patterns can be seen in these paintings, carvings, toys, and needlework.

Enter the DeWitt Wallace Decorative Arts Museum and the Abby Aldrich Rockefeller Folk Art Museum through the Public Hospital of 1773, a three-part exhibit on mental illness and treatment methods.

The Art Museums of Colonial Williamsburg are planning an expansion that will include an additional eight thousand square feet of gallery space to showcase the collections. A new entrance will allow guests to identify the museums more easily and to enter directly from the street. (The Public Hospital will remain an exhibition building but will not serve as an entrance to the museums.) The expansion plans also include a spacious lobby and grand course with portals into both the DeWitt Wallace Decorative Arts Museum and the Abby Aldrich Rockefeller Folk Art Museum, more space for programs and activities, and an expanded and updated café and museum store.

The following pages introduce a small sampling of the treasures to be found at the DeWitt Wallace Decorative Arts Museum and the Abby Aldrich Rockefeller Folk Art Museum.

▲ Rendering of planned museum façade

DeWitt Wallace Decorative Arts Museum

Peale's Portrait of Washington

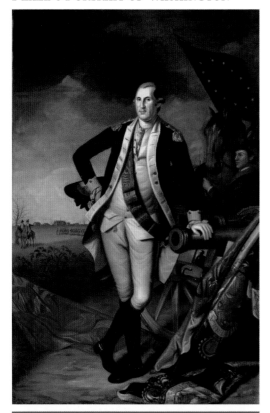

Portrait of George Washington, Charles Willson Peale, Philadelphia, Pennsylvania, 1780, oil on canvas, gift of John D. Rockefeller Jr., 1933-502

On January 18, 1779, the Supreme Executive Council of Pennsylvania, "Deeply sensible how much the liberty, safety, & happiness of America . . . is owing to His Excell'y General Washington," requested that the commander sit to painter Charles Willson Peale for a portrait. Washington posed in Philadelphia in late January.

Peale began receiving requests for replicas even before he completed the original painting. He varied the replicas, rendering both full-length and three-quarter-length versions and placing the commander variously on the battlefield of Princeton, Trenton, or Yorktown. A total of eight full-length versions are known to survive.

Peale used a state portrait formula in posing Washington, echoing the stance of George III in Allan Ramsay's coronation portrait of the British monarch, creating a statement that was satiric as well as earnest. Could anyone viewing Peale's painting doubt that America possessed heroic leaders on par with Europe's? The monumental scale of the painting provides further analogies with European state portraiture, as does the fact that one of Peale's likenesses was presented to the French king Louis XVI.

Light Dragoon Pistol

Pattern 1759 Elliot Light Dragoon Pistol, Board of Ordnance, London or Birmingham, England, 1760–1764, walnut, iron, steel, and brass, Museum Purchase, 1949-266

The Pattern 1759 Elliot Light Dragoon pistol was developed for use by the newly raised regiments of British Light Dragoons during the Seven Years' War. During the American Revolution, it was one of the most common pistols carried by mounted troops fighting on both sides. Other examples are known with markings for the Seventeenth Light Dragoons and the Sixteenth or "Queen's" Light Dragoons, which served here during the war.

One of many in Colonial Williamsburg's collection, this example was formerly part of an arms display at Stirling Castle, Scotland. It was dismantled at the beginning of World War II so the castle could accommodate soldiers preparing to head off to war.

1816 Grand Piano

Grand Piano, William Stodart, London, England, 1816, rosewood, mahogany, oak, white pine, ivory, ebony, brass, iron, cloth, and leather, gift of Irene Bernard Hilliard, 2000-67

The piano was purchased by Thomas Rutherfoord, a wealthy Richmond, Virginia, merchant, for his daughter Jane Rutherfoord Meade, most probably from Adam Stodart, a Richmond musical instrument dealer, and a relative of the maker of the piano. Adam Stodart is known to have imported pianos made by his London relatives William and Matthew Stodart.

Glass Dessert Stand

Sweetmeat Stand, England, 1760–1765, colorless lead glass and ormolu, gift of John V. Rowan Jr. in memory of Winifred Draco Shrubsole, 2001-853

With its original dishes and hanging baskets, this sweetmeat stand is a remarkably complete example of the most elaborate type of dessert glassware. The top glass would have held an orange or other preserved fruit; the baskets and dishes would have been filled with nuts and sweetmeats (candied fruits). The facets of the cut glass and the gilded metal mounts were designed to reflect the glow of candlelight, further enhancing the sparkling appearance of the whole. Although now quite rare survivals, glass sweetmeat stands once graced the dessert tables of many prominent colonial families. George Washington, John Randolph, and John

Marshall are among the prominent Virginians known to have owned such objects.

SOUTH CAROLINA CHEST

Double Chest of Drawers, Charleston, South Carolina, 1765–1780, mahogany, bald cypress, and tulip poplar, Museum Purchase, 1974-166

During the second half of the eighteenth century, the double chest of drawers was the most popular furniture form for clothing and textile storage in elite Low Country (coastal South Carolina and Georgia) households. It became fashionable in Britain about midcentury, which likely accounts for its almost immediate acceptance in Anglo-centric coastal South Carolina. The simplest Charleston-made double chests feature a flat top with a simple molded cornice, but other decorative and functional options were available at additional cost. With its enriched cornice, ornate fretwork pediment, and secretary (desk) drawer, this example is the finest of the known survivors.

The piece was first owned by Charleston merchant and planter John Deas, a Scottish immigrant, and his wife, Elizabeth Allen Deas. It is probably the "double Chest drawers" listed in the 1791 inventory of John Deas Sr.'s estate.

CEREMONIAL ARMCHAIR AND MATCHING BACK STOOL

Governor's Chair (left), England, ca. 1750, mahogany and beech, Museum Purchase, 1930-215; Back Stool (right), England, ca. 1750, mahogany, brown oak, cherry, beech, ash, and Scots pine, Museum Purchase, the Friends of Colonial Williamsburg Collections Fund, and the TIF Foundation in memory of Michelle A. Iverson, 2012-26

This impressive ceremonial armchair and matching back stool were likely part of a suite that included a matching footstool and at least twelve back stools. The furniture must have been ordered from England around 1750 for use in the Council Chamber of Virginia's

Capitol. The Council, consisting of twelve elite Virginians, met in the chamber to advise the governor on matters affecting the entire colony. As befit their position in society and government, these councillors sat in very expensive chairs made of highly carved tropical mahogany upholstered in red silk and adorned with polished brass tacks. Seating this costly was rarely seen in Virginia.

CHEROKEE CHIEF IN LONDON

Cunne Shote, the Indian Chief, a Great Warrior of the Cherokee Nation, engraved by James McArdell after Francis Parsons, London, England, ca. 1763, black-and-white mezzotint engraving, Museum Purchase, 2002-10

Cunne Shote was one of the three Cherokee men escorted to London in 1762 by Henry Timberlake, a British officer who had lived with the Cherokee. While in London, Cunne Shote sat for an oil portrait that was subsequently engraved in mezzotint.

Cunne Shote's combination of English and Native clothing and accoutrements was meant to suggest the harmonious unity between cultures. The medals around his neck commemorate the marriage of George III and Charlotte of Mecklenburg while the crescent-shaped silver gorget bears the initials "GR III." The most striking aspect of the portrait, however, is the forceful grip that Cunne Shote has on the scalping knife, a clear reminder of the tenuous relationship between the Cherokees and the European settlers living in the southern colonies.

SILVER-PLATE TURTLE SOUP TUREEN

Soup Tureen, probably Sheffield, England, ca. 1815, fused silver plate, bequest of Dr. Lowry Dale Kirby, 1991-693

The technique of fusing silver to copper was discovered by Thomas Boulsover of Sheffield, England, in 1742. Often known as Sheffield plate, this new metal rapidly attained great popularity both at home and abroad because of its success in mimicking sterling silver at a far lower cost. Manufacturers offered a wide array of goods in silver plate, from candlesticks to teapots to tableware. This tureen in the shape of a tortoise provided its original owner with a fanciful and elegant means of serving turtle soup, a popular and costly dish that might have been the first setting at a dinner with as many as five courses.

MASSACHUSETTS SAMPLER

Sampler, Mary Welsh, Massachusetts, ca. 1770, silk embroidery threads on a linen ground, Museum Purchase, 1962-309

Characteristic of Boston samplers worked between 1760 and 1790, this sampler features a reclining shepherdess figure, male "pole vaulter," spotted black dog, and trio of sheep—two white and one black—motifs typically found on "fishing lady" pictures, so-called because the dominant figure is of a lady fishing.

Despite their obvious complexity, most early American and British samplers were fabricated by young girls as a part of their education for "housewifery." This sampler is signed "Mary Welsh Her Sampler Wrought in the 12 Year of Her Age."

ENGRAVED PEWTER DISH

Dish, John Townsend and Thomas Giffin, London, England, 1768–1778, pewter, Museum Purchase, 1995-90

This dish, originally plain, was boldly engraved in 1782 for Hanna Feeshel of Shepherdstown, Virginia (now West Virginia). The design of the ornament and the use of hammer engraving strongly suggest that a local gunsmith decorated this dish, transforming a plain English dish into a highly individual piece of pewter. Gunsmiths were probably among the few in that area who had the requisite skills to accomplish it.

TALL CASE CLOCK

Tall Case Clock, attributed to Peter Rife and David Whipple, Pulaski County, Virginia, ca. 1810, mahogany, cherry, tulip poplar, oak, black walnut, holly, maple, bone, horn, silver, iron, brass, and steel, Museum Purchase, 1996-107

Visually arresting, this clock is distinguished by great height and an ambitious combination of colorful Germanic inlays, brass and silver mounts, and projecting ornaments. Sebastian Wygal of Montgomery (now Pulaski) County

in southwestern Virginia likely acquired it about 1810. The son of a German-speaking Swiss immigrant, Wygal owned a number of slaves and more than two thousand acres of land. Since his home was located on the wagon road from Baltimore to Tennessee, Wygal also operated a tavern and a wagon service to Richmond.

The clock case was probably fashioned by cabinetmaker Peter Rife, who was born in Rockland Township, Pennsylvania, and resided in southwestern Virginia by the 1770s. David Whipple signed the movement in a closely related clock. He was married to Wygal's niece.

SILVER CREAM POT

Cream Pot, Alexander Young, Camden, South Carolina, 1820–1830, silver, Museum Purchase, 2013-107

Camden, South Carolina, was the site of two key battles in 1780 and 1781. Departing British troops burned most of the city in the latter year, but Camden rebuilt and rose to prominence as a wealthy metropolis in the postwar years. Its rebirth was due largely to shipping on the Wateree River between Camden and Charleston.

More than half a dozen silversmiths worked in Camden prior to 1840. Alexander Young appears to have been the most prolific. Born in Scotland, he trained in Baltimore prior to settling in Camden by 1807. This cream pot, part of a now-disbursed tea set, is notable for its unusual patterns of milled banding and its winged animal-paw feet.

Pierced Stoneware

Gorge, James Morley, Nottingham, England, ca. 1700, brown salt-glazed stoneware, Museum Purchase, 1958-529

This finely carved gorge is attributed to James Morley's Nottingham pottery. The association of pierced wares with this potter and locale is based on a trade card issued by Morley around 1700. The card depicts a decanter and "mogg" (straight-sided tankard), flowerpot, teapot, "capuchine" (coffee cup), and jug. The last four items were carved in a style similar to this gorge, that is, constructed as double-walled vessels with foliate piercing cut through the outer walls of the pieces. The technique, which demands considerable skill in both throwing and carving, may be derived from Chinese

porcelain decorated in the so-called Ling Lung method of pierced decoration.

Although no extant teacups with this carved decoration are known, small yet unmistakable fragments of such a form were excavated at the Drummond plantation site near Williamsburg. The Drummond fragments are the only examples of this technique in brown stoneware found in America to date.

Early Map of the Chesapeake Bay and Environs

A Map of the Most Inhabited Part of Virginia Containing the Whole Province of Maryland with Part of Pensilvania, New Jersey and North Carolina, engraved by Thomas Jefferys after Joshua Fry and Peter Jefferson, London, England, 1768, black-and-white line engraving with watercolor on laid paper, Museum Purchase, 1968-11

In Virginia and Maryland, the Chesapeake Bay and its tributaries were the single most important factor in shaping the culture of the region. Thousands of miles of waterfront provided rich tracts of land, well suited for an agrarian economy supported by slave labor. The wealthiest colonists amassed large plantations along the shorelines. These waterways were critical to the tobacco trade, allowing ships to sail inland for miles to load tobacco directly at each plantation. This advantage spared planters the expense of transporting their crops over land.

The connection between the landscape and the slave-based economy was made clear in the cartouche of this map. The seated planter, being served a drink, is the only one for whom a chair was provided. The standing man in the foreground is presumably the ship captain. The scantily clothed laborers working in the background represent the labor force necessary for tobacco cultivation. These slaves were clearly depicted in a manner subservient to the Englishmen.

ABBY ALDRICH ROCKEFELLER FOLK ART MUSEUM

PAINTED CHEST

Blanket Chest, Johannes Spitler, Shenandoah (now Page) County, Virginia, 1800–1805, yellow pine, chestnut, brass, iron, and paint, Museum Purchase, 1990.2000.1

During the late eighteenth and early nineteenth centuries, furniture painter Johannes Spitler worked in the Shenandoah Valley's Massanutten area, where isolation facilitated the preservation of distinctive northern European cultural traditions. Using colors that were originally brilliant and saturated, he painted chests, clock cases, and other furniture forms made by local joiners with symbol-laden ornament that clearly reflected his Swiss- and German-American heritage. The stylized birds, hearts, vines, crescent moons, and compass-drawn flowers seen here signify a range of themes, including abundance, faith, love, fecundity, and spiritual growth. For instance, the flowers and vines bespeak the cycles of nature important to an agrarian society as well as the flowering and growth of the human spirit.

AFRICAN AMERICAN LIFE

The Old Plantation, attributed to John Rose, Beaufort County, South Carolina, 1785–1790, watercolor on laid paper, gift of Abby Aldrich Rockefeller, 1935.301.3

Arguably the best-known depiction of slaves in eighteenth-century America, *The Old Plantation* is remarkable for its sensitive, highly individualized depictions of enslaved men and women and for its objectivity in recording their efforts to maintain African cultural traditions within the context of plantation life. Depicted is a West African stick dance performed to the accompaniment of several African musical instruments.

The setting is likely artist John Rose's plantation on the Coosaw River about ten miles from Beaufort, South Carolina. Rose was educated in the classics, music, and art and devoted his free time to artistic pursuits.

PICTORIAL SIGNBOARD

Eagle Signboard, New England, 1821–1841, oil on wood panel, gift of Juli Grainger, 2008.707.1

Nineteenth-century signboards often combined symbols and texts, but many lacked wording altogether. Pictorial signage could be quite effective. Anyone seeking this proprietor's services would have been directed to "the sign of the eagle." Obviously, the business owner was a patriot, proud of that fact, and eager to attract a like-minded clientele. A spread eagle bearing a striped shield on its chest was the central motif of the Great Seal of the United States, adopted in 1782. Rapidly thereafter, the image gained recognition as a symbol of the new nation. As in many other cases, the eagle here is surrounded

by thirteen stars. The sign bears one alteration: the date at the bottom once read "1821," but the operation's 1841 owner apparently wished to signal a new beginning.

BALTIMORE ALBUM QUILT

Baltimore Album Quilt, Sarah Anne Whittington Lankford, Baltimore, Maryland, 1847–1853, plain and printed cottons with wool, cotton, and silk embroidery threads, ink, and metal and glass beads, gift of Marsha C. Scott, 1979.609.14

Like other appliquéd album quilts made in the vicinity of Baltimore, Maryland, this quilt consists of elaborately created blocks of appliquéd wreaths, baskets, and urns, in addition to representations of urban buildings and civic monuments. Inscribed "Ringgold," the second block in the top row depicts a memorial tribute to Major Samuel Ringgold, a brave Maryland soldier who died in the Battle of Palo Alto, the first engagement of the Mexican-American War. The building next to the Ringgold block represents the U.S. Capitol prior to the addition of the post-1850 wings. The bedcover is quilted in a wide variety of floral and foliage shapes, pinwheels, hearts, parallel diagonal lines, and ovals in about thirteen stitches per inch.

According to family tradition, Henry Smith Lankford purchased the quilt squares at a Baltimore auction. The prefabricated blocks were the work of professional artists. The assembly of the quilt squares and the quilting are attributed to his sister Sarah Anne Whittington Lankford prior to her marriage in 1853. Her initials SAWL are cross-stitched in the center of the lower left apple wreath. The bedcover descended through Henry's family.

SERPENT WEATHER VANE

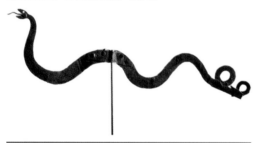

Weather Vane, New England, ca. 1850, iron, gift of Abby Aldrich Rockefeller, 1932.800.3

This snake's gaping mouth, serrated teeth, and ominous tongue perpetuate the stereotypical image of serpents as venomous aggressors. But the silhouette's rhythmic grace and sinuous beauty contrast markedly with conventional belief. Minute details of this vane, such as the teeth, the twisted-wire tongue, and the carefully placed eye are unusual considering that weather vanes were typically placed some distance from the viewer, often rendering such

details indiscernible. But the maker's skill at working iron and the pleasure taken in designing and fabricating the piece apparently outweighed such practical considerations.

PORTRAIT OF BABY

Baby in Red Chair, America, 1810–1830, oil on canvas, Collection of Abby Aldrich Rockefeller, gift of David Rockefeller, 1931.100.1

This endearing portrait was among the earliest acquisitions of pioneering folk art collector Abby Aldrich Rockefeller. Today, it is a widespread favorite of visitors to the museum named by her husband in her memory. The infant's innocence, contentment, and lack of self-consciousness seldom fail to elicit smiles from viewers. The sleeping baby appears oblivious to the world around, comforted and cradled by a soft white pillow and secure in the protective embrace of a sturdy, child-size armchair.

Despite the painting's popularity, little is known of its origin. Although long thought to have been created in Pennsylvania, no other works by the unidentified hand have been discovered there or in Boston, where the picture was discovered in the early twentieth century. There is, however, no doubt about the American origin of the work.

SCULPTURE OF YOUNG CHILD

Portrait of Amanda Clayanna Armstrong, Asa Ames, Evans, New York, 1847, polychromed yellow poplar, gift of Barbara Rice in memory of her grandfather Arthur T. White and her mother, Eleanor Rice, 2009.701.1

Asa Ames carved this portrait when his subject was three and a half years old. The informality of Amanda's pose is perfectly suited to a child's likeness. It also shows how little Ames was influenced by the theatrical attitudes in which high-style sculptors depicted their subjects. Amanda's attire is also realistic. Rather than presenting her in flowing neoclassical drapery, Ames showed her wearing what was, most likely, her own fashionable late-1840s frock. The familiar costume, Amanda's relaxed stance, and her outstretched hand provide a degree of spontaneity not seen in more academic likenesses. Besides being an exceptional achievement for a carver who was barely twenty-three years old, the sculpture reminds us of the importance Americans attached to images of children at a time when infant mortality rates were high.

George and Martha WASHINGTON

George and Martha Washington were prominent members of the Williamsburg community long before the outbreak of the American Revolution thrust them into the national, even global, spotlight. Although his home was more than one hundred miles north of the colonial capital, key moments in the life of George Washington (1732–1799) occurred here. In 1749, when he was only seventeen years old, he embarked on a career here when he was licensed to be a surveyor by the College of William and Mary. Those plans changed rather abruptly just a few years later when he was commissioned a major in the Virginia militia and ordered by the lieutenant governor, Robert Dinwiddie, to warn French troops out of British territory in the west. The result was the Seven Years' War and Washington's leap into transatlantic fame as he rose to the rank of colonel and commander of all Virginia forces. In 1758, Washington was elected to the House of Burgesses and resigned from the army. By then he had met Martha Dandridge Custis (1731–1802), a familiar face to many in Williamsburg. Martha was born and raised in New Kent County, just west of Williamsburg. In 1749, she had married Daniel Parke Custis, one of the wealthiest men in Virginia, with vast property holdings that included one of the largest houses in Williamsburg and several nearby plantations. Together Martha and Daniel had four children, but two of those children and her husband were dead by 1757 (they are buried in the Bruton Parish churchyard). George married Martha on January 6, 1759, at her home in New Kent.

Over the next fifteen years, George and Martha were frequent visitors to Williamsburg as George began his political career in the House of Burgesses and they did their best to manage the immense amount of property that they held in trust for her son, John Parke Custis, called "Jackie." The growing constitutional crisis with Great Britain drew the Washingtons into it as George came to believe that Parliament was increasingly invading the British rights of the Crown's American subjects. But domestic concerns were never far away as Martha's only daughter, Patsy, grew ill and died in the summer of 1773.

Washington retained hope that more moderate heads on both sides of the Atlantic would calm the political waters and protect American rights so that he could concentrate on family life at Mount Vernon, their northern Virginia estate. He even became friends with Virginia's last royal governor, Lord Dunmore, who shared Washington's interest in fox hunting and western land. In the spring of 1774, once news reached Virginia that Parliament had closed Boston's port in retaliation for the Boston Tea Party, Washington helped write the Fairfax Resolves, one of the strongest colonial condemnations of the act. After Dunmore dissolved the House of Burgesses (once he returned from spending several days with Washington at Dunmore's local farm, Porto Bello), Washington stood up in a meeting at the Raleigh Tavern and urged his fellow former burgesses to adopt a nonimportation association and call for a congress of representatives from all the colonies. His colleagues agreed and, several months later, elected Washington to represent them as one of Virginia's delegates to the Continental Congress in Philadelphia. After the Battles of Lexington and Concord in April 1775, the Congress appointed Washington commander in chief of the new Continental army.

Martha supervised affairs at Mount Vernon. She remained staunchly committed to George, visiting his camp six times between 1775 and 1781, spending a total of almost three years with her husband and the army during the war. Throughout the war, George maintained a regular correspondence with leaders and compatriots in Williamsburg, and Martha visited family and friends in August 1777, arriving "amidst the ringing of Bells, several discharges of artillery and vollies of small arms from the troops stationed here" as well as the "good wishes of all the inhabitants." In 1780, she enlisted the help of Martha Jefferson, wife of the then Virginia governor, to organize the ladies in a campaign to support the Continental troops by collecting money and making clothing for them. Moreover, Jackie was spending more time in Williamsburg after being elected to the new House of Delegates under the Virginia Constitution. The people of Williamsburg retained considerable respect and a growing affection for the general and his wife. One of the first children in America to be named for George was the son of Gabriel Maupin, the owner of the Market Square tavern, in October 1775. And one of the first public celebrations of Washington's birthday was held at the Raleigh Tavern on February 22, 1779. The party spilled onto Duke of Gloucester Street and became so raucous that soldiers had to be called in to ensure that it did not result in any property destruction.

Washington's return to Williamsburg was of monumental historical importance: On September 14, 1781, he arrived in command of the allied American and French army set to take on the British forces under Charles Cornwallis at Yorktown. An eyewitness reported that "Men Women & Children seem'd to vie with each other in demonstrations of Joy, and eagerness to see their beloved Countryman." With him, as a member of his staff, was his stepson, Jackie, who had strenuously lobbied his mother for the chance to be with the army for what might be the last campaign of the war. Martha agreed but only on condition that he remain close to her husband. Washington made a headquarters out of the house of his friend George Wythe and there spent two weeks planning the campaign to force the surrender of Cornwallis and, with the highest hopes, the end of the War for Independence. The whole army marched out of Williamsburg on September 28, reaching the outer fortifications of Yorktown that night.

Cornwallis surrendered less than three weeks later, which largely brought an end to the story of the Washingtons and Williamsburg. Grieving for Jackie who had caught a fever in the camp at Yorktown and died, they left Williamsburg. George was unanimously elected first president of the United States in 1789, which took him and Martha first to New York, as the nation's new capital, and then to Philadelphia, its successor, until his retirement from office in 1796. He died at Mount Vernon in 1799, freeing all his slaves in his will. Martha died in 1802.

RevQuest: Save the Revolution!

RevQuest: Save the Revolution! is an alternate reality game, a combined online and on-site experience for families and friends of all ages. You will be cast directly into a Revolutionary spy story in Williamsburg and challenged to help save the Revolution from a particular peril. All of the scenarios are based on rigorously documented historical events.

Players, or "questors," begin the mission online at colonialwilliamsburg.org /your-mission. You will be introduced to the world of eighteenth-century spy craft and explore the background history of Williamsburg and the Revolution in ways that prepare you for the on-site experience. After completing the initial online phase of the game, you continue the mission on-site in the Revolutionary City. You will use your cell phone to get clues, communicate with other spies, and complete the quest.

Playing RevQuest: Save the Revolution! immerses you in a different culture: the Revolutionary world of Williamsburg in the 1770s and 1780s. To succeed, you will have to learn manners and behaviors that are very different from those

More to EXPLORE

of the modern world. Your mission will take you through the city's neighborhoods, into its shops, houses, and public places, down its side streets, and into its backyards and hidden spaces. The experience does not end with solving the final clue. After texting in the last answer, you will have a final encounter with a costumed interpreter to receive your token of appreciation. The token will help unlock the final part of the mission on the website, where you can continue the game.

For many who choose to play, RevQuest: Save the Revolution! frames the entire Revolutionary City experience in unexpected ways. The Revolution required then—as citizenship still does—your full participation.

FOR FAMILIES

The Historic Area is full of exciting and kid-friendly activities. Be sure to pick up "This Week," available at any ticket sales location, for specific program information and schedules since times and activities change daily.

Consider walking, rather than taking the bus, the quarter mile from the Visitor Center to the Revolutionary City. The walk begins by crossing a five-hundred-foot pedestrian bridge. The plaques in the bridge illustrate how life has changed since colonial times and transition you back to the eighteenth century. Just across the bridge is Great Hopes Plantation, where children can sometimes work in the garden, visit the kitchen, and split wood as they learn about daily life and work on a rural plantation. From Great Hopes, it is an easy stroll into town.

Once in town, you can not only watch the Revolution—you can join it. Revolutionary City programming follows the collapse of royal government and the impact of war on the citizens of Williamsburg. Linger and talk to the characters after a scene is done. You can also play the alternate reality game RevQuest: Save the Revolution!, a combined online and on-site experience where you are cast in a Revolutionary spy story.

The Fifes and Drums of Colonial Williamsburg march daily through the streets of the Revolutionary City. Historically, fifers and drummers, usually boys between eleven and nineteen, supported the army in the field. Today, local boys and girls train and perform in this elite musical corps.

Some historic sites of special appeal:

Play Booth Theater. Weather permitting, the Virginia Company of Comedians presents scenes from eighteenth-century theater, musical entr'actes, and theatrical dances once performed during fair days at booths much like this one.

Magazine and Guardhouse. See guns, muskets, powder, and other military supplies.

Courthouse. Older kids can participate in mock trials based on colonial cases. In the pillory and stocks just outside the Courthouse, you can experience firsthand the punishment for stealing a pig.

Public Gaol. Here's where the pirate Blackbeard's henchmen were imprisoned.

Benjamin Powell House. One of the most interactive sites for children, where they can join in various eighteenth-century activities, such as singing and dancing, learning about children's duties in the kitchen and how to set a proper table, and trying out an eighteenth-century bed. Activities vary so check ahead.

James Geddy House. Kids can play with wooden hoops, tops, clay marbles, and other colonial toys.

Governor's Palace. Find your way through the boxwood maze.

The Historic Trades in general appeal to kids, with the specific trade depending on each child's interest. The blacksmith—with all the hammering and fire and smoke—fascinates kids. The milliner entices the fashion conscious. At the wigmaker, consider what you would have chosen in colonial times— human, horse, goat, or yak hair. Tradespeople at the foundry turn molten metal into spoons, candlesticks, and sword handles. At the Colonial Garden, kids may be enlisted to haul water from the well. The Brickyard may be the most kid-friendly site in the Historic Area—kids love the huge mud hole, the treading pit. There they can take off their shoes, step into the slippery mire, and mix clay and water with their feet to prepare the raw material of bricks.

Tickets for carriage and wagon rides are available on the day of the ride at any ticket sales location. Buy your tickets early as these often sell out.

Colonial costume rentals are available for boys and girls at the Visitor Center and at Market Square (open seasonally).

The DeWitt Wallace Decorative Arts Museum and Abby Aldrich Rockefeller Folk Art Museum offer family packs and family programs, including an audio tour for teens. Pieces at the Folk Art Museum and the *Down on the Farm* exhibit, which places folk art masterpieces in a farm setting, are especially child friendly.

A number of evening programs, including tours, plays, dances, concerts, and reenactments, draw families. "The Grand Medley of Entertainments," for example, is an eighteenth-century variety show. "Papa Said, Mama Said" is a delightful program where instructive fables come to life in celebration of the significance of oral African tradition. On the family-friendly Tavern Ghost Walk, enjoy spirited folklore about the ghosts that still haunt the historic buildings. In "Cry Witch," appropriate for older children only, you are part of the jury in this inquiry into the charges of witchcraft brought against Grace Sherwood in 1706.

In addition to the many formal sites and activities that appeal to children is the acreage itself. There are wide-open greens on which

to run and play, brooks to dabble in on a warm day, gardens to explore, tavern and trade signs to spy and decipher, and rare breeds of animals. Found in pastures, paddocks, chicken coops, and dovecotes, these aren't your ordinary farm animals. Red Devon cattle, Leicester Longwool sheep, American Cream Draft horses, and a variety of feathered friends are among the rare breeds of domestic animals preserved here, all of which bring another aspect of the past to life.

The taverns in the Revolutionary City offer a fun eighteenth-century dining experience. Chowning's Tavern has the most casual atmosphere. Weather permitting, you can enjoy lunch in the garden. Family entertainment at Chowning's runs from 5 to 8 p.m. and includes balladeers leading period sing-alongs and costumed servers teaching you to play period games. For southern favorites, try Shields Tavern. For a snack during the day, a favorite stop is the Raleigh Tavern Bakery, where you can take out gingerbread, queen's cake, ham biscuits, cider, and other goodies.

Restrooms are located in the Visitor Center and throughout the Historic Area. Most provide baby-changing stations. Family restrooms are located in the east yard of the Governor's Palace and near the bus stop behind the Magazine.

FIFES AND DRUMS

In the eighteenth century, the job of fifers and drummers was not to entertain but to communicate. They relayed commanders' orders to soldiers in camp and on the field of battle. The fifes and drums also communicated with enemy armies: When battlefields were choked with smoke from muskets and cannons and white flags did not always mean surrender, the fifes and drums spoke a language everyone could hear and understand. The rhythms and tunes of the fifes and drums also helped to keep the soldiers' minds off their tedious marching.

During the Revolution, the average age was eighteen for fifers and nineteen for drummers. Boys could enlist as young as eleven or twelve as long as they could keep up while carrying a drum. Colonial Williamsburg's fifers and drummers are the same ages as their Revolutionary counterparts. Since 1999, they have included girls as well as boys, though the girls portray boys when performing.

Today's fifers and drummers preserve the eighteenth-century traditions of military music, giving hundreds of performances a year, both in the Revolutionary City and elsewhere. The twenty-first-century corps represents the Virginia State Garrison Regiment, one of several raised in Williamsburg.

The Junior Corps represents a militia force of merchants' and farmers' sons who wore their own clothes, hence their different colored breeches and waistcoats. The Senior Corps represents fifers and drummers later in the war, from about 1778 when the American forces forged an alliance with the French, Spanish, and Dutch and received proper military gear. The Americans drew from European traditions, including that of dressing the fifers and drummers in the opposite colors of the regular infantry. American troops wore blue coats with red facing, or trim; American fifers and drummers wore red coats with blue facing.

The fife, a cylindrical, side-blown instrument with six finger holes and no keys, first appeared in the fourteenth century. It gained popularity in the 1750s, and the British and Americans adopted it to accompany the field snare drum. The high, shrill sound of the instrument carried well on the field of battle. The snare drums used by Colonial Williamsburg's corps are, like those used in the eighteenth century, made of wood shells and hoops with calfskin heads and gut snares. The bass drums became popular in the third quarter of the eighteenth century in Europe, and Americans began adopting them as the war continued.

GARDENS

Williamsburg has long had a reputation for fine gardens, a tradition that continues to this day. The Governor's Palace and the College of William and Mary employed professional gardeners throughout the eighteenth century, and Williamsburg shops offered a wide variety of seeds as well as the latest garden books imported from Europe for the benefit of Virginia gardeners. Gardening and botany were elements of a gentleman's education in eighteenth-century Virginia, and many prominent Virginians were renowned for their horticultural knowledge. The first American garden book, *A Treatise on Gardening,* was written in Williamsburg by John Randolph, the last royal attorney general for the colony of Virginia. John Clayton, clerk of courts for nearby Gloucester County, explored the Virginia frontier and compiled the herbarium specimens and documentation for *Flora Virginica,* published in Holland in 1739–1743.

Many Williamsburg residents kept gardens. Merchants such as William Pitt and Jacob Bruce regularly advertised the availability at their stores of "Garden PEASE, BEANS, and CABBAGE SEED of different Sorts, and the earliest and best Kinds." Professional, English-trained gardeners tended the gardens at the College of William and Mary and at the Governor's Palace throughout the colonial period. John Farquharson tended the Governor's Palace gardens for the last two royal governors and, in 1776, was appointed public gardener by the new Virginia state government. In that position he kept up the grounds of the Palace when it served as a residence for the first elected governors and then as a hospital, and he maintained the gardens created at the new local barracks for soldiers.

The Revolution and the constant demands of troops took its toll on the old capital. That is hardly the case today. Gardens across the Historic Area are maintained with period-appropriate plants and are among the most popular places for guests.

The most famous of Williamsburg's gardens, in Revolutionary times and today, are those of the Governor's Palace. The Bodleian Plate, a copperplate found in 1929, shows several landscape features that helped landscape architect Arthur Shurcliff re-create the complex of gardens. Features include the original eighteenth-century falling gardens (terraces) and canal. A yaupon holly maze was designed at the base of a mount because of English precedent. Originally envisioned by Governor Alexander Spotswood in the early 1700s, the gardens were so extensive and extravagant that members of the General Assembly, noting the gardens were being paid for by the public, complained about the expense.

Among the many other garden features of note in the Historic Area:

The garden at the David Morton House, based partly on a 1782 map and partly on archaeological excavations, features a wellhead as a central focal point.

The focal point in the shade garden next to Christiana Campbell's Tavern is the native yaupon holly.

The pleasure garden at the Elizabeth Carlos House is a typical four-square pattern using a wellhead as a focal point.

The kitchen garden at the Benjamin Powell House contains an assortment of fruits, vegetables, and herbs that colonists used in their daily lives.

Evergreens, nut trees, and old boxwood enclose the area behind the Coke-Garrett House and lead down to a flower border.

The symmetrical pleasure garden of the Palmer House is designed around a central sundial.

The pleasure garden at the Alexander Purdie House, a simple four-square design, has plants of seasonal interest, including shadblow trees, pomegranates, and oak-leaf hydrangeas.

The pleasure garden at the Alexander Craig House foregrounds the orchard's fruit trees, pleached arbors, and the original brickbat paths.

Behind the kitchen and adjacent outbuildings of Wetherburn's Tavern is a simple square kitchen garden filled with herbs and vegetables of the period.

The pleasure garden at the Prentis House features a small orchard balanced by the stable and paddock at the rear of the site.

The garden at the Orlando Jones House features boxwood topiary, a hornbeam aerial hedge, and seasonal flower beds.

The kitchen garden at the George Reid House has heirloom flowers, vegetables, and herbs and an orchard with heirloom fruit trees.

The gardens at the Bracken Tenement feature yaupon holly as an enclosing hedge, as topiary accents, and in a natural screen.

The parterre garden at the Custis Tenement features formal paths of crushed shell and brick partially enclosed by English boxwood.

At the Colonial Garden, historic gardeners demonstrate the tools and techniques of the professional eighteenth-century gardener.

A pleached American hornbeam arbor serves as the terminal focal point in the pleasure garden between the kitchen garden and work yard at the George Wythe House.

The Taliaferro-Cole House garden, like many in the Historic Area, is a riot of color from spring through fall.

The parterres in the Bryan House garden are based on patterns depicted on eighteenth-century maps of North Carolina towns.

The parterres in the John Blair House garden are planted with herbs that colonists used for their scents.

RARE BREEDS

Though Colonial Williamsburg is best known for preserving buildings, it also preserves animals. The Rare Breeds program is truly living history: These animals are like those that could have been present in eighteenth-century Williamsburg, some employed as they were over two hundred years ago. Some of these breeds have fewer than two hundred animals registered annually in North America; by helping prevent their extinction, the program is making a contribution to preserving genetic diversity in livestock.

Among the animals in the program, which you will find throughout the Historic Area:

Leicester Longwool sheep have long, lustrous coats that fall in ringlets. They are easy to feed, mature quickly, and provided a valuable supply of meat to the colonists. Colonial Williamsburg's original herd came from Tasmania, but now the sheep are bred in Williamsburg. George Washington raised Leicester Longwools at Mount Vernon, and his grandson used them to develop the first American breed of sheep.

American Cream Draft horses are a modern breed but very rare: just over five hundred exist in North America. They have a medium cream–colored coat, pink skin, amber eyes, long white manes and tails, and white markings.

The milk of American Milking Red Devon cows contains high butterfat content, prized in the eighteenth century for butter and cheese production. They also give quality meat, are very intelligent, and are good work animals. The milk from Colonial Williamsburg's Devons is used in Colonial Williamsburg's Foodways program. Descended from the Red Devon breed native to Devonshire, England, American Milking Devons now are bred here.

Canadian horses were developed from horses sent from France to Quebec between 1665 and 1670. Canadians were used for farmwork, transport, riding, and racing. They are solid and well muscled with well-arched necks set high on long, sloping shoulders. Canadians are primarily black or reddish brown with full manes and tails. They are energetic without being nervous and are adaptable for a variety of riding and driving disciplines.

Oxen are cattle trained to work. They were the trucks, tractors, and bulldozers of the eighteenth century. In the Historic Area, you will see Milking Shorthorns, or Durhams. Milking Shorthorns originated in England, can be red or white, and are used for milk, meat, and work. At the Great Hopes Plantation site, you can see a pair of Devon/Lineback crossbred oxen, which combine the attributes of Devon and Lineback cattle.

The Nankins are a foundation for many other breeds of bantam chickens, which were very popular in the nineteenth and twentieth centuries. Nankin hens are broody, meaning they like to sit on anything and were therefore used to hatch pheasant and quail eggs for large estates, where pheasants and quail were raised for organized shoots. They make good pets because of their gentle nature.

Dominique chickens were one of the first breeds of chickens developed in the United States. They are small to medium in size with a very hardy constitution. Their heavy plumage protects them in cold weather.

English game fowl were originally bred for cockfighting. Distinguished by their strength, agility, and aggression, these chickens lost popularity when cockfighting was banned. However, they produce high-quality meat and eggs. Eggs from the poultry in the Rare Breeds program are used in Colonial Williamsburg's Foodways program.

Robert
MUSH

Born at the Pamunkey Indian town in King William County in the mid-1700s, Robert Mush was a descendant of the once-powerful Powhatan peoples. As a boy, Mush (sometimes Mursh or Marsh) participated in the seasonal cycles of agrarian Virginia society—farming, fishing, and tending domesticated animals. By the eighteenth century, Pamunkey men were selling their hunting and fishing catch to "the neighboring gentry." Pamunkey women sold their bowls, milk pans, baskets, and other wares in Yorktown and Williamsburg. One English visitor to Williamsburg said the Pamunkey "commonly dress like the Virginians, and I have sometimes mistaken them for the lower sort of that people."

By the 1760s, Pamunkey headmen confirmed their tributary status to the Crown by delivering an annual quitrent, or land tax, of three arrows to the governor's residence. The former symbolic tribute of beaver skins had been remitted in favor of sending Pamunkey boys to be "brought up in the college." These Pamunkey were "more accustomed to the manners and habits of the English colonists" than of those Indian nations farther away.

Young Robert Mush arrived in Williamsburg in 1769 along with fellow tribesman George Sampson. They attended William and Mary's Indian school, residing in the Brafferton's third-floor apartments above the college library. Mush and the other Indian students attended Bruton Parish Church. Mush was one of three or four Pamunkey students listed by William and Mary's bursar between 1769 and 1775.

At the outbreak of the war, Mush and the other Pamunkey in Williamsburg were caught up in the Revolutionary fervor. When the Fifteenth Virginia Regiment mustered in Williamsburg in 1776, Mush enlisted. The Pamunkey fought at the Battles of Brandywine and Germantown. Mush survived the 1777 action, but his Williamsburg Pamunkey friend George Sampson died while in New Jersey, as did several other Pamunkey soldiers.

Mush served in the First Virginia Brigade during the British siege of Charleston, South Carolina. When the city fell in May 1779, Mush was among the five thousand American soldiers captured; he was held on the prison barges in Charleston Harbor for the next fourteen months. Released in early 1781, Mush returned to Virginia, was discharged, and then reenlisted. He fought at the Battle of Yorktown.

After the war, Mush returned to King William County and in 1783 married Elizabeth, "according to the form and solemnity of their Tribe." However, the Indian community had been moved by the tenets of the Great Awakening and a growing Baptist sentiment in rural Virginia. Mush "became Religious and attached himself to the [Baptist] Church and became a Minister of the gospeal." The Mushes were among thirteen baptized Pamunkey couples to help form Lower College Baptist Church in 1791.

Alexander HOY

What motivated men to join George Washington's army? Privates were far less likely than officers to record their reasons on paper, but circumstances can provoke speculation. Patriotism may have played a role but necessity did as well.

Alexander Hoy was a cutler, making and repairing metal tools, especially knives. Even before the war, Hoy struggled to pay his debts. Once the Revolution cut off trade with Britain, Virginia's economy deteriorated. Hoy may have tried hiring himself out as a laborer, but he must have found it increasingly difficult to support his wife, Barbara, and their children.

By April 1777, Hoy had enlisted in the First Virginia Regiment. If he had done so hoping for an easier life, he would have been disappointed. In October in Pennsylvania, the First Virginia took part in the Battle of Germantown. The regiment drove through the British line in a bayonet charge but then, with the rest of the American attack stalled, the Virginians found themselves surrounded by the enemy and forced to fight their way out. That winter, Hoy was at Valley Forge, where he and the other men of the First Virginia were drilled by Baron von Steuben. Hoy must have found some

solace knowing that, in December, some funds reached Barbara.

Von Steuben's drilling paid off at the Battle of Monmouth, in New Jersey, in June 1778. The First Virginia took part in an attack on the British. The two sides exchanged volleys at short range, resulting in the deaths of several men in the regiment but also in the retreat of the British. By December 1778, the hardships of the campaign had much reduced the strength of Washington's army. Fifteen Virginia regiments were consolidated into eleven.

In July 1779, the First Virginia took part in an attack on a British fort at Stony Point in New York. Using only their bayonets, the Americans captured the fort and four hundred British troops in just fifteen minutes. Fifteen Americans were killed in the attack.

In December 1779, the First Virginia, along with most of the Virginia troops in the north, began a long march south. In March, Washington wrote Lafayette that "the extreme cold—the deep Snows—& other impediments have retarded the progress of their March very considerable." In April 1780, the troops reached Charleston. Only seven hundred of the two thousand men who had started the march in December made it that far; others had fallen ill or deserted. Then, in May, after a siege of Charleston, the Americans surrendered.

Hoy may have been paroled or he may have escaped from the British. By 1782 he was back in Williamsburg, listed as the head of a household with six whites and no slaves.

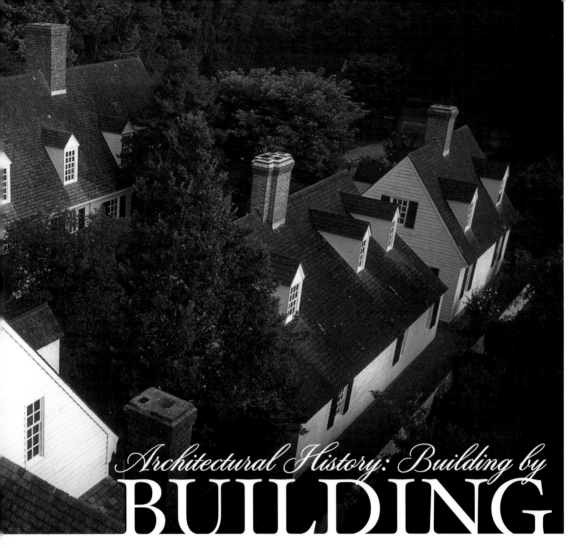

Architectural History: Building by
BUILDING

All of the buildings in the Historic Area were either restored or reconstructed based on archaeological evidence, documentary evidence, and historical precedence from surviving buildings in the region, other American colonies, or Great Britain from the same time period. More recently, tree-ring dating and microscopic paint analysis have provided the precise dates of the construction of many of the buildings and revealed the kinds and colors of coatings applied to surfaces. Documentary evidence includes written and visual period sources such as accounts, letters, newspapers, maps, deeds, inventories, insurance plats, and drawings. Early photographs documenting the exterior appearances of many

of the historic buildings enhanced the restoration efforts. Although the form and function of early buildings changed over time, each was restored or reconstructed to a particular time depending on the evidence available. The restoration of Williamsburg began in 1926 and continues to this day. Charlton's Coffeehouse was reconstructed in 2009. The reconstruction of the Public Armoury was completed in 2013. The most recent reconstruction is of the Market House.

The buildings are arranged in this section in the same order as the sites in the earlier section: west on Duke of Gloucester Street from the Capitol to the College of William and Mary and then from the Governor's Palace and

Palace Green east on Nicholson Street across Waller Street and west on Francis Street. This section includes every restored and reconstructed primary building in the Historic Area, including those not open to the public. Buildings currently used as residences, offices, other work spaces, and hotel facilities are marked in the following text as private. The name of each building can be found in front of or on the building. Typically, especially for private buildings, the name is on a small plaque on the lower left or right corner.

DUKE OF GLOUCESTER STREET

Capitol to Botetourt Street

CAPITOL

As a result of a fire in the first Capitol in 1747, eighteenth-century Williamsburg saw two Capitol buildings on this site. The building you see today represents the first. Like the originals, it forms an impressive vista down the town's main thoroughfare to the College of William and Mary.

The H-shaped plan of the Capitol reflects the division of colonial government between the lower and upper houses of the legislature. When completed in 1705, the west facade of the building, which faces Duke of Gloucester Street, was accentuated by a columned semicircular porch with a balustrade balcony above

it where public pronouncements were read. The west wing housed the General Courtroom on the first floor and the Council Chamber, the most ornate room in the building, on the second. The Council, made up of twelve leading colonists appointed for life by the king, constituted the upper house of the legislature. The east wing of the Capitol contained the House of Burgesses on the first floor and committee rooms for the burgesses on the second. The House of Burgesses, the lower house of the legislature, consisted of two members elected by the landowners of each county and one member each from Jamestown, Williamsburg, Norfolk, and the College of William and Mary. Each wing had its own staircase. If the two houses deadlocked, representatives from the Council and the burgesses met jointly in the second-floor chamber located over the piazza. In effect, this conference room formed a bridge between the two buildings. The architecture of the Capitol thus aided the process of mediation between the two houses. The projecting apsidal ends on the south side are one of the earliest examples of this feature in American architecture and may have reflected a conscious choice, like the name *Capitol,* to recall ancient Roman basilicas, or halls of justice, where magistrates sat in apses.

The foundations of the original building were laid in 1701. Virginia's lawmakers moved into the new Capitol in 1704, a year before its completion. As a precaution against fire, Williamsburg's first Capitol was designed without chimneys. In 1723, however, two chimneys were added to keep official records and documents from becoming damp, and, despite precautions, fire gutted the building on January 30, 1747, leaving "the naked Brick Walls only . . .

standing." Before rebuilding, Virginia's General Assembly seriously considered simply moving the entire government to a town further west; however, they eventually voted to remain in Williamsburg, and work on the new statehouse began in 1751. The second Capitol was completed in 1753. It incorporated parts of the surviving walls of its predecessor and retained the original layout of the building but differed in appearance. Foremost was the construction of a massive two-story pedimented portico on the front facade and the squaring off of the southern apses. It was in this second building that the stirring questions of the Revolution were debated.

The structure was last used as a Capitol on December 24, 1779. After Virginia's government moved to Richmond in 1780, it was used for a variety of purposes, including schools, a hospital, and a district court. The east wing fell into disrepair and was pulled down around 1800. In 1832, the west wing was destroyed by fire during a session of the district court. The Association for the Preservation of Virginia Antiquities (APVA), today known as Preservation Virginia, acquired the property in 1897 and marked the outline of the colonial foundations. The APVA gave the site to Colonial Williamsburg in 1928 for the reconstruction. In 1929, Colonial Williamsburg decided to reconstruct the first Capitol because it is more thoroughly documented than the second one. Reconstruction began in 1931, and the building opened to the public in 1934. Unfortunately, the restoration architects misread the evidence and placed the principal door on the west facade six feet to the north of where it was originally located and failed to reconstruct the semicircular front porch.

SECRETARY'S OFFICE

Constructed in 1748 after fire had destroyed the Capitol the previous year, this one-story brick building served as the office of the Secretary of the colony and as a storage space for provincial records, documents, and books. The Secretary ran the office and oversaw the training of future county court clerks, who were apprenticed to learn the procedures of the Virginia judicial system. To enhance its fireproof qualities, little decorative woodwork was used on the interior. The ceiling was unvaulted, and the original floor was paved with stones. The interior walls and window jambs were plastered directly onto the brickwork. Despite the potential hazards, the four fireplaces in the three-room structure were essential to provide heat in winter and drive off the damp and mold in summer. Over time, Tidewater humidity can be as destructive as fire to paper and leather. Reflecting the prestige of the office, the building's brickwork was laid in Flemish bond with glazed headers, and the exterior openings and corners are accentuated by rubbed bricks of a uniform orange-red color, a fashion that was popular throughout the Tidewater region in the middle of the eighteenth century. The entrance of the south facade has a glazed and rubbed Tuscan frontispiece, an exquisite example of the bricklayer's craftsmanship generally found on the largest houses and parish churches in the region. Two T-shaped chimneys pierce the hipped roof. Following the move of the state government to Richmond in 1780, the office served various uses, including government offices, a grammar school, and a residence. The small graveyard that sits between the Capitol and the Secretary's Office is that of the Jones family, who lived in the building well into the twentieth century but who had no connection to the building's colonial past. Restoration efforts in 1939–1940 addressed the various alterations that occurred over the years. Today, the building is used for special exhibitions and evening programs.

PUBLIC GAOL

Legislation passed in 1701 called for the construction of a "substantiall Brick Prison" twenty by thirty feet with an adjoining walled exercise yard. Henry Cary Sr., the builder of the Capitol, completed the structure with two cells two years later in 1703. Two debtors' cells were added in 1711, and quarters for the jailer and a larger exercise yard were constructed on the south (front) side of the building in 1722. In its present form, the Public Gaol has three criminal cells and two debtors' rooms on the first floor as well as a hall and chamber for the jailer and his family. The second-story east wing has a chamber in the attic for the jailer's use and two cells across a passage for the confinement of prisoners. The prison served the colony and then the commonwealth until 1780. The city of Williamsburg continued to use a portion of the building as its jail until 1910. Part of the brickwork of the Gaol's massive walls is original. Shackles were unearthed in the course of the building's restoration in the 1930s.

PALMER HOUSE

John Palmer, lawyer and bursar of the College of William and Mary, built this two-story brick house soon after an earlier structure on the site burned in 1754. The placement of the door near one end of the front facade indicates the interior arrangement: two rooms deep with a side passage serving a "hall," or principal entertaining room, in the front and a "chamber," or bedroom, in the rear. This plan type appeared in Williamsburg by the middle of the eighteenth century and remained primarily an urban phenomenon until late in the century when side-passage houses began to be seen in rural areas of Virginia. The holes in the brickwork, known as *putlog holes,* were left when the masons who built the Palmer House removed their scaffolding. In the late 1850s, the house was doubled in size with an addition to the east. During the Civil War, the dwelling served as a military headquarters, first for Confederate General Joseph Johnston and then for General George B. McClellan, the commander of the Union forces. The antebellum addition was removed when the building was restored in 1952. Private.

CHARLTON'S COFFEEHOUSE

This building was the first full reconstruction (2008–2009) on Duke of Gloucester Street in fifty years. Based on extensive archaeological research and the survival of original building elements, the Coffeehouse was built with traditional materials and methods. It is the only eighteenth-century coffeehouse in America and guests can sample authentic eighteenth-century coffee (though it is an exhibition site, not a working coffeehouse). The building that had once been Charlton's coffeehouse was built in 1749–1750 and stood until about 1889 when a large Victorian house was built on the site, using some of the original foundations, framing members, trim, and even several doors, windows, and shutters. That house was preserved and relocated to Henry Street, just outside the Historic Area, in the 1990s. Archaeological excavation and a photograph revealed that the building was one story tall and thirty-five feet square with a single, central chimney punctured with seven fireplaces. A porch projected across the front facade. Originally built as a store and dwelling, the building was converted into a coffeehouse by the early 1760s. (Buildings with porches became increasingly common in the late colonial period. The design was unusual for a store but ideal for a coffeehouse or tavern. Many of the taverns in Williamsburg, including the Raleigh Tavern and Wetherburn's Tavern, had such features by 1776.) Food probably was prepared in the cellar and carried to customers upstairs. As a gentry establishment that permitted no women, its sequestered rooms provided a place to conduct confidential business or to host exclusive gatherings. Its location served well for merchants who regularly gathered at "the Exchange," just across the ravine near the Secretary's Office, to trade and speculate in commodities. In 1767 Charlton advertised in the *Virginia Gazette* that his coffeehouse was now a tavern, which meant that he would offer lodging, perhaps in an attempt to generate

more business. By 1770, Charlton's tavern had moved from the site. From 1770–1772, Christiana Campbell appears to have rented the building, probably for a tavern. In 1772, Charlotte Dickson bought the building and converted it back into a store. She and her son Beverly, and his wife, lived in the building and ran the store as a haberdashery.

EDINBURGH CASTLE TAVERN

This early building had a plan similar to many early buildings constructed along Duke of Gloucester Street with an enclosed porch that opened into the larger entertaining room. Eventually these porches were seen as old-fashioned and were replaced with plans with central passages. Private.

JOHN CRUMP HOUSE

Originally constructed about 1719 by Francis Sharp as one of Williamsburg's smaller taverns, this building was extended to its present size before the end of the eighteenth century. Henry Wetherburn, one of the town's most successful tavern keepers, bought the establishment in 1742. His nephew Edward Nicholson inherited the property and rented it to various businessmen. John Crump, the town jailer, acquired it in 1789 and continued to operate a tavern through the first decade of the 1800s. During the nineteenth-century, the building gradually became so dilapidated that it was condemned as a fire hazard and razed in 1893. Reconstruction in 1941 was based on insurance plats dating from the ownership of John Crump and a late nineteenth-century photograph. Fedor Vasilevich Karzhavin, a Russian who visited Williamsburg during the Revolutionary era, sketched the John Crump House. Private.

NICOLSON STORE

Robert Nicolson, a tailor and merchant, insured a "Wood Store two Story 34 feet by 20 feet" (the size of the present building) on this site in 1796. The structure reflects the standard Virginia store layout of the period. The unheated front salesroom took up most of the first floor with a smaller, heated counting room at the back. The second floor was used for living purposes and storage. Despite the addition of a western extension in the early nineteenth century, only the front portion of the original roof framing was altered, and the rear facade remained to guide the restoration of 1949–1950. Evidence of the metamorphosis of the colonial building also existed in the original brick foundations that were laid in English bond, the newer portion being in common bond, which appeared in this area in the mid-nineteenth century. Clues to the existence of the central door were discovered in the framing as well as during archaeological excavations of the brick step foundations, still intact beneath the ground. Private.

SHIELDS TAVERN

Tavern keeper John Marot probably built the first part of this building in 1707. Within ten years he had extended the structure to the east in two successive phases; later a shed addition at the rear connected the first two phases with new rooms. In the early 1740s, James Shields, Marot's son-in-law, took over the tavern. Although located close to the Capitol, Shields Tavern attracted lower gentry and successful middling customers. After Shields died in 1750, the family retained ownership of the property until around 1770 and rented it out to various tenants. From 1772 to 1795, Dr. John de Sequeyra, first visiting physician at the Public Hospital and eighteenth-century Williamsburg's only known resident of Jewish descent, lived here. The original building was lost to fire in 1858. Today, a tavern once again operates on the site.

PASTEUR & GALT APOTHECARY SHOP

Dr. William Pasteur likely built his apothecary shop after he purchased the property in 1760. In 1775 Pasteur and Dr. John Minson Galt, who had run a competing apothecary shop, joined forces. The partnership lasted until 1778, at which time Pasteur retired from medicine. Galt continued in the business. Their reconstructed shop stands today where the original once did. It is stocked and furnished much as it was then, down to copies of Galt's medical certificates hanging on the walls.

SCRIVENER STORE

Merchant Joseph Scrivener bought this property in 1762. He lived in the house and operated a grocery-type business here until he died in 1772. Previous land values and the price that Scrivener paid indicate that the original house was built between 1745 and 1762. Torn down in 1906, Scrivener Store was rebuilt in 1941. The reconstruction was based on archaeological excavations, a photograph taken before demolition, and recollections of a neighbor who remembered the original structure. Private.

ALEXANDER CRAIG HOUSE

This two-story structure is a composite of various additions made to a small building. It is not clear when it was first built, though the lot was sold "with ye houses thereon" as early as 1712. The two doors at the front of the building suggest that at least in some periods it served as both a dwelling (on one side) and business (on the other). During the eighteenth century, a wide variety of tradesmen, including a goldsmith, a tavern keeper, a glazier, and a series of wigmakers, owned the property. Saddler Alexander Craig owned it from 1755 until his death in 1776. The east section at the right, which was used as a shop, is the oldest portion of the

building. The west wing was a very late eighteenth-century addition. It partially sits on top of the foundations of an earlier dwelling. Stone steps, indicated by archaeological excavation, were provided for the house entrance while wooden steps were thought more appropriate for the shop entrance. Although the type of business changed a number of times, the shop portion of the house continued to be used for commercial purposes until early in the twentieth century. Before Colonial Williamsburg restored the property, the eighteenth-century building was still standing but with many alterations, including both vertical and horizontal additions and changes in the windows and doors. Private.

JOHN COKE OFFICE

The building that originally stood on this lot may have been built by James Shields, an early owner of the lot along with the tavern next to it. Later in the eighteenth century, blacksmith John Draper seems to have used it sometime after his arrival in Williamsburg in 1768. During the Revolution he produced guns and nails for the patriot cause. Draper likely moved from this block when he purchased the George Davenport House in 1780. The building's name comes from a pair of insurance policies taken out by John Coke in 1806 and 1809, the first pieces of documentary evidence that make a clear reference to the building. Private.

ALEXANDER PURDIE HOUSE

The earliest record of a house on this lot dates to 1707 when James Shields conveyed the property to William Byrd with "one good dwelling house thereon building." Shields likely acquired the lot from the city of Williamsburg in an early act of land speculation building a house to secure his claim and then selling it at a profit. In 1749–1750 James Crosby, a merchant who was probably using the building as his home, sold it to Buchanan & Company, merchants of Glasgow. By 1753, Dr. Kenneth McKenzie had purchased the lot from Buchanan; he used the main part as his home and the eastern part as a medical shop. His first wife, Mary, may also have run a millinery business out of the house. Alexander Purdie purchased it in 1767. In 1774, the Scottish-born Purdie founded the third of three Williamsburg newspapers named the *Virginia Gazette*. He lived in the house until his death in 1779. No longer standing when Colonial Williamsburg acquired the property in 1927, the structure was re-created after archaeological excavations in 1951. Today, the reconstructed house serves as the east wing of the King's Arms Tavern; however, in 1776 the structures would have been two separate buildings.

KING'S ARMS TAVERN

Jane Vobe, one of Williamsburg's most successful tavern keepers, ran the King's Arms Tavern. In 1772, she announced her location as "opposite to the *Raleigh*, at the sign of the KING's ARMS," a name that she changed to the Eagle Tavern after the Revolution. Prior to the construction of the King's Arm's Tavern, a storehouse with a barrel-vaulted cellar stood on the site. This room, with the largest barrel-vaulted room in the region, was fitted out with racks for storing wine and beer, ideally suited to be integrated into the basement of the new building. Unfortunately, by the end of the eighteenth century, the arched ceiling had collapsed and the cellar filled in. The remnants were buried beneath new construction in the middle of the nineteenth century. Today's reconstructed King's Arms again operates as a tavern. The building is much longer than in the eighteenth century, connected as it is to the Alexander Purdie House.

KING'S ARMS BARBER SHOP

The building that stood on this site in 1776 may have been a new building constructed for Jane Vobe that year. Built as either a storehouse or a shop, it served various merchants as a store in the last quarter of the eighteenth century. In 1796, it was a barber's shop. The wigmaker works today in this reconstructed building.

CHARLTON HOUSE

A smaller house was originally built here

sometime before 1769, the year in which Edward Charlton, wigmaker and barber, moved in. Charlton himself, who carried on his business in a shop nearby, may have built it. The brick foundations and basement were later enlarged and incorporated into this building, firstly to the rear and then to the east. During the nineteenth century, the dwelling was bisected along its longitudinal axis, and the rear portion was taken down to ground level. Various additions were then made to the back of the house. During its 1929–1930 restoration, its rear half was reconstructed. Private.

RALEIGH TAVERN

Letters, diaries, newspaper advertisements, and other records indicate that the Raleigh was one of the most important taverns in colonial Virginia. Established in 1717, the tavern grew in size and reputation through the years. The original two-room structure, which was constructed around 1710 and would become the western corner of a much larger building, was expanded in the early 1730s with an east wing stretching across the lot along Duke of Gloucester Street and a semi-enclosed porch to form a front entrance. Around 1750, at the same time the Capitol was being rebuilt, a third phase of building took place in the form of a long rear addition, which housed two formal entertaining rooms—the Daphne and Apollo Rooms. This unusually large extension may be explained by the need to accommodate a building of significant size on a narrow lot.

In the fourth and final phase of construction, completed before 1773, an open porch was added facing Duke of Gloucester Street. Throughout this entire period, the building served as a tavern. James Southall took possession in 1771; earlier proprietors and tavern keepers included Alexander Finnie, Anthony Hay, and William Trebell. The tavern burned down in 1859. Fortunately, the exterior of the building and an interior view of the Apollo Room were depicted in 1848 in Benson Lossing's *Pictorial Field-Book of the Revolution*. The reconstruction, between 1929 and 1932, the first in the restoration of the city, was also aided by early insurance policies and archaeological excavations that revealed most of the original foundations of the tavern. The porch, which extended the length of the front facade, a feature typical of the best taverns in Virginia in the late colonial period, was not reconstructed. Inventories of the possessions of its eighteenth-century proprietors guided the refurnishing.

RALEIGH TAVERN KITCHEN

This large kitchen, behind the tavern, is where meals for tavern guests were prepared. The size of this building and the size of its cooking fireplaces reflect its commercial purpose and its association with one of the principal taverns of early Virginia. Today, the building houses the Raleigh Tavern Bakery, which serves sandwiches and other light refreshments.

THE UNICORN'S HORN AND JOHN CARTER'S STORE

This double, brick structure was built in 1765 by three brothers. Dr. James Carter and Dr. William Carter used the west portion as an apothecary shop under the sign of the unicorn's horn. The unicorn's horn was used as a symbol of an apothecary based on the myth that unicorn, and rhinoceros, horns held magical healing powers. John Carter ran a general store in the other half and also lived here with his family. Under different owners, the building served as a store until it burned down, along with the Raleigh Tavern, in 1859. Colonial Williamsburg excavated the site in 1931 and completed a reconstruction of the building in 1953. Private.

THE GOLDEN BALL

James Craig, a jeweler and silversmith from London, established his business at this location in 1765. In 1772, Craig began advertising his shop as "the Golden Ball," a trademark commonly used by jewelers and goldsmiths. Craig lived and worked on these premises with his family of five and one slave until he died in the early 1790s. The original building on this site, used as a tavern early on, was built in 1724. Craig extended the building by six feet to the east into the passage between his shop and the newly built Carter store next door.

The building survived until 1907. It was reconstructed in 1948. Today, one side of the Golden Ball houses the silversmiths, and the other side a retail store selling silver hollowware and gold and silver jewelry.

MARGARET HUNTER SHOP

Typical of commercial buildings, this shop has a gable-end facade, and its interior is divided between a large unheated storefront with shelves lining the long windowless side walls and a smaller counting office with a fireplace in the rear. Like many buildings, it served as both workplace and home. Probably built by Harmer and King, merchants, who occupied the site until 1746, the building was later occupied by the physician-apothecary George Gilmer. Milliner Margaret Hunter rented and then purchased the shop shortly after 1770. The building was a filling station and garage when restoration began in 1930. During additional work that occurred in 1951, the pre–Civil War memories of John S. Charles, a local resident, aided in reconstructing the entrance steps and returning the main floor to its original higher level. Today, the milliner, mantua-maker (gown maker), and tailor share the space.

RUSSELL HOUSE

Named after a family who lived here in the eighteenth century, this residence was built by

1745, modified with a rear addition and a cellar by 1776, likely razed by 1815, and reconstructed in 1949. Private.

The Prentis family owned this residence, built sometime before 1725 and expanded by 1765, for much of the eighteenth century. The house burned to the ground in 1842 and was reconstructed in 1938. Private.

WETHERBURN'S TAVERN

This structure, which survives from the eighteenth century, is one of the most thoroughly documented buildings in Williamsburg—architecturally as a carefully studied original building, archaeologically through extensive excavations, and historically by surviving deeds, accounts, and a room-by-room inventory taken after the death of Henry Wetherburn, its long-time owner-operator, in 1760. Wetherburn erected the original, eastern portion of this building in the 1730s. The plan consisted of a central stair passage with two rooms on either side. Due to a thriving business, he added the west extension with a large fashionable entertaining room by 1752. The junction between the two sections is marked by the beaded corner board near the west, or right, doorway and by a break in the brick foundation directly below. Wetherburn's "great room," which measures

twenty-five feet square and occupies most of the west end of the first floor, occasionally served as an informal town hall in which scientific lectures, political gatherings, and balls took place. The tavern depended on the enslaved to cook, serve, clean, tend the garden, and groom customers' horses. Wetherburn's twelve slaves lived in the attics over the kitchen and stable. The outbuildings, vegetable garden, and yard form one of the most thoroughly researched work spaces in Williamsburg. The dairy survives with its original framing. The other outbuildings, including the kitchen in which there is a huge fireplace, were reconstructed on their eighteenth-century locations. During the 1966–1967 restoration, the window and door locations were returned to their original positions, and the east entrance porch was reconstructed, though the porch that extended across part of the front facade from door to door at the time of the Revolution was not. The exterior was painted in the original Spanish brown.

TARPLEY'S STORE

James Tarpley bought this subdivided lot from Henry Wetherburn in 1759. He erected and operated a commercial establishment at this location until his death in June 1764. Over the years, Tarpley had various business partners. He took up with John Thompson after his previous partner died in 1761. After advertising its sale for a couple of years, Thompson finally sold and left the property in 1767. The reconstructed Tarpley's Store is again today a mercantile establishment. Tarpley, Thompson & Company features reproduction tavern ware.

DUKE OF GLOUCESTER STREET

Botetourt Street to Queen Street

BRICK HOUSE TAVERN

This lodging house was built as a two-story, six-unit rental property in the early 1760s. Itinerant tradesmen and others with services or goods to sell would arrange for lodging here, advertise in the *Virginia Gazette*, and show their wares to customers in their rooms. If business seemed promising, they might settle down elsewhere in town; if not, they would move on. Over time, a surgeon, a jeweler, a watch repairer, a milliner, a wigmaker, and several tavern keepers, to name a few, called the Brick House Tavern home. Today, it is a hotel facility, as is the Brick House Tavern Shop behind it. Private.

JAMES ANDERSON HOUSE

This site served at various times as a residence and place of business for a tavern keeper, a milliner, a barber and wigmaker, and a chandler and soap boiler before James Anderson purchased the property in 1770. During the Revolution, Anderson operated a public armory behind his home. Private.

JAMES ANDERSON'S BLACKSMITH SHOP AND PUBLIC ARMOURY

Extensive archaeological excavations on this once-prosperous industrial site revealed the foundations of the forges and workshop in 1975. Subsequent work, including documentary research, revealed the site to have been the location of Williamsburg's public armory, begun in 1778 to support the War for Independence. The design of the principal work building with its four working forges is based on comparable trade sites in England and America as well as records in James Anderson's and Humphrey Harwood's account books for the purchase of bricks and other construction materials. Its sheathed and weatherboarded walls reflect the significant investment made in its durability and security. At one point during the war, more than forty men worked at this site, which included a kitchen, a workshop, a privy, two storage buildings, and a tin shop. The reconstruction of the site was completed in 2013.

MARY STITH HOUSE

Mary Stith, daughter of William Stith, president of the College of William and Mary from 1752 to 1755, owned this small structure. In her will of 1813, she left this lot, its buildings, and much of her estate to her former slaves in gratitude for past services. Private.

WILLIAM PITT STORE

Once the apothecary shop of Robert Davidson, a "Practitioner in Physick" and mayor of Williamsburg in 1738, this building now houses the William Pitt Store, Colonial Williamsburg's gift shop of children's products.

WILLIAM WATERS HOUSE

Reconstructed in 1942, this house is named for the wealthy planter from the Eastern Shore who bought the dwelling when he moved to Williamsburg about 1750. Private.

WATERS STOREHOUSE

This structure and the next two form a fine collection of reconstructed eighteenth-century commercial properties, all of which present their gable ends to the street. By 1760 a storehouse was located on the site where Waters Storehouse now stands. Private.

HOLT'S STOREHOUSE

The three sugar loaves hanging outside this building are the traditional sign of the grocer. John Holt also sold dry goods and china. Private.

HUNTER'S STORE

Tenant grocer M. Dubois conducted business here in the late 1770s. Today, the store carries sweet treats and beverages.

POST OFFICE, PRINTING OFFICE, AND BOOKBINDERY

These three services were housed in two buildings: the post office on the street level with the printing office below and the bookbindery in a separate building on the lower level with the printer. The boxlike protruding windows allowed for product displays, as they still do today. Several hundred pieces of type, probably Dutch, were unearthed at this site during archaeological excavations that also uncovered bookbinder's ornaments and crucibles in which a printer may have melted lead. Archaeologists also found lead border ornaments used in printing paper money during the Seven Years' War. Today, the Post Office sells books, inkwells, quills, prints, pamphlets, stationery, and maps and posts mail; pressmen set type and print newspapers and other materials; and the bookbinder stitches together and covers gathered pages, just as it was all done in Revolutionary times.

GEORGE PITT HOUSE

Although built as a residence, this house sometimes served as a combination shop and dwelling in the eighteenth century. In 1731, Sarah Packe, a young widow, had her millinery business here and also took in lodgers. When she died in 1757, Dr. George Pitt inherited the property through his wife and opened an apothecary shop, the Sign of the Rhinoceros, in part of it. Dr. Pitt sold the property to printer John Dixon in 1774. Private.

PRENTIS STORE

In Williamsburg's best surviving example of a colonial store, the firm of Prentis and Company operated a highly successful store from 1740 until the Revolution. A classic example of store architecture, the building is long and narrow, and its gable end faces the street. Through the door above, merchandise could easily be lifted into the loft. Sizable windows that flank the front doorway throw light into the sales space. Windows along the sides were located toward the rear of the building to light the counting room and to leave long, blank walls for ample shelving in the sales area. Dating from 1738, the building survived well into the twentieth century as an automobile service station, which partially explains why so few changes were made. The building was initially restored in 1928–1931; in 1972, after new

evidence was discovered, the porch design was changed to accommodate a single side stair, and the cellar cap was rebuilt. Today's Prentis Store offers customers handcrafted items made by Colonial Williamsburg tradespeople.

ORLANDO JONES OFFICE AND HOUSE

Born in 1681, Orlando Jones was the grandfather of Martha Custis, who married George Washington. The house (right), office (left), and kitchen (not pictured) are now hotel guest accommodations. Private.

GEORGE REID HOUSE

A merchant who operated a store near the Capitol built this house possibly as late as 1790. Archaeological excavations revealed that a path near the house was paved with fragments of clay pipes that might have been broken in shipment to Williamsburg. Matching pieces have also been found at the Prentis Store across the street. Private.

WILLIAM LIGHTFOOT KITCHEN AND HOUSE

William Lightfoot, a planter, merchant, and attorney, probably built this town house (right) between 1733 and 1740. With its side passage and two back-to-back rooms per floor, it resembles the Palmer, Orrell, and Tayloe Houses in plan. The reconstructed entrance steps and landing are based on evidence from the original foundation excavated beneath. Two of the exterior louvered shutters are early and served as models for the others. Shutters with fixed louvers appear to have come into common usage at the end of the eighteenth century. They allow air circulation and, even when closed for privacy, still allow a moderate amount of light. The house was restored in 1931. The kitchen (left) was reconstructed in 1948–1949. Private.

PETER HAY'S SHOP

In April 1756, the *Maryland Gazette* reported a fire broke out in this shop "and in less than Half an Hour entirely consumed the same, together with all the Medicines, Utensils, & c." Fortunately, "the Assistance of a Fire Engine" prevented damage to nearby buildings. The kitchen behind the shop is now part of Colonial Williamsburg's hotel facilities. Private.

LUDWELL-PARADISE HOUSE

Although an earlier structure existed on this site, Philip Ludwell III built this elegant two-story brick house as a rental property in 1752–1753. In the 1760s and 1770s, William Rind—and later his widow, Clementina—operated a press on the premises. The

Ludwell-Paradise House was the first property John D. Rockefeller Jr. purchased for the restoration of Williamsburg. When it was restored in 1931, the entrance steps, still outlined against the exterior cellar wall, resumed their original double flight configuration. The arches and sills of the first-floor windows were raised to their original positions, which could be easily discerned in the rubbed and gauged brickwork. Basement window grilles were also returned to their original form. Private.

THE RED LION

The west end of Duke of Gloucester Street was less commercially attractive than the end closer to the Capitol. This block, on which the Red Lion stands, was already far enough to be adversely affected by the distance, and half-acre lots on this block were rarely subdivided. The Red Lion suffered many failures and a rapid turnover of its tavern keepers, including Josiah Chowning at one time. Private.

DUKE OF GLOUCESTER STREET
Queen Street to the College of William and Mary

CHOWNING'S TAVERN

The structure was built about 1750. In 1766, Josiah Chowning advertised the opening of his tavern "where all who please to favour me with their custom may depend upon the best of entertainment for themselves, servants, and horses, and good pasturage." Today, Chowning's Tavern once again serves food and drink to hungry travelers.

MARKET SQUARE TAVERN

Although taverns and shops could not compete with the more profitable establishments farther down Duke of Gloucester Street toward the Capitol, this area's proximity to the courthouse and market house provided potential customers, and a number of businesspeople tried their luck here. John Dixon leased this site from the city in 1749 and built a store on it by 1751, the core of which survives just to the east of the main door with its porch. Ten years later, Robert Lyon doubled the size of the building, adding the principal entrance passage and two rooms to the west. Thomas Craig, a later tenant, began to operate it as a public house in 1767. Thomas Jefferson rented rooms here while he studied law with George Wythe. In 1771, Gabriel Maupin bought the building, added nine feet to the east of the original store, and made various improvements. Besides boarding customers, Maupin ran a saddler and harness-making business in the buildings at the back of his property. Today, Market Square Tavern and the Market Square Tavern Kitchen are two of Colonial Williamsburg's hotel facilities. Private.

GUARDHOUSE AND MAGAZINE

The Magazine (right) was erected in 1715 after Lieutenant Governor Alexander Spotswood urgently requested a "good, substantial House of Brick" in which to store the arms and ammunition for the defense of the colony. Spotswood himself is credited with the Magazine's unusual octagonal design. Although a magazine was the type of utilitarian structure that typically would be located at the edge of a town, the central, park-like location of Williamsburg's magazine called for a more picturesque structure. The pleasing octagonal shape would have been common in English garden buildings. A high wall and a guardhouse (left) were added for increased security at the time of the Seven Years' War (1754–1763). From the 1790s through the 1830s and again in the late 1850s, the Magazine was used as the public market house. The Baptists worshiped here from the mid-1830s until their church was completed in 1856. The Association for the Preservation of Virginia Antiquities (today Preservation Virginia), recognizing its historical importance, purchased the deteriorating building in 1889 and stabilized it. Colonial Williamsburg restored it and reconstructed the perimeter wall and the Guardhouse, both of which had been pulled down in the nineteenth century, in 1934–1935.

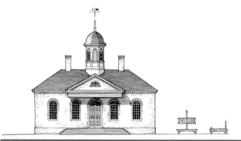

COURTHOUSE

Like many Virginia courthouses, this one is T-shaped with a central courtroom and side jury and storage rooms. Built in 1770–1771, its formal design elements—brick walls, round-headed windows, a cantilevered pediment, columned portico, wide stair platform, and an octagonal cupola with the original weather vane crowning the hipped roof—add to and reinforce the building's official appearance. Although the building is the same height as some two-story buildings, it looks like a one-story building since the door and window openings are enlarged to fit the tall proportions of the walls. It is likely that four stone Ionic columns were intended to support the projecting portico. The original red sandstone steps from St. Bee's quarry in the northwest of England were received from a London merchant in 1772. Inside are a series of zones. Just inside the door is the public space where the eighteenth-century public would have stood. A balustrade, or railing, marks the end of the public space. In raised boxes to either side of the balustrade sat the sheriff and a constable. The presiding justices sat even higher on a curved platform at the far end of the courtroom, with the chief justice at the center in an elaborate chair with arms, a higher seat, and a pediment overhead, the pediment repeating the classical reference at the front exterior of the courthouse. The private rooms in front for jurors and justices had fireplaces, but public spaces, like the courtroom, seldom had heat. Fire gutted the courthouse in 1911. Aware of its historical significance, the community repaired the building rather than demolish it. It continued to serve as a courthouse until 1931 when the exterior was restored and a new building erected nearby to house the local courts. In 1991 the colonial courtroom fittings were restored.

MARKET HOUSE

The marketplace (what we today call Market Square) was laid out in the 1720s. Its large size anticipated the growth of a much larger town than actually developed. In the late 1750s, the city erected a market house, a one-story wooden structure on a raised brick foundation, on the south side of the square where butchers, bakers, and country people sold basic foodstuffs and other items. Stalls and makeshift stands were arrayed around the market house. A clerk of the market rang a bell early in the morning signaling the opening of business and then closed the session several hours later with a second bell. The paved brick area defined the official limits of the marketplace. How long the market house stood is unknown, though it appears on a 1781 map. By 1796 the market was housed in the magazine.

ROSCOW COLE HOUSE

Completed between 1809 and 1812, this house was built on the foundations of an earlier colonial frame structure. The brickwork of the building contrasts with its eighteenth-century neighbors in the parapets that terminate the roof, the absence of a water table course, the use of 1:3 bonding on the rear facade, and the articulation of the jack arches over the windows and stringcourse between the first and second floors, which are stuccoed in imitation of stone. Architectural stone detailing is scarce locally since good building stone was not readily available in Tidewater Virginia. Other characteristics of the early republic period are the semicircular fanlight over the door and the large window panes that are separated by thin muntins, or wooden members of the window sash. The house, named for a merchant who operated a store in an adjoining building, was restored in 1939 and 1956. Private.

MARY DICKINSON STORE

Mary Dickinson, who rented her shop from her neighbor James Geddy Jr., advertised millinery, jewelry, and other goods for sale *"next Door to Mr.* JAMES GEDDY'S *Shop, near the Church"* in an October 1771 issue of the *Virginia Gazette.* Today, an assortment of items similar to those sold by an eighteenth-century milliner is available in the store.

JAMES GEDDY HOUSE

From about 1737 to 1777, gunsmith James Geddy Sr. and his sons lived at or operated shops on this site. A good deal more than gunsmithing went on here. An inventory taken after Geddy's death lists shop equipment including brass work for guns, a turner's lathe, bullet molds, and gunsmith's, cutler's, and founder's tools. In 1751, Geddy's sons David and William advertised that they were carrying on these trades at the shop. In 1760, the widowed Anne Geddy sold the property to her son James Jr., who set up shop as a silversmith, goldsmith, and watch repairer. This white, weatherboarded, relatively large and fashionable house, befitting the Geddys' rising social standing, was built in 1761–1762 by James Jr. The parlor and a chamber of this two-story, L-shaped dwelling flank the central stair passage with a large dining room forming the rear wing. In the eighteenth century, several busy forges in the foundry behind the house resulted in a yard littered with piles of coal, mounds of slag, and assorted iron and brass waste. Geddy was cited by the city magistrates for dumping his refuse on the public property just outside his own. Modified very little over the years, the Geddy House was restored first in 1930 and again in 1967. The house retains much original woodwork. The door from the rear dining room onto Palace Green was not restored. Evidence for the reconstructed porch was taken from a ghost outline on the exterior weatherboarding. The neoclassical design of the porch was adapted from that of the late eighteenth-century example still in place at the William Finnie House. The one-story retail shop extension to the east was rebuilt on its original foundations. A foundry and a gunsmith once again operate on the property. Here founders cast and finish metal objects, usually of brass, silver, or pewter. Gunsmiths also cast metals, and they demonstrate the skills of other trades in order to create and maintain guns and other weapons.

GREENHOW TENEMENT

Merchant John Greenhow, who had a large house and store a few doors to the west, owned this frame structure from sometime before 1782 until about 1800. An 1801 insurance plat identifies the building as a tenement, which simply meant a rental property, belonging to his son Robert and shows a wooden shed addition at the back. Printer and newspaper publisher Joseph Repiton acquired the property around 1810, and many have operated a store on this site, demonstrating the ease in which many of the buildings in Williamsburg in the colonial and early national periods could be converted from domestic to commercial use. Reconstruction in 1938 was aided by a late nineteenth-century watercolor of the property and by a photograph taken shortly before the twentieth-century demolition of the building. With its shed additions at the rear and east, the Greenhow Tenement, especially the part facing Market Square, is another example of a structure that grew over time. Private.

GREENHOW BRICK OFFICE

Behind the Greenhow Tenement, facing the Magazine, this modest brick structure was once the property of merchant John Greenhow, whose house and store are located around the corner on Duke of Gloucester Street. It may have been built as a combined store and dwelling. Restoration in 1948 involved the reconstruction of the brick entrance steps and the dormers on the upper floor, which were indicated by structural framing and localized patching of plaster. As at the George Wythe House, pockets in the brickwork indicated wooden nosings for brick steps descending from three sides of the top landing step. There was also evidence that the original transom had been bricked up and the door height lowered. Private.

SHOEMAKER'S SHOP

In 1773, George Wilson & Company advertised the arrival of a "choice Cargo of the best Sorts of ENGLISH LEATHER for all Manner of Mens Shoes and Pumps." Wilson must have had more business than he could handle since he encouraged two or three journeymen shoemakers to apply to him "next Door to Mr. *Greenhow*'s Store in *Williamsburg*." By the end of the next year, however, the household furniture and working materials of George Wilson, deceased, were offered for sale. Today, tradespeople once again make shoes here.

JOHN GREENHOW STORE AND HOUSE

John Greenhow was a merchant in Williamsburg from about 1755 to his death in 1787. Viewed from the street, this building, which combines store and house, appears to be in three segments. From left to right, there are a sloped-roof counting room or office, the entrance to the store, and the doorway to the house. The store is the most completely reconstructed eighteenth-century commercial space in Williamsburg. From the counting room in back to the arrangement of the counters and shelving to the sign above the front door, the store is a re-creation of its eighteenth-century counterpart. Advertisements in the *Virginia Gazette* from 1766 to 1780 enabled researchers to identify the wide variety of goods that John Greenhow and his sons sold in their general store. Some similar items are for sale here again today. The size, layout, and exterior finish of the combination store and home, as well as the lumber house next door, are indicated on several early nineteenth-century fire insurance policies. One contemporary account described Greenhow's home as a "large and commodious Dwelling house." Private.

JOHN GREENHOW LUMBER HOUSE

Gable end facing the street, this building functioned as a stockroom for furniture, barrels, and odds and ends too bulky to keep in the store itself. In eighteenth-century parlance, *lumber* meant "items in storage." Today, the building serves as a ticket office.

CUSTIS TENEMENT

John Custis acquired this lot in 1714. He also purchased two lots to the immediate west, built structures on all three of them, and rented the properties. Martha Custis, the widow of Daniel Parke Custis, John's son, inherited the property. The widow Custis later married George Washington. Private.

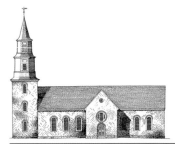

BRUTON PARISH CHURCH

In the late seventeenth century, before the college was built, Bruton Parish Church was the center of a loose amalgam of plantations at what was then called Middle Plantation. Named for a town in Somerset, England, Bruton Parish was established when several smaller parishes were joined together in 1674. Three years later, the vestry ordered that a new church be built in Middle Plantation. A buttressed brick church was completed in 1683 by Francis Page, the son of John Page, who provided land for its construction. Francis Louis Michel, a Swiss traveler who visited Williamsburg in 1702, left a sketch of the first Bruton Parish Church that shows it had curvilinear end gables done in the artisan mannerist style that was then fashionable in England. Its foundations remain and are marked by granite posts northwest of the present building.

The small church was badly in need of repair by the early 1700s. Furthermore, when the capital moved from Jamestown in 1699, the numbers of worshippers increased significantly. In 1706 the vestry decided to build a new church. The project was partially funded by the parishioners and the provincial government, and in 1711 Governor Spotswood, an architectural enthusiast, provided a "platt or draught" for a cruciform structure with two wings projecting from the main body of the building. The form arose not from religious symbolism but from a desire to have separate seating sections. The north and south wings provided space for the pews reserved for the governor, members of the Council and House of Burgesses, and provincial officials. The parishioners sat in the pews in the west end of the church—originally the men seated on the north side and the women on the south side of the central aisle. William and Mary students were consigned to the west gallery, the only surviving original feature in the church today. The new building was begun in 1713 and has been in continuous use since 1715.

The private gallery in the south wing was erected in 1720 for a few families. The one on the south wall of the nave was added in 1721 and extended eastward to the corner of the south wing in 1744. The north gallery along the nave was erected in 1762. The gallery in the north wing was constructed as late as 1852 as a slave gallery long after the building had been subdivided and reoriented and the other galleries demolished. In 1752, the chancel was extended twenty-two feet to the east, making the length of the chancel equal to that of the nave. The brick perimeter wall around the churchyard also was added that year. An organ loft was erected in the northeast corner of the church in 1755, and an English pump organ was installed the same year. The vestry hired Peter Pelham as the organist, a position he held for more than forty years. The stone baptismal font reportedly was brought from an earlier church at Jamestown about this time. In 1769, local contractor Benjamin Powell was awarded the contract to build a tower and steeple. The much darker shade of the bricks used in the tower contrasts with the soft salmon color of the brickwork of the main building. The bell, given to the parish by merchant James Tarpley in 1761, is still in use.

The interior was substantially changed in the nineteenth century. The tower, for example, was turned into a coal bin to fuel new heating stoves. From 1905 to 1907, under the direction of then-rector Dr. W. A. R. Goodwin, nineteenth-century changes were stripped from the church to return the interior to the way it had looked in the colonial period. A more complete restoration occurred in 1938–1939. The building's walls and most of the windows are original, as is the west gallery where students from the college sat. The initials some students carved in the handrail are still discernible.

Many graves are located in the churchyard. Governor Francis Fauquier is buried inside the church along with more than two dozen other individuals. In the eighteenth century, however, it was more often the custom for people residing in the countryside to be buried at home in private cemeteries. Because of the absence of stone in the area, the early table tombs in the churchyard were imported from England. Privately owned, visitors welcome.

HARTWELL PERRY'S TAVERN

Hartwell Perry owned and operated an "ordinary," as colonial taverns were sometimes called, on this site from the mid-1780s until he died about 1800. The sign hanging out front is a rebus. It depicts a deer, a well, and several pears. *Hart* is another name for a deer, and an alcoholic beverage made from pears is called *perry*. Private.

TALIAFERRO-COLE SHOP

Coachmaker Charles Taliaferro practiced his trade in Williamsburg for more than thirty years. He also operated a brewery and a warehouse, hired out boats, and sold foodstuffs and other supplies to outfit ships at nearby College Landing. He purchased this property, including the house next door, in the early 1770s. In 1804, Jesse Cole purchased the shop, which he used as a post office and general store, and the house. The gable-roofed section is the older portion of the shop. An insurance policy indicates that the shed addition existed by 1809. The shop evolved over time to meet changing commercial needs, but, despite a late nineteenth-century facade and earlier additions to the rear, the original shop had remained essentially intact when restoration of the building began in 1940. The iron hardware on the cellar entrance was among the early features retained. Today, the building houses the weaver's shop.

A sign on the inside of the gate identifies this site as the weaver's, but there is no sign identifying the building as the Taliaferro-Cole Shop.

TALIAFERRO-COLE HOUSE

The western section of this house dates from Charles Taliaferro's period of ownership, starting in the 1770s, but the restored house reflects the early 1800s when Jesse Cole acquired the house and shop. The original structure—the half immediately on the corner—had a door between the two far windows and was probably built as a store before 1769. The eastern half of the house was added between 1815 and 1825. The house was restored in 1940–1941. The reconstructed porch was based on an 1836 watercolor, excavated foundations, and the paint line of the original porch pilasters, cornice, and roof as revealed on exterior weatherboards. Private.

BOWDEN-ARMISTEAD HOUSE

Completed in 1858, this house is an example of Greek Revival architecture. Lemuel J. Bowden purchased the land on which the house stands from Bruton Parish. The smooth, machine-made bricks of the front facade were imported from Baltimore. In 1874, Robert T. Armistead purchased the house from the Bowden estate. The Armistead family still owns it. Private.

BRYAN HOUSE

By the late 1700s, a house existed where this house now stands. By the end of the century, William Bryan owned it, and it survived until early in the twentieth century, at different times serving as a grocery store, school, and residence. In reconstructing the gable-roofed house, architects were guided by photographs and recollections of Williamsburg residents as well as archaeological records. Private.

CATHERINE BLAIKLEY HOUSE

William Blaikley and his wife, Catherine, lived in this house. When he died in 1736, William bequeathed to Catherine "all my whole estate of lands, houses, Negroes, goods & chattels." Catherine, who never remarried, remained at this address until her death in 1771 at the age of seventy-six. She was renowned as an "eminent Midwife . . . who, in the Course of her Practice, brought upwards of three Thousand Children into the World." The house was reconstructed in 1952. Private.

DURFEY SHOP

In April 1773, tailor Severinus Durfey announced his move to the Catherine Blaikley

House, and he used the Durfey Shop to the west for his tailoring activities and for other commercial purposes. The golden fleece of the signboard is the traditional symbol of a tailor's shop. Private.

JOHN BLAIR HOUSE AND KITCHEN

This house is one of the oldest in Williamsburg. The original, easterly part was built in 1720–1723 with a center passage and exterior end chimneys. The front door opened onto a passageway with rooms to either side. The larger room, on the left, with two front windows, probably served as a parlor. The walls and roof were covered originally with tarred clapboards. The twenty-eight-foot extension, to the left, with its own wider door was added in 1737 to serve as a new entertaining room replete with an imported marble chimneypiece. The stone steps at both doors were added at the time. The stone, imported from England, was typical of the period. The house is named for its early owner, John Blair Sr., a nephew of the Reverend James Blair, minister of Bruton Parish Church and first president of the College of William and Mary. John Blair was a burgess, a member of the governor's Council, and auditor general of the colony from 1728 until his death in 1771. He oversaw the extension of Bruton Parish Church and the reconstruction of the second Capitol in the early 1750s. As president of the Council, Blair twice served as acting governor of the colony. His son John Jr. signed the U.S. Constitution. President Washington named the younger Blair to the Supreme Court in 1789. Colonial Williamsburg acquired the property in 1928. During the restoration, an unaltered dormer on the back facade provided an example for the pedimented dormers in hipped form. The west entrance door is original and served as the model for the one on the east. The kitchen, with its huge chimney, has been reconstructed. Private.

Merchants Square

The 1782 Frenchman's Map shows quite a few buildings on the last block of Duke of Gloucester Street, the area that is now called Merchants Square, but little is known about the people who resided here or the structures in which they lived and worked. Likely a tavern and other businesses catered to the needs of the faculty and students at the College of William and Mary. Today, Merchants Square is again a commercial and shopping district. Many of the stores displaced by the restoration at the eastern and central parts of town were moved to this new commercial district. The stores are modeled after eighteenth- and early nineteenth-century structures from outside Tidewater Virginia. More than seventy years old, Merchants Square is listed by the National Register of Historic Places as an important example of an early planned shopping district.

College of William and Mary (Wren Building)

The orderly and almost symmetrical area of the College of William and Mary yard at the western end of Duke of Gloucester Street forms an architectural unit in itself, similar to the plan of many large gentry houses of the period that had important service buildings flanking the main structure. The central structure is the U-shaped main college building, the so-called Wren Building, with its massive chimneys and lofty cupola. The north wing contained the original great hall, and the south wing the college chapel. Flanking it to the north and south are the President's House and the Brafferton. The narrow, many-paned windows and steeply pitched roofs of these two buildings give a strong vertical accent to the architectural composition.

The Wren Building is the oldest academic structure in English-speaking America in continuous use, and the College of William and Mary is the second oldest institution of higher education in the United States. It received a charter from King William and Queen Mary in 1693 after the General Assembly sent the Reverend James Blair to England to persuade the royal couple to found an Anglican college in the colony. In the eighteenth century, higher education was not easily acquired in the colonies, so the few who attained it enjoyed considerable prestige. Although the average enrollment at William and Mary during the eighteenth century was less than one hundred, the college greatly influenced the intellectual life of Virginia. Students received a classical education, including Latin, Greek, mathematics, geography, logic, rhetoric, ethics, and physics. Largely through the influence of alumnus Thomas Jefferson, the curriculum was broadened in 1779 with law, chemistry and medicine, and modern languages. Since the 1920s, the college building bears the name of distinguished English architect Sir Christopher Wren, who is erroneously credited with its original design. Construction began in 1695. Inspired by the arrangement of many of the ancient colleges in Oxford and Cambridge, the original plan of William and Mary envisioned a quadrangle central courtyard enclosed by buildings, of which approximately half, including the Great Hall, classrooms, and dormitory space, had been erected by 1697. The south chapel wing, which matched the form of the north wing, was added in 1732. As late as 1772, at the royal governor's request, Thomas Jefferson, an accomplished amateur architect, drew plans for completing the design, and foundations had been laid when the outbreak of the Revolution put an end to the project. Some of those foundations still exist.

The Great Hall, in the north wing, held the dining room for the college. The kitchen was directly below. The second-floor common room where the professors and masters gathered to converse and relax would today be called the faculty lounge or library. The president and masters conducted college business in the convocation room, familiarly known to generations of students who were called there for commendation or censure as the "blue room." Above the lower cellar plinth, the west front brick wall of the building was laid for a number of courses in the newly fashionable Flemish bond, but bricklayers reverted further up to the more traditional English bond. Innovative, however, was the use of sliding sash windows rather than pivoting casements. Their use here is the earliest recorded instance of this new window form in the colony. Although fires in 1705, 1859, and 1862 did serious damage, the massive exterior walls of the Wren Building are largely original. They have withstood not only flames but also the architectural modifications

and structural alterations that were part of each rebuilding. The first major structure Colonial Williamsburg restored, in the late 1920s, the building now has the outward appearance that it showed from early in the eighteenth century until the fire of 1859. The building still houses classrooms and faculty offices.

PRESIDENT'S HOUSE

This building, on the north side of the college yard, was built in 1732–1733 and continues to serve its original function as the official residence of the college's president. It is slightly larger than the Brafferton across the yard. The building suffered fire damage at the end of the Revolution from bivouacked French troops, but the French government generously contributed funds to restore it a few years later. Private.

BRAFFERTON

Completed in 1723, this building, which faces the college yard on the south, was built to be used for the education of Christianized Indian boys. Funded through the estate of scientist Robert Boyle, the school educated and housed a dozen or so Indian boys at a time until the Revolution cut off revenue. The boys typically returned to their native homes and ways although some became guides, traders, and interpreters. The building suffered remarkably little damage over the years, although federal troops ripped its interior woodwork from the walls and used it for firewood during the Civil War. The Brafferton today houses college offices. Private.

AT GREAT HOPES PLANTATION

WINDMILL

Windmills were a common sight in colonial Virginia. In the early 1720s, lawyer William Robertson operated a mill in the vicinity of the Peyton Randolph House. The 1782 Frenchman's Map also shows a post windmill located south of the Public Hospital. This windmill, completed in 1957 to commemorate the 350th anniversary of the Jamestown settlement, stood for fifty-three years behind the Peyton Randolph House. As the Windmill and current configuration of the Peyton Randolph House never coexisted, and the likely historic location of the Windmill was further to the north, the decision was made to move the structure to Great Hopes. Based on the 1636 Bourn Mill in Cambridgeshire, England, this form, called a *post mill*, has the superstructure revolving on top of a single timber post. The upper floor holds the main wind shaft and millstones; the lower floor holds the bolting, or sifting, apparatus. Windmills required constant attention to ensure that they faced the wind and that the grinding and bolting operations ran properly. For post mills, if the wind changed direction, the miller lifted the stairs and pushed on the

tail-pole and wheel to turn the mill to face the wind. This reconstructed post mill is one of the most accurate representations of an eighteenth-century mill in the United States.

GOVERNOR'S PALACE AND PALACE GREEN

GOVERNOR'S PALACE

By the time it was finally completed in 1722, the home of Virginia's royal governor was considered one of the finest residences in British America. The majority of Virginians at the time, even many who were relatively well-to-do, lived in one-story houses composed of no more than two or three rooms. Sited at the end of a broad, imposing thoroughfare, the governor's residence terminated the primary north-south axis of the town, one that had not been conceived when the town was first laid out. The high visibility, scale, and symmetrical formality of the house and its two front offices enclosed by a brick wall and iron gates did much to reinforce the importance of the governorship. So too did the elaborate gardens with a canal and falling terraces, the heraldic gate piers, the impressive displays of arms in the entrance hall, and the elegant appointments of the upper middle room where the governor received petitioners. From the foot of the green at Duke of Gloucester Street to the inner sanctum of the governor's receiving rooms, the Palace complex was a carefully orchestrated procession of spaces moving toward and culminating in the presence of the man sworn to uphold the authority of the English monarch in Virginia.

Construction began in 1706, during the administration of Governor Edward Nott. In June of that year, following repeated exhortations from the Crown, the General Assembly voted to build a residence for the governor and appropriated three thousand pounds toward its erection. Henry Cary Sr., the builder of the Capitol, oversaw the construction based on specifications outlined by a building committee. Construction proceeded slowly, and the house was little more than a shell when the money ran out. When Lieutenant Governor Alexander Spotswood arrived in June 1710, the new resident dismissed the builder and took charge of fitting out the interior and laying out the formal gardens. It was almost certainly at his urging that the General Assembly enacted additional legislation providing for the enclosure of the forecourt and gardens and considered further recommendations for "rendring the new House Convenient as well as Ornamental." Spotswood had moved into the house by 1716 although the work continued for another six years. During his tenure, Spotswood created the formal arrangement of the gardens, including a series of terraces known as a falling garden that descend to a canal below. The house was finally completed by 1722 after Spotswood had left office. Ironically, the final work was done by Henry Cary Jr., son of the man whom Spotswood had dismissed.

The Palace had fallen into such poor condition by 1751 that Lieutenant Governor Robert Dinwiddie was forced to take up quarters next door at the Robert Carter House while expensive repairs were undertaken. By 1752, the Palace had been sufficiently rehabilitated to receive the governor and his household. During the ensuing months, a rear wing encompassing the present ballroom and supper room was erected under the supervision of Richard Taliaferro. The creation of two large rooms for public entertainments coincided with the construction of similar spaces elsewhere in Williamsburg, such as the great room at Wetherburn's Tavern and the Apollo and Daphne Rooms at the Raleigh Tavern. Such rooms were being added to private residences as well, such as in the Peyton Randolph House. This trend echoed a similar one in England. In 1756, English architect Isaac Ware noted that the addition of a "great room" to private residences had become commonplace, complaining that such an addition "always hangs from one end, or sticks to one side, of the house, and shews to the most careless eye, that, though fastened to the walls, it does not belong to the building."

After the completion of the ballroom wing, few important changes occurred at the Palace until the arrival of Norborne Berkeley, Baron de Botetourt, in 1768. Shortly after assuming his post, the royal governor launched a thorough program of redecoration including decorating the ballroom with a plain blue wallpaper that quickly caught the attention of the wealthy, who emulated the stylish finish. The arrival of the last royal governor, John Murray, fourth Earl of Dunmore, with his wife and six of their children changed the use of several of the rooms and also necessitated additional upgrades. The Palace eventually served as a residence for the first two governors of the Commonwealth of Virginia, Patrick Henry and Thomas Jefferson. During his residence, Jefferson prepared a series of drawings to guide in remodeling the Palace. His proposed changes were never carried out because the seat of government—and the governor's residence—moved to Richmond in 1780. Following the siege of Yorktown, American forces used the vacant Palace as a hospital to house their sick and wounded, more than 150 of whom are buried in the garden behind the building. On the night of December 22, 1781, fire broke out in the Palace, and in three hours it had burned to the ground. Shortly afterward, all that remained of the central structure's charred hulk was pulled down, and the bricks were sold. The two front ancillary buildings survived and were converted into dwellings before they were pulled down during the Civil War.

In the colonial period, large quantities of muskets, swords, and pistols were impressively displayed on the walls of the entrance hall. First installed by Governor Spotswood in 1715, this arms arrangement served not only as a symbol of royal authority but also as a supplementary arsenal to the magazine. The hall functioned as a screening area where the butler, whose office was in the pantry to the left of the front door, "sorted out" visitors wishing to see the governor. From this vantage point, he also managed the household staff, which consisted of more than two dozen servants and slaves. Hanging on the door is a ring of keys, a reminder that the butler along with the housekeeper also controlled access to the governor's valuable collection of silver and to his stocks of wine and food in the cellar. At least during Dunmore's tenure, the parlor on the right served as a business area, with a small space reserved for his private secretary, or chief of staff, Edward Foy. The majority of official business was carried out in one of the advance buildings. The ornamental display of firearms and swords extended up the stairs to the second story of the Palace. Beyond these stairs, a formal receiving room was part of the grand progression of spaces required for eighteenth-century aristocratic protocol. The earl and the countess probably had separate bedchambers. While "levees," formal ceremonies to welcome and entertain guests, had traditionally been held in the upper middle room, this receiving room also might have been used by the family when the countess visited with her children during the day. Those who enjoyed a close friendship with the governor or countess might be invited into their bedchambers, each of which also would have contained a dressing closet. The six chambers on the third story were occupied by children; the nurse, Mary Thompson; and perhaps the governess, Francotte Galli. An additional story over the ballroom might also have contained chambers for family and other servants. The dining room was perceived as a masculine domain, from which ladies typically withdrew after meals. Food brought over from the kitchen on covered pewter platters was transferred to china and silver serving pieces and garnished in the little middle room before being taken into the dining room across the passage. Dances, or "assemblies," took place in the ballroom, through the set of double doors in the entrance hall. The ballroom and supper room were among the most fashionable and up-to-date rooms in the building. At the far end of the supper room, a last pair of doors leads into a formal garden resembling those found on many English estates during the early eighteenth century. A "park," a distant landscape that encompassed, in this case, sixty-three acres, complemented the formal gardens. The service yards are located to the east and west of the advance buildings that flank the Palace. The kitchen, scullery, laundry, and other support buildings involved in the task of maintaining the household are in the west yard. Of special interest is the hexagonal "bagnio," or bathhouse, a luxury rarely found elsewhere in Virginia. The kitchen was among the finest in Virginia. Today, Historic Foodways staff demonstrate the high style of cooking there. The stables and carriage house in the east yard served the transportation needs of the household.

Excavation of the Palace complex began in 1930, and the reconstruction of the site was completed and opened to the public in 1934. The archaeological work uncovered the original cellar walls and floor paving largely intact, together with the foundations of the ancillary buildings. Research was aided in particular by the measured floor plan drawn by Jefferson (which included room dimensions, ceiling heights, wall thicknesses, window placements, and chimneys) along with information in colonial records and graphic sources such as the Frenchman's Map and the Bodleian Plate (which includes an engraving of the eighteenth-century exterior of the Palace). Colonial records show that "handsome gates" to the forecourt were specified for the new residence in 1710. The design of the present wrought-iron gates was based on excavated fragments and eighteenth-century English examples. The Portland stone lion and unicorn atop the gate piers were sculpted in London in the early twentieth century. Similar figures at Hampton Court Palace inspired their general character.

ROBERT CARTER HOUSE AND OFFICE

Constructed in the late 1740s, the house served as a temporary residence for Governor Robert Dinwiddie while the Palace underwent repairs in 1751 and 1752. Robert Carter Nicholas, a member of the House of Burgesses and treasurer of the colony, purchased it in 1753 and sold it in 1761 to Robert Carter III, his cousin. Robert Carter III made immediate alterations to the house, including papering several rooms with fashionable English wallpaper. He probably also altered the roofline to the hip-on-hip configuration, covering over the two central valleys of the old M-shaped roof, which may have been prone to leaking. Carter and his family lived in the house for twelve years. Six of his seventeen children were born here. After three of his young daughters died within a year of each other, the Carter family returned to their plantation, called Nomini Hall, in 1772. A brick vault located beneath the north passageway appears to date from the third quarter of the eighteenth century. Accessible from the basement of the main house, it was used to store wine and produce. Such storerooms were not uncommon in the better houses in colonial Virginia. Restored in 1931–1932 and 1951–1953, the house and the brick outbuilding are original. Other structures—including the office (to the far right in the drawing) and the covered way—are reconstructions. The Robert Carter Kitchen is now one of Colonial Williamsburg's hotel facilities. Private.

McKenzie Shop

At midcentury, Dr. Kenneth McKenzie owned and lived on this property with his family. He operated his shop on the site. McKenzie died in 1755. Among other bequests, he left a skeleton to his "good friend Doctor James Carter having behaved in a very kind manner to me in my sickness." Colonial Williamsburg rebuilt the McKenzie Shop in 1951–1953. Light refreshments are now sold here.

Elkanah Deane House

This house was named for the Irish coach-maker who paid seven hundred pounds for four lots and the original dwelling, shop, and garden on this site in 1772. Elkanah Deane may have been encouraged to move to Williamsburg from New York by royal governor Lord Dunmore. Deane advertised in the *Virginia Gazette* that he "had the honour of making a coach, phæton, and chaise, for his Excellency the Right Honourable Earl of DUNMORE." Private.

Elkanah Deane Shop

Behind the Elkanah Deane House is the shop. In the eighteenth century, the shop was the scene of carriage making on a considerable scale. Wheelwrights, blacksmiths, and harness-makers were among the artisans who worked together to make carts, wagons, riding chairs, and carriages. Today, Colonial Williamsburg's wheelwright practices his trade in the shop.

George Wythe House

George Wythe's father-in-law, Richard Taliaferro, a planter and amateur architect, is believed to have designed and built this elegant brick house around 1752–1754. In his will, Taliaferro gave George and Elizabeth Wythe use of the property for life. Wythe lived in the house from about 1755, around the time he married Elizabeth Taliaferro, until 1791, when he moved to Richmond to serve as a judge on Virginia's Court of Chancery.

One of the grandest and most impressive private dwellings in town, the Wythe House is one of the most sophisticated examples of the architectural aspirations of the Virginia gentry during the second half of the eighteenth century. The plan of the house consists of four rooms on each of two full stories, with both floors centrally divided by a large stair passage. Two great chimneys rise between the paired rooms, thus affording a fireplace in all eight. The smaller windows in the second story exemplify the clever use of proportioning used in the building. Most colonial builders used a rule of thumb to determine the height of a window to its width—often a variant of two to one. In two-story Virginia houses, the second-floor windows lighting the more private bedroom chambers are slightly shorter in height than those on the ground floor, which open into the common rooms. At the Wythe House, the architect narrowed as well as shortened the openings on the second floor compared with those below, a subtlety that was seldom used elsewhere in the colony. The exterior exhibits some of the best masonry work in town, featuring Flemish-bond brickwork framed with rubbed jambs, corners, and water table and gauged-brick stringcourse and splayed brick arches. The walls eschew the systematic display of glazed headers, a decorative conceit that was going out of fashion in Williamsburg in the 1750s. Although little is known about the specific personal property of George and Elizabeth Wythe, the house has been furnished with objects typically found in comparable Virginia gentry homes. Architectural and documentary evidence suggests that this dwelling was once wallpapered virtually throughout. The yellow ocher trim color, discovered through paint analysis, complements the brightly colored wallpaper exhibited in the house. A comprehensive study of wallpaper usage in colonial Virginia provided the documentation for the wide variety of patterns and colors used throughout the building.

The Wythe property stands on several lots. Behind the house, a symmetrical garden plan divides the property into distinct areas. Archaeological excavations established the locations of major outbuildings in the service yard. Among the reconstructed frame outbuildings are a smokehouse, kitchen, laundry, lumber house, poultry house, well, dovecote, and stable. Two privies are nearby. The orchard and the kitchen garden are on the south side of the property.

The house passed through a succession of owners until 1926 when Bruton Parish Church acquired it and used it as the parish house. After transference of the property in 1938, Colonial Williamsburg restored it in 1939–1940.

THOMAS EVERARD HOUSE

John Brush, gunsmith, armorer, and first keeper of the public magazine, originally constructed this house in 1718 as a timber-framed one-story building typical of the houses built here in the early years of the eighteenth century. Dendrochronological testing of the framing timbers indicates that the north wing was part of the original construction, which created an L-shaped plan. The exterior was finished with beaded weatherboards, and the roof was originally covered with oak clapboards rather than shingles. Parts of that earlier covering survive beneath modern materials. After Brush died in 1726, the house had several different owners, including Thomas Everard. Everard added the south wing in the early 1770s to give the house its current U-shaped configuration. The central passage and original staircase with its molded handrail and turned balusters are part of Brush's original plan, but subsequent owners embellished the house by adding wainscoting, wallpaper, and new mantels. Fine paneling and rich carving are evidence of Everard's affluence and taste. Everard, who arrived in Virginia as an orphan apprentice in the 1730s, acquired the property about 1755 and lived here for twenty-five years. He was the clerk of the York County Court for nearly forty years, twice served as mayor of Williamsburg, was on the vestry of Bruton Parish Church, and was deputy clerk of the General Court from the 1740s until the Revolution. The work yard between the house and the outbuildings is paved with the original bricks discovered during the course of archaeological excavations. The wooden smokehouse and the brick kitchen are original buildings that have been restored. The kitchen began its existence as a frame structure on brick foundations, with only the chimney end being brick. In 1774 the building was extended, the wooden portions were rebuilt in brick, and dormers were added, probably to ventilate sleeping areas for slaves in the loft. Everard's nineteen slaves lived and worked in these outbuildings. The house was restored in 1949–1951.

Play Booth Theater

This open-air theater is located on the site of the first purpose-built theater constructed in the American colonies, which was active in the 1720s and 1730s. Archaeologists unearthed fragmentary foundations likely related to the playhouse built by William Levingston, who bought three lots at the corner of Palace and Nicholson Streets in 1716 and who managed the theater. The two-story wooden structure may have measured as much as eighty-six feet in length by about thirty feet in width, the same general size as many English provincial theaters of the period. In 1718, to celebrate the birthday of King George I, Governor Spotswood sponsored the first play known to have been staged at the theater. In 1745 the theater was remodeled and used as the city courthouse until 1770, and the old playhouse was subsequently demolished. Today's Play Booth Theater is similar to temporary outdoor stages erected for fairs and race days in England.

Although performances sometimes attracted a boisterous, rowdy audience, the gentry frequently filled the seats of provincial playhouses. Actors at the Play Booth Theater present scenes from eighteenth-century comedies.

Levingston Kitchen

Soon after buying three lots at this location in 1716, William Levingston built a house, a kitchen, and other outbuildings. He also constructed a theater and laid out a bowling green. To date, only the kitchen has been reconstructed. Levingston briefly operated a tavern at the house. When he encountered financial difficulties, he had to mortgage the property, though it continued to be used periodically. By the mid-1730s, Dr. George Gilmer, a successful apothecary-surgeon, had acquired the property, moved into the house, and built an apothecary shop on the corner. In 1788, St. George Tucker bought the house that Levingston had built, moved it to face Market Square, and enlarged it. Private.

Nicholson Street

St. George Tucker House

St. George Tucker, who attended the College of William and Mary and later became professor of law there, bought the property in 1788. He moved an older building, the one-story dwelling built in 1716–1717 on the Palace green by William Levingston, manager of Williamsburg's first theater, to this site, re-oriented the house toward Market Square, enlarged it, and placed it on new raised brick foundations. Over the next six years, Tucker added a second story, flanking one-story wings, and a kitchen connected to the house by a semi-enclosed "covered way." Accounts for all this work survive, making its construction the best documented building in Williamsburg. A 1798 agreement between Tucker and local painter Jeremiah Satterwhite even specifies the paint scheme to be used on the house and kitchen: "Spanish brown," "pure White," "Chocolate," "dark brick Colour," "pale Stone colour, or straw Colour," and "yellow Ochre." The house was renovated in 1930–1931 but not restored to its eighteenth-century appearance. In the late 1830s, Nathaniel Beverley Tucker had raised the roof slope of the two wings to create bed-rooms, which were lit by dormer windows. The roof height and dormers were left in place but retrimmed. Many of the Greek Revival details of his renovations were changed to imitate colonial ones, but the form of the building was not changed. Unfortunately, the first floor windows in the center part, which had been doubled in number in the 1790s, were thought to be later additions and were altered during the restoration of 1930–1931. Rare, triple-hung sash installed by St. George Tucker that had once lit the parlor to the left of the front door were removed. The kitchen at the west end of the complex was reconstructed based on the archaeological footprint of the original 1790s

building. Today, the house is Colonial Williamsburg's donor reception center.

Grissell Hay Lodging House

The core of this house, probably one of the first houses on Market Square, may date from around 1720, when it belonged to Dr. Archibald Blair, a Scottish physician and a partner in Williamsburg's leading mercantile business, the Prentis store. The present symmetrical, five-bay, fairly sizable exterior probably dates from the second half of the eighteenth century. Apothecary Peter Hay lived here in the 1760s. After Hay's death, his widow, Grissell, operated the dwelling as a lodging house. During the house's 1930–1931 restoration, sash windows of an eighteenth-century type, which had been replaced during the nineteenth century with larger paned two-over-two light sash, were installed. The early nineteenth-century front porch with its Doric columns and pediment was retained because it continued the classical eighteenth-century architectural tradition. Archaeological excavations disclosed the original three-sided stone steps beneath the porch. Their unusual design also exists at Scotchtown, the Hanover County home of Patrick Henry, and Tuckahoe, a Randolph family seat in Goochland County. The Grissell Hay dairy, smokehouse, and privy, which date from the early nineteenth century, are among the few surviving early outbuildings extant in the Historic Area. Private.

PEYTON RANDOLPH HOUSE

The home of one of the most prominent families in colonial Virginia, this dark red house has three sections. William Robertson, clerk of the Council, erected the corner portion in 1715–1718 as a two-story house built around a central chimney that faced west onto North England Street. Sir John Randolph and his family were living here in 1724 when he bought the lot and the one-story house next door. In 1754–1755, son Peyton Randolph linked the two with a two-story central section that features a grand stairway, a monumental round-headed window, and an elegant dining room with bedchamber above. Peyton and his wife, Betty, also had the old kitchen torn down and replaced with a much larger one that contained laundry facilities, slave quarters, a cellar, and a covered way that connected it to the main house. Inside the house is the best series of surviving paneled rooms in Williamsburg. Although most of the paneling is the usual yellow pine, the northeast room on the second floor of the oldest section is paneled completely in oak. The wood stringcourse girding the house at the second-floor level is a decorative feature imitative of a similar feature often seen on brick houses. The reddish brown exterior paint enhanced the illusion of a masonry structure. A telltale sign of the building's growth over time is the roofline of the main block, which is hipped on the west and gabled to the east, indicative of two periods of construction. The frame, shingles, and wood guttering for an earlier

M-shaped roof over the original section of the house survive beneath the present roof.

Colonial Williamsburg restored the home in 1938–1940 and in 1967–1968. Today, the Peyton Randolph House is furnished with English and American antiques, including several pieces of Randolph family silver. And the Randolph yard is again alive with activity since carpenters, starting in 1997 and using eighteenth-century materials, tools, and techniques, reconstructed the kitchen, the passageway connecting it to the main house, a smokehouse, a milk house, and other service buildings.

LUDWELL TENEMENT

This house reaffirms another characteristic of Williamsburg's back streets: rental property and smaller houses coexisted with the homes of well-to-do residents such as the Randolphs and the Tayloes. Private.

TAYLOE HOUSE, OFFICE, AND KITCHEN

It appears that this frame house (left) was built between 1752 and 1759 when Dr. James Carter, who operated the Unicorn's Horn apothecary shop, owned the property. John Tayloe, a prominent planter who was about to undertake the construction of a great stone mansion at his plantation Mount Airy, bought the house and lot in 1759 for three times the amount Carter had paid. Tayloe purchased the house to serve as his town residence after he was appointed to the governor's Council two years earlier. The "Dutch," or gambrel, roof has two separate slopes to provide more headroom in the upper story. A distinctive architectural refinement is the elongated kick, or upturn, on the lower eaves. The house is also noted for its fine interior woodwork and the original marble console table supported on wrought-iron brackets near the front door. This building is largely original, but the platform of the reconstructed porch is paved with fragments of English Portland stone found on the site during excavations. Most of the brick foundations are original and still retain their colonial mortar, which, due to the local unavailability of limestone, was made with ground oyster shells. Remains of original brick drips, or ground gutters, were excavated along the north and south walls and were restored. They broke the force of rainwater falling from the roof, prevented erosion, and carried moisture away from the house. The most conspicuous of the surviving Tayloe House outbuildings is the office (middle) with its ogee, or bell-shaped, roof. Located just east of the main house, it is the only example in Williamsburg of this roof form. The office is largely original. The kitchen (right) was reconstructed in 1951. Private.

LUDWELL-PARADISE STABLE

The stable was reconstructed in 1932 based on precedents found at the Botetourt Hotel in Gloucester County and the tavern stable at the King William County Courthouse, both of

which have since been torn down. Today, coopers demonstrate their trade in this building.

HAY'S CABINETMAKING SHOP

This shop occupied low ground between two substantial residences. Here cabinetmakers made some of the finest furniture in the colonies. Anthony Hay, who had been a cabinetmaker in Williamsburg for several years, bought this lot in 1756. Hay gave up the business in 1766 when he purchased the Raleigh Tavern, after which he leased the building to former workmen. Subsequent renters include cabinetmakers Benjamin Bucktrout and Edmund Dickinson. Carver and gilder George Hamilton worked here, too. Archaeologists found the remains of a fence rail in the streambed under the shop. The seven-foot-long artifact showed both the crude form of the wood rail and the spacing between the pales that had been nailed to it. The fence in front of the shop reproduces these details. Archaeological discoveries also provided evidence of clay roofing tiles like those that now cover the shop. The building was reconstructed in 1965. Today, tradespeople once again fashion fine furniture and musical instruments.

ELIZABETH REYNOLDS HOUSE

This house is one of the few structures on Nicholson Street that faces north. In 1777, *Virginia Gazette* printer William Hunter deeded a narrow strip of land containing a house and garden to his mother, Elizabeth Reynolds. Hunter was illegitimate, and, although his father had acknowledged William in his will, he failed to provide for the boy's mother. In addition to the house and lot, Hunter agreed to pay his mother an annuity of forty pounds. Private.

WILLIAM RANDOLPH LODGINGS

This small rental property, built on the north edge of the lot facing the back street, is unusually narrow—only twelve feet deep (and forty-six feet long), near the minimum depth of a dwelling house. The building was rented in 1735 to William Randolph, the uncle of Peyton Randolph. A burgess and later a councillor, William apparently considered this modest structure an appropriate residence when he came to Williamsburg on government business. It was reconstructed in 1949. Private.

BOOKER TENEMENT

This small one-story tenement, which lacks a sign identifying the building, is typical of a Williamsburg house of the "middling sort." An analysis of the tree growth rings in its timbers showed that the wood was cut in 1823–1824. Although modest in size, this center-passage house had a heated cellar and two heated chambers in the garret. Documentary evidence indicates that Richard Booker, carpenter and

town constable, had begun to rent out rooms in his newly built tenement by the spring of 1826. Private.

COKE-GARRETT HOUSE

This long, rambling house is made up of three sections. In 1755, John Coke, a goldsmith and tavern keeper who already owned a house and three lots immediately to the east, bought the two lots on which the one-story west section stands. He probably built that section in the late 1750s or early 1760s. Coke died in 1767. His widow, Sarah, continued to operate or rent out the house as a tavern. Her son, Robey, repaired wagons, mounted cannons, and helved axes during the Revolution. The Garrett family acquired the property in 1810 and owned it for well over a century. The two-story center portion was built in 1836–1837, and the one-story east section, an eighteenth-century structure, was moved to this site from an unknown location around the same time. The brick office (far right) that served as Dr. Robert Garrett's surgery after the Battle of Williamsburg in 1862 apparently dates from about 1810. Dr. Garrett treated the wounded of both armies here. The subdued Greek Revival architecture of the center section merges easily with the colonial styles of the east and west wings. The brick office bears full evidence of the Greek Revival style in its columned and pedimented porch. The restoration of the house was carried out in stages from 1928 through 1961. Little was changed on the exterior. A nineteenth-century porch was removed, and a third dormer, which existed originally, was added between the two still in place on the middle section. One of only a few such surviving examples of eighteenth-century work, the Chinese-style railing on the west entrance porch duplicates the dilapidated original that was still in place before the restoration. Private.

WALLER STREET

BENJAMIN POWELL HOUSE AND OFFICE

Benjamin Powell, a successful builder, bought this house and property in 1763 from Benjamin Waller, a prominent local lawyer and owner of much of the land east of the Capitol, and sold it in 1782. It changed hands several times before Benjamin Carter Waller, son of the early owner, bought it in 1794. The front frame portion of the house was added before 1782 to the original brick house that lies behind facing south. The small brick building next to the large house probably served as the office of Waller's son, Dr. Robert Waller, to whom he deeded that part of the property in 1814. The temple-style brick office is similar to the one at the Coke-Garrett House across the street. The kitchen was built between 1820 and 1840 while the smokehouse and dairy may be slightly earlier. During the house's restoration in 1955–1956, everything above the present eaves level was reconstructed. The first floor of the house is original. Open seasonally.

ELIZABETH CARLOS HOUSE

In 1772 Elizabeth Carlos bought this lot with a one-story frame house. Typical of Williamsburg's more modest dwellings, the dusky brown color of this reconstructed house would have been familiar to early residents. A manuscript account book that records purchases of gloves, hose, ribbons, thread, and fabric from Carlos in 1777 and indicates that she made aprons and gowns suggests that Elizabeth Carlos was a milliner and dressmaker who carried on her business in her home. Private.

CHRISTIANA CAMPBELL'S TAVERN

Christiana Campbell announced in October 1771 that she had opened a "TAVERN in the House, behind the Capitol" where she promised "genteel Accommodations, and the very best Entertainment," by which she meant food and drink. A distinguished clientele patronized her tavern. When George Washington came to town to attend the House of Burgesses in the spring of 1772, he recorded in his diary that he dined here ten times within two months. Washington and his friends often gathered at the tavern for refreshments and discussions of everything from horse races to politics. The building was reconstructed in 1954–1956. Today, Christiana Campbell's Tavern once again entertains guests with food and strolling balladeers.

The Blue Bell

Little is known about this site, which probably had a building on it around 1707. At various times beginning in the 1760s, the Blue Bell (the name was mentioned in a 1770 letter) housed a tavern, a lodging house, a store, and a gunsmith's shop. After being informed in 1771 that their Williamsburg property was in bad repair, absentee owners Hannah and William Lee of London tried to sell it but failed to find a buyer. After archaeological excavations in 1932 and 1946, Colonial Williamsburg reconstructed the Blue Bell. Private.

Powell's Tenement

In the eighteenth century, there was a house and a shop on this site. Wheelwright and riding chair maker Peter Powell rented a shop here from 1755 to about 1770. Later, in 1779, the tenement was rented by the keeper of the Public Gaol. The reconstructed building now houses the heating plant for the Capitol. Private.

George Davenport Stable

Today, the Presbyterian Meetinghouse is staged in this large reconstructed building behind the George Davenport House.

Isham Goddin Shop

Militiaman Isham Goddin acquired this small shop in 1778 for two hundred pounds. In 1783 he sold his plot and building for only ninety pounds, a decrease that reflects both wartime inflation and the collapse of Williamsburg property values after the capital moved to Richmond in 1780. The building, reconstructed in 1954, now serves as a hotel accommodation. Private.

David Morton House and Shop

In 1777 tailor David Morton purchased this lot for four hundred pounds, a sum that indicates that the transaction included the house and the shop next door. Morton, an active member of the Williamsburg Lodge of Masons, served as treasurer of the lodge from 1780 to 1786. The house was reconstructed in 1953 and today is a hotel facility. Private.

York Street

George Jackson House and Store

This property was once owned by a merchant who risked his life as well as his fortune during the Revolutionary War. George Jackson chartered a ship, sailed it to Bermuda, and returned with a supply of much-needed gunpowder for the American forces. Jackson acquired the property shortly after he moved to Williamsburg from Norfolk in 1773 or 1774. The different roof slopes indicate that this building was, in effect, two buildings. The window and door arrangements of the east wing (right side of the drawing) are typical of shops in the eighteenth century, and the rear chimney would have heated a small counting room. Jackson probably used this part of the structure as his store. The property now serves as hotel accommodations. Private.

COGAR SHOP

This small eighteenth-century building was moved from King and Queen County, Virginia, to this lot in 1947. Colonial Williamsburg acquired the property in 1964. Private.

ROBERT NICOLSON HOUSE

Robert Nicolson, a tailor and merchant, built this gambrel-roofed house about mid-century. The off-center entrance door testifies to two periods of construction, the eastern part possibly as early as 1752 and the western part a little later. For several years thereafter, Nicolson took in lodgers. Nicolson initially had his shop across the street. When his eldest son, William, joined him in the tailoring business in

1774, they opened a shop and store on Duke of Gloucester Street, a much better location for commercial purposes. During the Revolution, Nicolson served on the local committee of safety. He and William provided uniforms to the American army. Private.

FRANCIS STREET

BENJAMIN WALLER HOUSE

Benjamin Waller acquired this lot before 1750, and the property remained in the Waller family for over a century. A prominent Williamsburg attorney, Waller was George Wythe's law teacher. He held a variety of offices during an impressive career: burgess, city recorder, clerk of the General Court, judge of the Court of Admiralty, and vestryman of Bruton Parish. Waller probably used the office, which is adjacent to the house on the east, as a clerk's office for his many posts and also for his private law practice. The smokehouse is an original structure. Behind the house is a formal garden that has been re-created with the help of a sketch drawn in the early 1800s. Like many old houses, this house is the product of several building phases. The earliest portion is the single large room to the left of the front door. Later on, a center stair passage and then a large formal room for entertaining were added to the west end. This was followed by a gambrel-roofed extension in the rear. The horizontal weatherboards, some of them original, on the dormer cheeks are unusual because such boards are generally attached at an angle that matches the roof slope. The ornamental fence pales at the east end of the yard are copies from a surviving eighteenth-century specimen that had been used in reroofing the house during the nineteenth century. The house and outbuildings were restored between 1951 and 1953. Private.

BASSETT HALL

This property was the Williamsburg home of Abby Aldrich and John D. Rockefeller Jr. The Rockefellers acquired Bassett Hall in October 1927, although it was several years before they took up residence. The Bray family owned the property from the early seventeenth century until 1753 when it was transferred to Philip Johnson, husband of Elizabeth Bray. Johnson probably built the present house soon after; the front portion is believed to date from the mid-eighteenth century. The estate then consisted of 950 rural acres and four contiguous lots. Richard Corbin, the next owner, refurbished the house in the 1790s. From 1796 to 1839, Burwell Bassett, a Virginia legislator and the nephew of Martha Washington, owned the property. Despite various owners in the interim, it has carried the Bassett name ever since. The restoration of Bassett Hall began in 1928, but a fire in 1930 destroyed part of the building's roof and stair passage and delayed the renovation of the house. An officer of Colonial Williamsburg saved the stair handrail, balusters, and newel post when he tore them out of the building. Colonial Williamsburg's architects were involved in the restoration, but the Rockefellers oversaw the work and also planned the interior decoration. In furnishing Bassett Hall, the Rockefellers drew on their many interests in the arts: Chinese porcelain, Oriental carpets, European tapestries, and modern American art. Abby Aldrich Rockefeller also formed an unprecedented collection of early American folk art, creating a rich mixture of inviting and relaxing furnishings. Outside, the Rockefellers realigned the three historic outbuildings (smokehouse, kitchen, and dairy) near the house to allow for a better view of the property and landscaped fourteen acres of gardens. John D. Rockefeller Jr. was especially fond of a mammoth great oak tree, which was about four hundred years old when it collapsed in 1998. Following Abby Aldrich Rockefeller's death in 1948, Rockefeller deeded Bassett Hall to their son John D. Rockefeller 3rd, reserving a life interest in the property. After his father's death in 1960, John D. Rockefeller 3rd and his wife assumed responsibility for the property. At John D. Rockefeller 3rd's death in 1978, the property was left to family members who presented it to the Colonial Williamsburg Foundation. The next year, the John D. Rockefeller 3rd Fund gave Bassett Hall furnishings to the Foundation. A complete restoration of the Bassett Hall complex, including the gardens and historic interiors, was undertaken in 2000–2002 and funded by Abby O'Neill, granddaughter of Abby and John D. Rockefeller Jr., and her husband, George O'Neill.

Today, the house and grounds look much the way they did in the late 1930s and 1940s. The decorative arched heads of the second-floor windows are unusual in an eighteenth-century frame building. The reconstructed entrance porch follows the general form—with greatly simplified detail—of the original example still in place at the William Finnie House.

GEORGE DAVENPORT HOUSE

George Davenport and his descendants owned this property until 1779. In 1780 John Draper, a blacksmith who had come to Virginia with royal governor Lord Botetourt in 1768, bought the property. Draper operated a blacksmith and farrier business on Duke of Gloucester Street. The house has been reconstructed. Private.

JAMES MOIR SHOP

The tailor James Moir operated his business in this shop next to his home. Private.

JAMES MOIR HOUSE

This house is named for the tailor who owned this property from 1777 to about 1800. In an effort to supplement his income, James Moir opened his home to lodgers. In 1784, when Walker Maury, a 1775 graduate of the College of William and Mary, established a grammar school in the old Capitol, Moir advertised that he had furnished his house to accommodate eight or ten pupils and would lodge, board, wash, and mend for them at a low price. Private.

AYSCOUGH HOUSE

Christopher Ayscough, a former gardener, and his wife, Anne, who had been the head cook for Lieutenant Governor Francis Fauquier at the Palace, purchased this house and established on this site in 1768 a tavern, which probably stood west of the present structure. The funds probably came from a bequest of £150 that Governor Fauquier left Anne "in recompence of her great fidelity and attention to me in all my Illness, and of the great Economy with which she conducted the Expenses of my kitchen during my residence at Williamsburg." The Ayscoughs' tavern-keeping venture proved to be short-lived. Within two years, Christopher Ayscough, deeply in debt, offered to sell his dwelling along with furnishings, Madeira wine, slaves, and horses. A succession of commercial establishments occupied the building in the eighteenth century. Original framing was revealed during the 1932 restoration. A large shop window and the gable-end entrance attest to the structure's early commercial use. The shed at the rear was a late eighteenth-century addition. Joiners now ply their trade in the house.

WILLIAM FINNIE QUARTERS

This small building just east of the William Finnie House is an original structure. Private.

WILLIAM FINNIE HOUSE

This house was probably built around 1769–1770 by William Pasteur, one of the town's leading apothecaries. He opened his first shop in 1759 and later went into a partnership with Dr. John Galt. The two erected a new premise on Duke of Gloucester Street in 1775. The entrance porch was added between 1791 and 1801, requiring a reduction in the size of the second-story windows in the central pavilion. Called "the handsomest house in town" by St. George Tucker in 1809, it is a precursor of the neoclassicism that began to change the American architectural scene after the Revolution. The two-story central block with its pedimented gable and flanking one-story wings became the prototype of a house form that gained currency in Virginia and neighboring states in the following decades. The house passed through a number of owners in the late eighteenth and nineteenth centuries, though the form of the building was little altered. From the 1770s to the mid-1780s, Colonel William Finnie, quartermaster general of the Southern Department during the Revolution, and his family lived here. James Semple, a judge and professor of law at the college, acquired the property in 1800 and insured the house and outbuilding for two thousand dollars. This largely original house was restored in 1932, with further work completed in 1952. The porch piers were returned to their original fluted Doric form, and the decorative guilloche fret pattern of interlaced bands on the porch architrave was restored. This geometric design became a very

popular decorative motif most often associated with the neoclassical style of architecture that became popular in the late eighteenth and early nineteenth centuries. Private.

NELSON-GALT OFFICE

This small office near the Nelson-Galt House is original. In the eighteenth century, the word *office* described any outbuilding not otherwise designated as to use. Private.

NELSON-GALT HOUSE AND KITCHEN

This house is the oldest dwelling in town and among the oldest frame houses in Virginia. The framing members encased in the central part of the present house date to 1695. The chimneys and flanking shed closets are later additions probably made when William Robertson, clerk of the Council, bought the property and remodeled the house about 1709. He appears to have moved the building to its present site in the second decade of the eighteenth century. Thomas Nelson Jr., a member of a prominent Yorktown family, owned the house later in the century. Nelson signed the Declaration of Independence, commanded Virginia's forces during the Yorktown campaign, and succeeded Thomas Jefferson as governor of the Commonwealth of Virginia. Dr. Alexander Dickie Galt, visiting physician at the Public Hospital, purchased the house in 1823. Descendants of the Galt family, residents of Williamsburg since colonial days, continued to live here into the twentieth century. The house (left) was restored and the kitchen (right) was reconstructed in 1951–1952. Private.

CHISWELL-BUCKTROUT HOUSE

In 1766 John Chiswell, a planter, businessman, and former burgess, became the center of a scandal that "put the whole country into a ferment." Accused of killing Robert Rutledge during a tavern brawl, Chiswell was arrested for murder. As was customary in such cases, bail was refused, but three of Chiswell's friends, who were judges of the General Court, reversed the decision and released him on bail. The less privileged attributed this unusually lenient procedure to Chiswell's political and family connections. He died the day before his trial—by his own hand, it was rumored. Cabinetmaker Benjamin Bucktrout resided and worked here by the 1770s. A study of the surviving roof timbers provided the evidence for the reconstruction of this elongated hipped-roof dwelling. Today, the house and its freestanding kitchen are hotel facilities. Private.

EWING HOUSE

When Ebenezer Ewing, a Scottish merchant, died in 1795, he left his house to Elizabeth Ashton, the mother of their illegitimate son,

Thomas, with the proviso that "the moment she marries . . . [it] becomes the property of my said son Thomas." Elizabeth remained single until her death four years later, when young Thomas inherited the dwelling. In 1805, the Williamsburg Hustings Court ordered the boy's legal guardian to bond him out for three years to learn the art of seamanship; Thomas disappeared before completing his apprenticeship. The Ewing House and the Ewing Shop behind are today hotel accommodations. Private.

MOODY HOUSE

Josias Moody, a blacksmith, owned this one-story frame house from 1794 until he died about 1810. The house, which likely dates from 1725 to 1750, was altered several times before reaching its present size and appearance by 1782. The long lean-to roof on the back indicates that additions were made to an earlier structure. The kitchen behind the house is now a hotel facility. Private.

DR. BARRAUD HOUSE

This house was erected in the third quarter of the eighteenth century. The original brickwork and framing indicate that the house was built in two distinct phases. The earliest was a double-pile section closest to the corner of Francis and Botetourt Streets. A smaller ten-foot section was added to the west. Though the early history of the site is ambiguous, it seems likely that apothecary William Carter or blacksmith James Anderson erected the building as rental property in the 1760s or early 1770s. The house reached its present dimensions by 1796. The owner at that time was Dr. Philip Barraud, who had served in the army during the Revolutionary War and later was a visiting physician at the Public Hospital. Like most buildings in eighteenth-century Williamsburg, the Barraud House was altered to suit changing needs and fashion. As originally built, the front of the house probably looked much like the asymmetrical facade of the Moody House standing on the other side of Francis Street. The original plan most likely consisted of two front rooms and two smaller back rooms. The front door remains in its original location and had two windows flanking it on the east and a single one on the west. However, it opened directly into a large room instead of the present central passage. With the ten-foot addition to the west, the passage was created and the two west rooms enlarged with a new chimney to heat them. No major exterior changes were necessary when the house was restored in 1942. New window sash and frames follow the design of original windows in the gable ends while the shutters are based on local precedent. Weatherboarding is new and the chimney stacks were rebuilt above the roof ridge while the cornices are repaired original features. The entrance porch was rebuilt to conform to the old foundations as well as to traces of the original framing against the exterior wall. A fanciful Chinese fret railing was installed though no evidence for it appeared at this site. However, some versions of railings done "in the Chinese taste" appear in contemporary

Virginia examples, including the Coke-Garrett House. Stone paving found on the site was used in the reconstructed walk flanking the entrance steps. A ground-level brick gutter, meant to catch and carry away rainwater falling from the eaves, was unearthed almost intact along the south front. A similar original example was excavated in place at the Palace. The dwelling was slightly modified in 1987. Private.

LEWIS HOUSE

Charles Lewis owned the property until 1806 and is believed to have built the house that stood here. Initially the lot was part of the Orlando Jones property, which extended from Duke of Gloucester Street to Francis Street. The side-passage house was reconstructed on its eighteenth-century foundations in 1948–1949 and now serves as hotel accommodations. Private.

ORRELL HOUSE

Probably built between 1750 and 1775, this house takes its name from John Orrell, who acquired the property about 1810. The plan of this gambrel-roofed dwelling is similar to a number of other structures in town, such as the Lightfoot House, with a passage on one side that provides access to front and back rooms heated by a shared chimney on the other side of the house. The gambrel roof provides additional space on the second floor. The house forms on plan an exact square whose sides measure twenty-eight feet, and because the roof ridge is twenty-eight feet above the top of the basement wall, it is proportioned as an ideal geometric cube. Today, it is a hotel facility. Private.

THE QUARTER

This small, early nineteenth-century cottage was named "The Quarter" during the restoration in the 1930s when an oral informant described it as having been occupied by a black family around the time of the Civil War. Though it is clearly a modest building, its prominent location on the street argues against its interpretation as a slave quarter. No known purpose-built slave quarters have been identified in Williamsburg. Whatever its history, the chimney shows evidence that there was once another section that stood against the east side of the present structure. The addition of a shed portion at the rear of the building has resulted in an unusual and attractive roofline. It is now a hotel facility. Private.

RICHARD CRUMP HOUSE

Richard Crump owned this house in the late eighteenth century. The Reverend John Bracken also owned the house briefly. Today, it is a hotel facility. Private.

BRACKEN KITCHEN

Once owned by the Reverend John Bracken, the kitchen today is a hotel facility. Private.

BRACKEN TENEMENT

This one-story rental structure has a steep gable roof and massive T-shaped exterior chimneys laid in English bond. By the end of the eighteenth century, it was in the possession of the Reverend John Bracken, who had extensive real estate holdings along Francis Street. His rise to social and financial prominence began in 1776 with his marriage to Sally Burwell of Carter's Grove plantation. He was the rector of Bruton Parish Church for forty-five years, mayor of Williamsburg in 1796, and president of the College of William and Mary from 1812 to 1814. In 1815 one observer recounted how Bracken kept a couple waiting at the altar. Apparently the "Round Bellied Vicar" imbibed a drop too much en route to the wedding. He lost his way, "upset the Gigg and broke it," and arrived—wet and muddy—an hour late for the ceremony. Private.

MASONIC KITCHEN

Today, the Masonic Kitchen is a hotel facility. Private.

MASONIC LODGE

The "ancient and loyal Society of free and accepted Masons" leased a portion of this lot and met in a building on this property from the 1780s onward. In the 1770s, the lodge held its regular meetings at Market Square Tavern and patronized Christiana Campbell's tavern for balls and special entertainments. The Williamsburg chapter, which had been meeting at local taverns since midcentury, received a new charter in 1773. It members included Peyton Randolph, Peter Pelham, Bishop James Madison, St. George Tucker, and James Monroe. Reconstructed on the site of an earlier frame structure, the brick Masonic Lodge was built in 1931. Private.

LIGHTFOOT HOUSE

Built in the mid-1700s probably as rental property, this house was brought to its final form by 1750 as a town house for the prominent Lightfoot family of Yorktown. This fine brick residence is unusual in having a second floor as high as the first. It is adorned by a stringcourse in molded brick and by a wrought-iron balcony suggestive of the one at the Governor's Palace. The decorative front fence shows the Chinese, or chinoiserie, influence popular about 1750. The Lightfoot family owned this property during much of the eighteenth century. In 1783, Philip Lightfoot advertised the house for

sale, describing it as "a large two story brick dwelling house with four rooms on a floor; its situation is esteemed one of the most pleasant in the City, lying on the back-street near the market." The Reverend John Bracken bought the property in 1786. During restoration in 1940–1941, the ornate wrought-iron balcony was reconstructed based on evidence in the brickwork, particularly the enlarged size of the middle second-story window and the projecting stringcourse, which left a flat indentation over the door. If this interpretation is correct, this embellishment is indicative of the Lightfoot family's wealth since the form is occasionally seen on public buildings but not domestic ones in this region. Semicircular stone steps were reconstructed following the outline of old foundations; they duplicated the design of the original north steps to the Brafferton still in place at the college. Private.

LIGHTFOOT TENEMENT

The Reverend John Bracken also bought this tenement, a term that meant a rented house. It is now a hotel facility. Private.

NICHOLAS-TYLER OFFICE AND NICHOLAS-TYLER LAUNDRY

Reconstructed on their original foundations, these two buildings mark the site of the Nicholas-Tyler House. Robert Carter Nicholas, treasurer of the colony of Virginia and later a judge of the Chancery Court, bought the property in 1770 and built a large frame house with numerous outbuildings near the site of the earlier James City County courthouse. John Tyler, tenth president of the United States, and his family were living here when two horsemen reined up in front of the house early on April 5, 1841. They delivered the news that President William Henry Harrison had died and the duties of the presidency rested on Tyler's shoulders. The office (left) and laundry (right) are now hotel accommodations. Private.

CUSTIS KITCHEN

This building, now standing alone on a rise at the far side of a pasture, is the sole survivor of a series of remarkable buildings and landscape owned by John Custis—scholar, planter, and gardener—who settled in Williamsburg about 1715. Custis built a substantial brick house and a number of outbuildings and cultivated his celebrated garden, one of the most ambitious ornamental and experimental gardens in early America. Correspondence that records Custis's exchange of plant specimens with the great English natural history enthusiast Peter Collinson has been helpful in planting Colonial Williamsburg's gardens. When Custis died in 1749, his son, Daniel Parke Custis, inherited the property. Daniel's widow, Martha, subsequently married George Washington, who administered it until his stepson, John Parke ("Jacky") Custis, came of age in 1778. Private.

PUBLIC HOSPITAL

Francis Fauquier, one of the colony's most popular royal governors, first proposed the establishment of the Public Hospital to the House of Burgesses in 1766. Until that time, the insane in Virginia were cared for at home, maintained in a neighbor's house in exchange for money from tax revenues collected by church vestries for poor relief, or confined with vagrants in parish workhouses. Some were even incarcerated. The General Assembly enacted legislation "to make provision for the support and maintenance of ideots, lunatics, and other persons of unsound minds" in 1770. The hospital, the first public institution in British North America devoted exclusively to the care and treatment of individuals with mental disorders, opened in 1773. Well-known Philadelphia architect Robert Smith designed the building. George Wythe, John Blair Jr., and Thomas Nelson Jr. were among its original trustees. After a disastrous fire in 1885 destroyed the colonial building, the facility was rebuilt. In the mid-1960s, the hospital, which had expanded to form a sizable campus, removed to the outskirts of Williamsburg, and the buildings were torn down. The hospital was reconstructed on its original site in 1985 following the form and details of the original building. It contains an interpretation of its use and serves as the entry to the contemporary Art Museums of Colonial Williamsburg.

TRAVIS HOUSE

This seventy-foot-long, gambrel-roofed house was built in three distinct periods. Edward Champion Travis, a member of the House of Burgesses, erected the western portion, sometime between 1762 and 1765. It consists of a side passage and a room to the west. Sometime later a second room was built to the east of the passage, possibly by Travis, creating a two-room center-passage plan. In 1794–1795 an additional room was constructed to the east. In the early nineteenth century, a small room under a shed roof was added, perhaps by Champion Travis, son of the first builder. The additions are marked today by the vertical boards of their respective sections. Superintendents of the Public Hospital lived here until early in the twentieth century. At the beginning of the restoration, Colonial Williamsburg moved the house to the south side of Duke of Gloucester Street opposite Palace Green and opened it as a restaurant. The building was later moved back to its present location when it was decided not to move buildings off their original foundations. Private.

Gowan PAMPHLET

Hemmed in by law, fear, and prejudice, Gowan Pamphlet nevertheless became a Baptist minister and preached a message of equality before God to a congregation of black people.

Pamphlet was an enslaved man in the household of tavern keeper Jane Vobe. Vobe probably allowed and may even have encouraged some or all of her slaves to attend Bruton Parish Church in Williamsburg. Parish registers show that at least four of her slaves were baptized.

Pamphlet, like many other Virginians, enslaved and free, was moved by the Great Awakening, during which itinerant preachers spread the message that all people were in need of repentance and spiritual renewal. In Williamsburg, slaves first gathered to hear a preacher known only as Moses, and Pamphlet followed in his footsteps. Preaching

was extremely risky since authorities were quick to associate slave gatherings with rebellion and the law allowed patrols to lash anyone caught meeting secretly. Oral tradition suggests that Pamphlet first preached hidden in arbors made of saplings and underbrush at Green Spring plantation, several miles from town. By 1781 the congregation numbered two hundred and may have been gathering in a wooded area on the outskirts of Williamsburg.

Pamphlet might have had a chance to escape slavery that year when British troops occupied Williamsburg. But he stayed with his congregation until 1785 when Vobe moved her tavern (and her workers) to Chesterfield County. After Vobe died, David Miller, her son and Pamphlet's new owner, returned to Williamsburg in 1791, and Pamphlet returned to preaching to a black Baptist congregation that by that time numbered around five hundred.

Pamphlet's situation remained precarious. In 1793 William Nelson Jr. claimed that Pamphlet had accidentally dropped a letter in Yorktown. Nelson saw this as evidence that Pamphlet was a messenger for a network of armed slaves involved in what came to be known as the "Secret Keeper Plot." Nothing came of the accusation.

That same year, Miller drew up a deed to "manumit emancipate and set free a Negro man named and called Gowin Pamphet." Also in 1793, amid gradually increasing but by no means universal acceptance of black people's Christianity, Pamphlet attended the annual meeting of the Dover Association, a regional association of white Baptist churches. The association's minutes record that "the Baptist church of black people at Williamsburg; agreeably to their request, was received into this Association, as they could not have done better in their circumstances than they have."

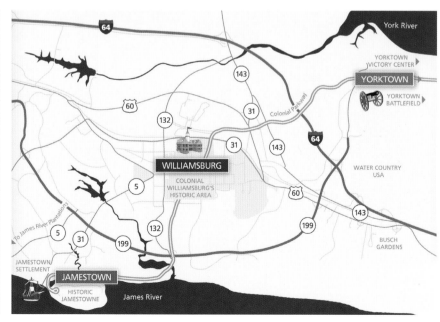

The Historic TRIANGLE

The story told in the Revolutionary City is not solely the story of Williamsburg. Two other sites that played crucial roles in the creation of the American Republic are within thirty minutes of Williamsburg. Jamestown, Williamsburg, and Yorktown, linked by the scenic Colonial Parkway, together form America's Historic Triangle.

It was at Jamestown, in 1607, that the English established their first permanent settlement in the New World. Twelve years later, the colonists took a crucial step toward democracy when they elected the first representative assembly in English North America. Jamestown, like the later United States, was an experiment in diversity: Here Indian, English, and African people interacted, each playing a vital role in shaping the New World.

It was at Yorktown, in 1781, that the Revolution—so many of its ideas formulated in Williamsburg—achieved decisive military victory. After marching from Williamsburg, General Washington's troops, aided by French allies, defeated the British troops under Lord Cornwallis and assured American independence.

JAMESTOWN

HISTORIC JAMESTOWNE

A land bridge takes you onto Jamestown Island, where the settlers arrived. On the island you can see the site of the fort the settlers built. The fort's remains were long thought to be lost to the James River, but in 1996 a team of archaeologists led by William Kelso discovered an outline of the fort with only one corner washed away. The Jamestown Rediscovery Archaeological Project not only unearthed the site of the original fort but also more than 1.8 million artifacts. These have changed the way we think about the original settlers, whom we now understand to have been remarkably industrious and resourceful in confronting extreme hardships, including a devastating drought. Split-log palisades have been reconstructed above the original remains to give a sense of how the fort looked.

▲ Facial reconstruction of "Jane."

The Nathalie P. and Alan M. Voorhees Archaearium showcases the findings of the Jamestown Rediscovery Archaeological Project with displays of more than 1,500 artifacts excavated at James Fort. Built above the remains of Jamestown's last statehouse, it includes an exhibit on a recent remarkable discovery at Jamestown: the remains of a fourteen-year-old English girl whom archaeologists named "Jane." Her remains exhibit signs of cannibalism and were discovered among other evidence of "the starving time" winter of 1609–1610. This is the first forensic evidence of survival cannibalism in the American colonies.

Also at Historic Jamestowne, you can see the Jamestown church tower, the only remaining aboveground seventeenth-century structure on the island. The tower recently received extensive repair and research by Colonial Williamsburg experts. The tower stands adjacent to the 1907 Memorial Church, which was built over the site of the 1617 church. The 1617 church hosted the first legislative assembly in English North America in 1619. Foundations of the 1617 church are still visible inside the Memorial Church.

You can also walk to New Towne, where the settlement expanded beyond the fort, and you can drive around the entire island, much of which is still a swampy wilderness. Before the entrance to the island is the Glasshouse, where the colonists built a glass factory in 1608 and where today, in a reproduction building, glass-blowers demonstrate their trade.

Historic Jamestowne is jointly administered by the National Park Service and the Colonial Williamsburg Foundation (on behalf of Preservation Virginia).

JAMESTOWN SETTLEMENT

At Jamestown Settlement, on the mainland next to the island, you can explore re-creations of the Jamestown fort, an Indian village, and the settlers' ships. The fort is based on a 1610 description by settler William Strachey. Several of the buildings in the fort are based on early seventeenth-century archaeological sites, including Historic Jamestowne. The Indian village is based on archaeological research at nearby Powhatan sites as well as settlers' descriptions. You can board the full-size replicas of the three ships that carried the settlers to Jamestown: the *Susan Constant*, the *Discovery*, and the *Godspeed*.

Galleries, many of which are interactive, chronicle the cultures of the Indians, Europeans, and Africans that converged in seventeenth-century Virginia and the legacies those groups left at Jamestown.

Jamestown Settlement is operated by the Commonwealth of Virginia.

YORKTOWN

YORKTOWN BATTLEFIELD

The National Park Service has preserved four thousand acres of battlefield at Yorktown. From the field outside the Visitor Center, you can see the earthworks Cornwallis's men built and, in the distance, the siege lines built by French and American troops. You can walk to Redoubts No. 9 and No. 10, two earthen forts the French and American troops captured on the night of October 14, 1781, allowing them to finish their second siege line and fire point-blank on the British position.

Self-guided driving tours take you to battle-field sites, including the Moore House, where surrender negotiations occurred, and the site of Washington's headquarters.

VILLAGE OF YORKTOWN

Yorktown includes a mix of historic sites and private residences and businesses. Among the former is the Nelson House, once home to Thomas Nelson Jr., a signer of the Declaration of Independence.

YORKTOWN VICTORY CENTER

The Yorktown Victory Center is undergoing a transformation and will be renamed American Revolution at Yorktown when the project is complete in late 2016. In addition to galleries, there are outdoor exhibits—a Continental army encampment and a Revolution-era farm.

The Yorktown Victory Center is operated by the Commonwealth of Virginia.

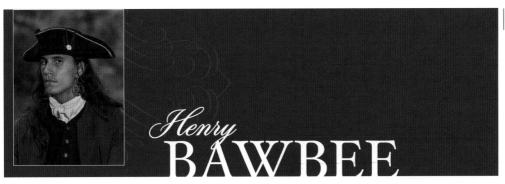

Henry BAWBEE

During the summer of 1775, Virginia officials and British representatives scrambled to secure Indian loyalties in the Ohio Country. Virginia sent a delegation from Williamsburg to Fort Pitt in order to negotiate with the Shawnee. At the conclusion of the negotiations, one member of the delegation returned to Williamsburg and informed the citizenry "that all the different nations who attended the treaty are peaceably disposed." Returning with the delegation was "a young Indian (son of the famous Bawbee) to be educated at the college."

Henry Bawbee, son of the Wyandot Chief Bawbee, or Odinghquanooron, was possibly descended from the seventeenth-century French Canadian trading family of Jacques Bawbee (Bâby/Baubee/Babie). Chief Bawbee may have been the son of a French Indian trader from the Bawbee family and a Wyandot woman. The chief's son was described by American officials as "half Indian."

On Henry Bawbee's arrival in Williamsburg, he was enrolled in the College of William and Mary's Brafferton Indian school. For the next three years, he resided in the third-floor apartments of the brick Georgian building alongside classmates from the Pamunkey and Catawba tribes. Bawbee was instructed in reading, writing, mathematics, and the Book of Common Prayer and attended Bruton Parish Church. As Bawbee became anglicized and fluent in English, Governor Patrick Henry and other Williamsburg officials hoped he would prove useful in the diplomacy of the Ohio frontier. Former Brafferton alums had acted as guides, Indian traders, and interpreters.

Bawbee had a growing taste for the trappings of Virginia society. Governor Henry approved allocations for Bawbee from the public store, including textiles for clothes, buttons, hats, handkerchiefs, shoes and buckles, blankets, pillows, bed sheets and ticking, paper, and bookbinding.

By the summer of 1778, Bawbee was preparing to return to the Ohio Country and likely left Williamsburg during the fall of that year. Indians such as Bawbee and other middlemen often switched sides in the war for various reasons. On Bawbee's arrival in the Ohio Country, he reportedly spread unfavorable opinions about the Americans, but he soon after created a map of the network of British forts for them. When he traveled to Fort Pitt in 1780 to deliver it, however, he was identified as a British spy and held captive. In early 1781 he escaped back to Wyandot country where his father, a principal chief, remained allied to the British.

On to YORKTOWN *and* VICTORY!

The allied American and French armies under George Washington had been in Williamsburg for two weeks, preparing for an attack at Yorktown on Lord Cornwallis and his army of British regulars, Hessians, loyalists, and former slaves. The stakes could not have been higher for the Americans because the French, whose navy had sealed the Chesapeake Bay and cut off Cornwallis's escape route, would not commit to operations past October, and British reinforcements might have arrived at any time. Through spies, the allies knew that Cornwallis was at his breaking point, with supplies running perilously low and disease depleting his ranks. Washington was painfully aware that this was his best—and perhaps last—chance to bring the war to an end.

The spirits of the townspeople were running high as people celebrated Washington and a moment of impending victory that many had thought would never come, since British armies had controlled most of the Williamsburg area for much of the year. The entire combined army, swelled by new recruits, then marched on to Yorktown, arriving that evening.

To Washington's lasting credit, his plan worked. The allied forces surrounded Yorktown and compelled Cornwallis's surrender on October 19—just days before the French navy left and British reinforcements arrived. News of the surrender reached London in December, and the next time Parliament met, in February 1782, it declared an end to offensive operations in America and opened talks on a peace treaty that recognized the independence of the United States of America.

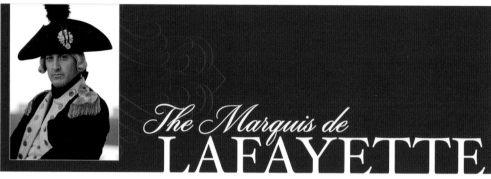

The Marquis de LAFAYETTE

Marie-Joseph-Paul-Yves-Roch-Gilbert du Motier (1757–1834), the marquis de Lafayette, was the most important of the French volunteers who joined the American Revolutionary cause. His father was a soldier who was killed in action in 1759 against a British army that included some of the son's future foes, Charles Cornwallis for one. Heir to a vast fortune, Lafayette expanded his wealth when he was sixteen years old by marrying a relative of the French royal family. The same year he received his first commission as an officer in his grandfather's regiment, the Black Musketeers. By 1776 Lafayette was a captain of cavalry and enthralled with the Enlightenment ideals of liberty and equality contained in the Declaration of Independence. He arranged a meeting with an American representative in France, who wrote a letter of introduction for Lafayette to the Continental Congress. Lafayette then purchased a ship and left for the United States in April 1777 in open defiance of his family and the French king.

Although Lafayette had no battlefield experience, Congress appointed him a major general on July 31, 1777—a decision made easier when Lafayette made it clear he did not expect pay or a command. He and George Washington formed a close bond that would last the rest of their lives. Lafayette first saw field action at the Battle of Brandywine on September 11, 1777, when the young Frenchman helped stave off a complete rout and was wounded in the left leg, which gave him credibility in the eyes of his American compatriots. Several months later Congress gave him his own command: a division of Virginia infantry. During

the winter of 1777–1778, Lafayette demonstrated great loyalty to Washington by frustrating an attempt to remove Washington from command instigated by a brigadier general malcontent. He then endured the hardships of winter at Valley Forge. When the British turned their attention to defending the West Indies from the French, Lafayette took the opportunity of the lull in fighting on the mainland to return to France. He persuaded his government to increase its military aid to the United States, which led to a French expeditionary force joining Washington in 1780. Lafayette returned to America in April 1780 and provided valuable service as intermediary between Washington and the French commander, the comte de Rochambeau.

In March 1781, Washington sent Lafayette to Williamsburg when news of Benedict Arnold's invasion of Virginia raised alarms about the vulnerability of the Chesapeake region. In the remarkable Virginia campaign of 1781, Lafayette and one thousand men faced Charles Cornwallis's much larger army and avoided the British commander's efforts to trap them until more Continental troops could arrive. Lafayette then advanced on Cornwallis, engaging him in a skirmish near Williamsburg on June 26 and attacking what he thought was a rear guard of Cornwallis's forces at Green Spring on July 6. Instead, Lafayette encountered the main body of Cornwallis's reinforced army of seven thousand men. Disaster was avoided due to a well-timed charge by Anthony Wayne's troops, Lafayette's own skillful handling of the retreat, and Cornwallis's failure to press his advantage. By August, Cornwallis had moved his exhausted and ill troops to Yorktown while Lafayette shifted his base of operations to Williamsburg to keep the British army confined on the Peninsula. A month later, the combined French-American army of Washington and Rochambeau rendezvoused in Williamsburg on their way to Yorktown and the ultimate engagement of the war.

In 1782, Lafayette returned to France to help organize its direct efforts against Britain, but peace was declared before he could act. He visited America briefly in 1784 and then, back in Paris, assisted the American ambassador to France, Thomas Jefferson. Lafayette embraced the burgeoning revolution in France, hoping that the American experiment in liberty could be extended to his country. In 1789 he proposed a French Declaration of Rights, and he advocated for the abolition of the titled aristocracy and slavery. He soon recognized that the leaders of the French Revolution were not interested in taking gradual steps towards building a stable republic. Lafayette withdrew from public life in 1791 but was soon recalled to defend France against an Austrian invasion. He had other ideas, however, and intended to use the army to restore the monarchy on a constitutional footing. He was charged with treason by the National Assembly in August 1792 and recalled to Paris to stand trial. Rather than face the guillotine, Lafayette attempted to return to America. He was taken prisoner by the Austrians while on his way to the coast. He was put in prison, where he remained until 1797. After his release and two subsequent years in exile in Holland, Lafayette retired again, removing to his wife's estate near Paris.

In 1824, Lafayette accepted James Monroe's invitation to visit America. He arrived in New York City in August and began a tour of the country. At one stop after another, he was greeted with a level of enthusiasm that contemporaries believed was without precedent in American history. In October he arrived in Williamsburg. At the Raleigh Tavern, a grand banquet was held in his honor. Lafayette returned to France in September 1825 and was again elected to the Chamber of Deputies. He took command of an army in the field once more in 1830 during the July revolution and helped restore the French monarchy. He died in Paris on May 20, 1834. To this day, an American flag flies over his grave.

Be Our GUEST

COLONIAL WILLIAMSBURG HOTELS

Guests who stay at an official Colonial Williamsburg hotel receive discounted prices on admission tickets and passes; unlimited use of the Revolutionary City shuttle buses; preferred reservations for spa services, dining, tennis courts, and tee times for golf; and complimentary delivery of purchases at Colonial Williamsburg stores to the hotel. Colonial Williamsburg offers a selection of hotels from the luxury of the Williamsburg Inn, Williamsburg Lodge, Colonial Houses, and Providence Hall Guesthouses to the family-friendly Williamsburg Woodlands Hotel & Suites located adjacent to the Visitor Center and the value-priced Governor's Inn. For reservations and hotel package information, call 855-368-3287 or visit colonialwilliamsburg.com.

WILLIAMSBURG INN

The Williamsburg Inn, the landmark property conceived by John D. Rockefeller Jr. and opened in April 1937, has been the crown jewel of Colonial Williamsburg's hotels for more than seventy-five years. Under the direction of renowned Boston architect William Perry, the Inn was designed and decorated in the Regency style of nineteenth-century England, giving it a style very distinct from the colonial architecture in the Historic Area.

The Inn's striking whitewashed brick facade

is marked by a generous balcony with tall Ionic columns, wrought-iron railings, and a graceful arched portico entrance. The Regency style is evident in neoclassical architectural features ranging from interior cornices and chair rails to the exterior pediments, arches, and columns. Guest rooms are exquisitely decorated in three distinctive styles: floral, classic, and restoration. All rooms feature period furnishings of Honduras mahogany, original artwork, and handmade silk window treatments that have been a Williamsburg Inn signature for decades.

Rooms offer views of the golf course, lawn bowling green, gardens, and terrace. Some rooms feature canopy beds with separate sitting areas and wood-burning fireplaces. Spacious bathrooms feature twin marble vanities, Italian marble–enclosed soaking tubs, and large marble showers in shades of salmon and rose.

While the rooms are rich in history, hotel amenities also address the needs of today's travelers. If he were alive today, Rockefeller would surely applaud the addition of more spacious writing desks and delight in the concierge staff, twenty-four-hour room service, and wireless Internet connectivity. Inn guests have access to one indoor and two outdoor pools and the Spa fitness quarters.

Nestled on the Inn's grounds are the Providence Hall Guesthouses, large contemporary accommodations with breezy balconies in a garden setting. Some rooms include a fireplace and overlook a serene pond.

The Williamsburg Inn's culinary team serves the elegant Regency Room as well as the Restoration Bar, the Terrace Room, catering, and room service. The Inn's history includes a succession of masterful chefs who have delighted heads of state, celebrities, VIPs, and guests who return time after time to celebrate special occasions or simply enjoy superb meals served in style. The Regency Room offers classic regional American cuisine with traditional European roots and a wine list of more than three hundred selections. Breakfast and dinner are served daily.

The Terrace Room overlooking the Inn terrace is the perfect retreat for lunch, cocktails, hors d'oeuvres, and a light dinner. Both the Terrace Room and the Goodwin Room across the hall provide a refined, informal setting. The Restoration Bar with its classic club-like setting is the perfect spot to enjoy cocktails and specialty drinks any time.

WILLIAMSBURG LODGE

Opened in 1939, the Williamsburg Lodge was, like the Inn, constructed under the guidance of John D. Rockefeller Jr., the first benefactor of the town's restoration. From the original blue stone floors to the cypress accents and reproduction folk art, in every cozy nook and spacious expanse, the Williamsburg Lodge reflects its Virginia setting.

With its 11,200-square-foot Virginia Room and 45,000 square feet of meeting and banquet space, the Lodge is a premier conference choice in the mid-Atlantic, a prime location for meetings, banquets and weddings as well as for a family vacation or couples getaway. All guests receive a generous helping of Southern hospitality, impeccable service, and amenities including access to the fitness quarters at the Spa of Colonial Williamsburg, two outdoor pools, and one indoor lap pool. The Lodge is fully Wi-Fi capable, and a business center provides a fax, computer, and printer.

Accommodations at the Lodge total 323 guest rooms with furnishings inspired by the collections of Colonial Williamsburg's Abby Aldrich Rockefeller Folk Art Museum. Four new guesthouses—the Ashby and Custis houses, with thirty rooms each, and the Nicholas and Tyler houses with thirty-eight rooms each—complement the renovated South Hall and Tazewell guest rooms. The entire Lodge complex is connected by a series of covered walkways.

The culinary team at the Lodge's Traditions dining room has created innovative menus that are an ode to the bounty of Virginia with local oysters, beef and pork from regional farms, and, in season, vegetables grown in the gardens of Colonial Williamsburg. Virginia wines are always in season. For lighter fare, the Lodge Lobby Lounge offers salads, soups, sandwiches, hamburgers, desserts, beer, wine, and specialty cocktails.

COLONIAL HOUSES—HISTORIC LODGING

Located throughout the Historic Area, Colonial Houses combine eighteenth-century accommodations with twenty-first-century resort amenities. Guests can wake up to the sound of sheep in a pasture, take a morning walk on Duke of Gloucester Street, enjoy Spa services or golf, and return to the charm of a wood fire and a tavern dinner. The lodgings range from a room in a tavern to a full house with multiple bedrooms or a tiny eighteenth-century dependency that might have been a detached kitchen or laundry. Each house is furnished with period reproductions, and some have canopy beds, some have working fireplaces, and some overlook private gardens.

WILLIAMSBURG WOODLANDS HOTEL & SUITES

The Williamsburg Woodlands Hotel & Suites is the right spot for an old-fashioned getaway, business conference, or family vacation. The contemporary, three-story hotel offers 96 suites and 202 guest rooms, all accessed from secure, interior hallways. The hotel features a spacious lobby finished in heart pine bathed in natural light from cathedral ceiling skylights. A hospitality suite just off the lobby provides an informal gathering spot.

Guest rooms at the Woodlands each have two full-size beds, a sitting area with a desk and two chairs, a coffeepot, a comfortable lounge chair (that converts to a single bed), and cable television. Each suite has a sitting room with queen sofa bed, desk, and cable television as well as a convenience counter with a small refrigerator, microwave, sink, and coffeemaker; the separate bedroom has a king-size bed and second television. A full complimentary breakfast is served daily at the hotel.

The Woodlands offers a number of recreational options, including a heated pool open from April to November and an adjacent splash zone with interactive water toys, cascading canoes and barrels, water trees, and geysers. During the summer months, a poolside snack bar open in the evening serves drinks, snacks, and sandwiches from Huzzah! BBQ Grille. Miniature golf, table tennis, volleyball, shuffleboard, storytelling around the fire pit, pool parties, and games round out the fun activities available at the Woodlands.

Huzzah! BBQ Grille, across the promenade from the hotel, is a family-friendly restaurant where kids can create their own pizza. All selections on the menu are made from scratch, including the selection of barbecue sauces. Outdoor seating is available, and the full-service bar is a great spot to watch sports on flat-screen televisions.

GOVERNOR'S INN

Located a short walk from the Historic Area and a convenient shuttle ride from the Visitor Center and Woodlands complex, the Governor's Inn offers Colonial Williamsburg quality at an economical price. The spacious guest rooms are served with the same Southern hospitality found at all Colonial Williamsburg hotels. The hotel has a daily complimentary continental breakfast and an outdoor swimming pool. Guests have access to the fitness center at the Woodlands. Summer programs are offered for Governor's Inn guests ages five to twelve.

RECREATION

GOLF

Colonial Williamsburg's Golden Horseshoe Golf Club includes forty-five holes on three courses. Designed by the legendary Robert Trent Jones Sr., the Gold Course, located behind the Williamsburg Inn, is one of the best examples of traditional golf course architecture in the world. The course is a Certified Audubon Cooperative Sanctuary and has been named one of *Golf Magazine*'s Top 100 You Can Play, *Golf Digest*'s 75 Best Golf Resorts in North America and America's 100 Greatest Public Courses, and *Golfweek*'s Best Resort Courses.

Jones Sr. called the Gold Course, opened in 1963, his "finest design." In 1998, Rees Jones, Jones Sr.'s son, was the architect of a course renovation that remained faithful to the original design but expanded the appeal of the course for higher-handicap players while simultaneously lengthening the course from the back tees. The Gold Course celebrated its fiftieth anniversary in 2013 with a tribute to Rees Jones and the Jones family's contributions to Colonial Williamsburg's golf history and legacy.

Rees Jones designed the Green Course, which opened in 1991 and has been acclaimed by national and regional golf magazines. The layout is carved from the same terrain as the Gold Course and is more typical of contemporary trends in golf course architecture. The two courses stand out as the first father-son tandem of side-by-side layouts.

Named for colonial governor Alexander Spotswood, the nine-hole Spotswood Course is the elder Jones's 1964 update of the Williamsburg Inn's 1947 original nine-hole course. *Golf Magazine* called it the "best 9-hole short course in the country."

The Golden Horseshoe Gold Course Clubhouse Grill offers casual dining overlooking a tranquil pond and the serene finish of the eighteenth hole while the Golden Horseshoe Green Course Clubhouse Grill provides a sweeping view of the amphitheater eighteenth finish. Menus include sandwiches, wraps, salads, desserts, and cocktails. Golf pro shops at both courses include an apparel line featuring resort ware from Fairway & Greene, Cutter & Buck, Ahead, and FootJoy. The golf equipment is from leading vendors including Ping and Titleist. The Golden Horseshoe Golf Club is open to the public and also offers memberships, tournaments, and instruction for juniors and adults.

What *was* "The Golden Horseshoe"? Daring adventures are part of Virginia's history, but few are as significant as Governor Alexander Spotswood's 1716 expedition to explore the far reaches of the Virginia Colony. Spotswood, aware of the frontier's economic potential and bent on encouraging westward settlement, led a party of sixty-three men on the arduous journey.

In *The Present State of Virginia*, published in London in 1724, Hugh Jones offered his account of the toll taken by the rocky soil of the Piedmont and the Blue Ridge: "For this Expedition they were obliged to provide a great Quantity of Horse-Shoes; (Things seldom used in the lower Parts of the Country, where there are few Stones:) . . . the Governor upon their Return presented each of his Companions with a Golden Horse-Shoe, (some of which I have seen studded with valuable Stones resembling the Heads of Nails)." The recipients became known as the Knights of the Golden Horseshoe. Although several people in the nineteenth century claimed to have seen them, none of the small, golden horseshoes described by Jones have been found.

For information and to reserve tee times, call 757-220-7696.

SPA

The Spa of Colonial Williamsburg offers relaxing, rejuvenating, and healing therapies inspired by five centuries of wellness practices. The twenty-thousand-square-foot spa, located in a Georgian Revival building on South England Street, radiates Southern charm, harmonizing with its historical surroundings and the personality of its colonial heritage. A few steps from the Williamsburg Inn and Williamsburg Lodge, directly adjacent to the Golden Horseshoe Golf Club, the spa is open to guests of Colonial Williamsburg hotels and to day visitors. Guests enter via a wisteria-draped brick pathway alongside a fountain and formal garden.

The spa includes twelve private treatment rooms and two couples' suites, and a full-service conservatory salon with three pedicure, five manicure, four hair salon, and two makeup stations. Separate locker rooms for men and women feature private changing rooms and aromatherapy steam rooms. The men's locker room includes a large-screen TV and a cold plunge pool while the women's has an experiential shower with multiple shower heads.

Rain-head showers and large whirlpools are inviting aspects of both locker rooms. Separate elevators transport guests to their designated treatment rooms. Separate men's and women's lounges and one coed lounge provide quiet, relaxing spaces to read, relax, or enjoy the spa cuisine before or after services.

Conveniently located in a wing adjoining the Spa of Colonial Williamsburg reception area, the Spa fitness center contains a selection of the latest free weights, weight-training stations, treadmills, recumbent bicycles, elliptical machines, and rowing machines. Group exercise classes, from stretch and strengthening and water aerobics to yoga and Pilates, are also offered. Wellness memberships are available and include access to the fitness center, classes, locker rooms, and indoor and outdoor pools.

For information and reservations, call 757-220-7720.

Swimming and Fitness

Guests of the Williamsburg Inn, Williamsburg Lodge, Providence Hall Guesthouses, and Colonial Houses–Historic Lodging have complimentary access to the swimming pools and the fitness center at the Spa of Colonial Williamsburg. Guests of the Williamsburg Woodlands Hotel & Suites and the Governor's Inn have pools on location, and guests of the Governor's Inn may use the fitness center located in the Woodlands.

Walking and Biking

Colonial Williamsburg is a delight for walkers. The Historic Area offers one of the most picturesque locations in America for a brisk walk or a leisurely stroll, and a hiking trail through the woods behind Bassett Hall is also available. For those who wish to bicycle through Williamsburg or on the nearby

Colonial Parkway, Schwinn single-speed cruisers are available for daily rental at the Spa of Colonial Williamsburg. Rental includes helmet, lock, and basket.

Tennis

Tennis enthusiasts can enjoy six Har-Tru clay and two premier surface courts at the Williamsburg Inn Tennis Club, located on the grounds in front of Providence Hall on Francis Street. The full-service pro shop features men's and women's tennis attire and offers racket stringing, racket and ball machine rentals, and changing facilities. Lessons are available for youths and adults.

Lawn Bowling

The Williamsburg Inn Lawn Bowling Club hosts lawn bowling, a game that dates to thirteenth-century England, Sundays from April through the fall at the green behind the Williamsburg Inn. In 1966, Colonial Williamsburg built the lawn bowling green—the only professional one in Virginia—for guests and visiting teams. In addition to hosting hotel guests, members of the Williamsburg Inn Lawn Bowling Club play regularly and hold tournaments. The club has sixty members, making it second in size only to Central Park's New York Lawn Bowling Club in the Northeast Division of the United States Lawn Bowls Association.

DINING

COLONIAL WILLIAMSBURG DINING

Dinner reservations are required at all historic dining taverns and recommended at all other Colonial Williamsburg restaurants. Lunch reservations are required only for groups of twenty or more and for dining in the Regency Room. Afternoon tea at the Inn also requires reservations. Reservations may be made at the Visitor Center Dining and Lodging Reservations Desk or by calling 855-368-3287.

Historic Dining Taverns and Other Historic Area Eateries

In the eighteenth century, taverns provided lodgings for travelers and served as community gathering places for meals, conversation, and entertainment. Today's tavern guests experience the flavor of the Revolution through atmosphere, entertainment, food, and beverages. The taverns offer craft beers, carefully selected wine pairings, foods prepared with fresh local ingredients, and specialty desserts.

Christiana Campbell's Tavern

George Washington loved the seafood in this tavern, and today's diners do, too. Guests can enjoy a visit with Mrs. Campbell and tap their feet to the sound of eighteenth-century musicians. Dinner is served Tuesday through Saturday beginning at 5 p.m. Capitol bus stop.

Chowning's Tavern

This eighteenth-century alehouse features period-inspired foods and specialty brews. Dine inside or out under the grape arbor (weather permitting) and enjoy lively eighteenth-century music and visits from people of the past. Lunch is served daily from 11:30 a.m.–2:30 p.m. and dinner from 5 p.m. Magazine bus stop.

Gambols at Chowning's

Enjoy music, sing-alongs, eighteenth-century games, and entertainment from 9 p.m. nightly. No reservations.

McKenzie Apothecary

On Palace Green next to the Robert Carter House, this quick stop offers snacks and beverages to warm or refresh. Refillable souvenir mugs are available for purchase from 10 a.m.–5 p.m. Palace bus stop.

M. Dubois Grocer

 The grocer has Mars candy, fountain beverages, ice cream, and other sweet treats. Souvenir mugs can be purchased and refilled. Open daily 11 a.m.–5 p.m. Tavern bus stop.

Raleigh Tavern Bakery

The Bakery has fresh sandwiches, salads, and baked treats along with beverages to warm or refresh. Souvenir mugs are sold and refilled. Casual seating is available in the courtyard and rear garden. Open daily 9 a.m.–5 p.m. Tavern bus stop.

King's Arms Tavern

 The town's premier tavern offers a chophouse menu featuring peanut soup, prime rib, pork chops, and game pye. Music from the period entertains while citizens of the Revolutionary City bring news of the day. Lunch is served from 11:30 a.m.–2:30 p.m. and dinner from 4 p.m. Tavern bus stop.

Shields Tavern

 The home-style menu at Shields offers selections for every taste, including lunch favorites like hot dogs and hamburgers. Belowstairs is relaxing and intimate with music to complement the atmosphere and visits from historical characters. Dinner theater is offered seasonally. Tavern bus stop.

Other Colonial Williamsburg Restaurants

Golden Horseshoe Gold Course Clubhouse Grill

The Gold Course Clubhouse Grill, which overlooks the eighteenth green of Robert Trent Jones's famed Gold Course, offers sandwiches, salads, light entrees, desserts, and cocktails served from 11:30 a.m.–3 p.m. daily when the course is open. Williamsburg Lodge bus stop.

Golden Horseshoe Green Course Clubhouse Grill

The Green Course Clubhouse Grill has a full lunch menu of favorites such as hot dogs, chicken tenders, salads, and appetizers served from 11:30 a.m.–3 p.m. daily when the course is open.

Museum Café

Located in the Art Museums of Colonial Williamsburg, the café offers a light lunch, including soups, sandwiches, and freshly prepared desserts. Open daily from 11 a.m.–4 p.m. Museum bus stop.

Regency Room in the Williamsburg Inn

Balancing cuisine and techniques from around the world with regional American flavors in a beautiful contemporary setting, the Regency Room has a wine list with more than three hundred selections. Breakfast and dinner served daily. Magazine bus stop.

Terrace Room in the Williamsburg Inn

Afternoon fare and dinner are served daily. Magazine bus stop.

Restoration Bar in the Williamsburg Inn

Cocktails and beverages are served in a classic club-like setting. Magazine bus stop.

Afternoon Tea at the Inn

Tea is served Thursday through Saturday seasonally. Location varies. Magazine bus stop.

Traditions at the Williamsburg Lodge

Prepared with the freshest ingredients from the region, the menu is sure to please from breakfast through dinner. Wine Spectator Award of Excellence. Seafood buffet served Friday nights. Williamsburg Lodge bus stop.

Williamsburg Lodge Lobby Lounge

Sandwiches, soups, salads, and light fare are served in a casual setting by the fireplace or large-screen television. Beverage specials. Williamsburg Lodge bus stop.

Huzzah! BBQ Grille

Specializing in barbecued chicken, pork, and beef, Huzzah! also offers pizza and other favorites. Full bar. Located on the promenade next to the Williamsburg Woodlands Hotel & Suites, steps from Colonial Williamsburg's Visitor Center. Open daily.

Visitor Center Café

Located next to WILLIAMSBURG Revolutions, the café has baked treats, fruit, sandwiches, and beverages. Souvenir mugs sold and refilled. Open daily.

MERCHANTS SQUARE DINING

Aromas Coffee and Café

Gourmet coffee roasted on location, teas, smoothies, pastries, wine, and beer are served in the lively and welcoming atmosphere of an old world coffeehouse. Full breakfast, lunch, and dinner served daily. 757-221-6676

Baskin-Robbins

Choose from a variety of ice creams, milk shakes, malts, sundaes, and frozen yogurt. Daily. 757-229-6385

Berret's Restaurant and Taphouse Grill

Specializing in fresh regional seafood, Berret's has seasonal outdoor dining and live music. Lunch and dinner served daily. 757-253-1847

Blackbird Bakery

Enjoy fresh baked goods from the kitchens of the Trellis Restaurant, Blue Talon Bistro, and DoG Street Pub, including yeast rolls, cinnamon sticky buns, fruit tarts, chocolate mousse, turtle bars, peanut butter pie, homemade granola, candies, and chocolate-covered coffee beans. Daily. 757-229-8610

Blue Talon Bistro

Chef David Everett serves his "serious comfort food" in a relaxed bistro atmosphere. Intriguing wine list, Illy coffee. Breakfast, lunch, and dinner served daily. 757-476-BLUE

The Cheese Shop

This Williamsburg institution offers two hundred imported and domestic cheeses, charcuterie, freshly baked breads, specialty foods, and more than four thousand bottles of wine in the wine cellar. Patio tables offer a relaxed setting to enjoy famous Cheese Shop sandwiches, a cheese plate, and a beer or glass of wine almost year round. Daily. 757-220-1324

DoG Street Pub

In this American gastropub, Chef David Everett delivers delicious food with American flair inspired by the uncomplicated dishes of an English pub. The pub features draft and bottled beers from around the globe in the relaxed setting of a neighborhood tavern. Outdoor dining in season. Lunch, dinner, and late-night dining served daily. 757-293-6478

Fat Canary

Executive Chef Thomas Power Jr. is a graduate of the Culinary Institute of America. Since opening in 2003, the Fat Canary has earned awards and accolades for its innovative menu, service, and wine list. Reservations highly recommended. Dinner served daily. 757-229-3333

Seasons Restaurant & Tavern

Seasons offers a wide variety of food and beverages to suit the entire family, including steaks, ribs, seafood, sandwiches, salads, pasta, burgers, fries, specialty coffees, desserts, a children's menu, and a full-service bar. Lunch and dinner served daily; brunch served Saturday and Sunday. 757-259-0018

Stephanos Pizza and Subs

For a quick bite, try Stephanos New York–style pizza and oven-baked sandwiches, salads, dessert, and ice cream. Lunch and dinner served daily. 757-476-8999

The Trellis Restaurant

Chef David Everett offers contemporary American dining with a focus on local, responsibly raised products and small-scale artisan farmers to bring the best of the region's flavors to the table. Outdoor dining in season.

Breakfast, lunch, and dinner served daily. 757-229-8610

SHOPPING

Colonial Williamsburg offers nearly six hundred items made in the USA—from glass stemware to Virginia peanuts to bird bottles to drums to sterling-silver bracelets. WILLIAMSBURG products are available in nineteen retail stores located in Merchants Square, the Historic Area, the Visitor Center, and Colonial Williamsburg's hotels and museums. Revenue from the sale of all products supports the restoration, preservation, and educational mission of the Colonial Williamsburg Foundation.

williamsburgmarketplace.com or 1-800-446-9240

IN THE HISTORIC AREA

Colonial Nursery

Heirloom seeds and plants, herbs, flowers, seasonal greens, wreaths, eighteenth-century clay flowerpots and bird bottles are offered for sale in this working garden, where colonial gardening techniques are practiced daily. Weather permitting.

James Craig Jewelers/The Golden Ball

Colonial Williamsburg's silversmiths are hard at work hammering, sculpting, and plying brass, pewter, and sterling silver to create fashionable one-of-a-kind pieces of jewelry. Reproduction gemstone rings, earrings, pendants, and charms in sterling silver and 14-karat gold join handcrafted sterling hollowware pieces made next door at the silversmith shop. Hand-cut and machine engraving are available on-site. Many of the same jewelry pieces advertised by James Craig in the eighteenth century are available today.

John Greenhow Store

Willow baskets, fine imported porcelain, floorcloths, fabrics, cooper's items, tinware, and craftsmen's tools similar to what Mr. Greenhow offered in the eighteenth century are sold today in this shop.

Market House

This open-air market sells toys, hats, pottery, and baskets and rents eighteenth-century costumes for boys and girls. Weather permitting.

Mary Dickinson Store

The petticoats, short gowns, cloaks, mitts, caps, and decorated straw hats available in this shop are all made in Williamsburg and are similar to the products eighteenth-century milliner Mary Dickinson sold. The jewelry and toiletries also reflect eighteenth-century fashion.

Post Office

The Post Office features reproduction prints, maps, leather-bound books, stationery, quill pens, ink, inkwells, and sealing wax. Many of the forms and other printed materials are set by hand and printed "below stairs" on an eighteenth-century press. Guests can also purchase stamps, letters, and postcards and mail them here, where they will be canceled by hand with a reproduction eighteenth-century Williamsburg postmark.

Prentis Store

This shop sells one-of-a-kind items made by Colonial Williamsburg's skilled tradespeople using eighteenth-century tools and techniques. These include richly handcrafted leather goods, iron hardware, reproduction pottery, furniture, and baskets.

Tarpley, Thompson & Company

Those who want to bring the look of Colonial Williamsburg taverns into their own homes will enjoy the tavern ware, pewter, and glassware from the King's Arms, Shields, Chowning's, and Christiana Campbell's. The shop also offers mixes, jams, candies, cold beverages, and twenty-first-century gifts.

William Pitt Store

This children's shop offers toys, games, historic apparel, publications, and other products such as stuffed animals based on Colonial Williamsburg's Rare Breeds program. The store is also a source of information for the RevQuest: Save the Revolution! interactive spy game.

VISITOR CENTER SHOPS

Learning Resource Center

Teacher, student, and parent educational videos, books, and internet classroom materials are sold in the Learning Resource Center.

WILLIAMSBURG Booksellers

This bookstore carries a wide selection of books, CDs, and DVDs about the Revolutionary War and other history and Colonial Williamsburg–related topics, plus gifts and general-interest publications.

WILLIAMSBURG Revolutions

Treasures for all are available in this shop—games, toys, gifts, food, and logo apparel as well as costume rentals.

OTHER COLONIAL WILLIAMSBURG SHOPS

Museum Gift Shop

Folk art, decorative accessories, books, recordings, and items inspired by the collections and exhibits in the DeWitt Wallace Decorative Arts Museum and the Abby Aldrich Rockefeller Folk Art Museum make wonderful gifts and keepsakes.

Regency Shop at the Williamsburg Inn

The gift shop in the Inn offers an exquisite selection of jewelry, gifts, and decorative accessories, reflecting the elegance of the Inn.

Williamsburg Lodge Gift Shop

The Lodge gift shop carries newspapers, sundries, toys, books, wine, and unusual gifts and home accents crafted by Virginia artisans.

Williamsburg Woodlands Hotel & Suites Gift Shop

Gifts, souvenirs, logo apparel, and guest service items such as sundries, cameras, and film are available in the Woodlands gift shop.

Spa Boutique

The Spa offers premium spa products and related goods, including robes, candles, skin and hair care products, and signature lavender lemongrass and colonial mint products.

Golden Horseshoe Gold Course Pro Shop

Golfers can choose from a wide selection of top golf equipment, custom and personalized golf bags, resort ware, and Golden Horseshoe logo apparel for ladies and men.

Golden Horseshoe Green Course Pro Shop

Golfing essentials, including custom and personalized golf bags, gloves, balls, hats, polo shirts, and footwear, are available in the pro shop at the Green Course.

MERCHANTS SQUARE SHOPS

Bella Fine Lingerie & Loungewear

Elegant lingerie from around the world is available in this intimate shop. 757-220-8440

Binns

Binns is a boutique department store that carries dresses for the mother of the bride, proms, and special occasions as well as shoes, accessories, fine gifts, and cosmetics. 757-229-3391

Campus Shop

Owned by the Wallace family since 1994, it's Tribe headquarters for the College of William and Mary apparel and gifts. 757-229-4301

The Carousel Children's Clothier

This shop carries classic children's clothing and accessories. 757-229-1710

Chico's

Women can find everything from casual clothing to elegant eveningwear in this nationally known shop. 757-564-7448

The Christmas Shop

Owned and operated by the Wallace family since 1964, the Christmas spirit is alive and well in this festive shop that carries ornaments and decorations all year round. Many ornaments are made locally and in the USA while others are imported from Europe. 757-229-2514

Closet Envy

Women will give their friends "closet envy" when they shop in this store that carries designs by Diane Von Furstenberg, Nanette Lepore, Michael Stars, Theory, Trina Turk, and others. 757-220-0456

The College of William and Mary Bookstore and Café by Barnes and Noble

In addition to textbooks and school supplies, this college bookstore carries Williamsburg clothing, books, souvenirs, William and Mary merchandise, greeting cards, stationery, newspapers, and periodicals. The café serves coffee, tea, sandwiches, pastries, and juices with tables located inside and out. 757-253-4900

Danforth Pewter

This locally owned shop carries jewelry, oil lamps, housewares, ornaments, and more, merging a colonial craft with contemporary design. 757-229-3668

Everything WILLIAMSBURG

From T-shirts to tavern ware to toys, a broad selection of exclusive Colonial Williamsburg logo products and souvenirs are sold in this shop. 757-565-8476

Gallery on Merchants Square

Paintings and sculptures by established artists are on display for browsing or purchase. 757-564-1787

The Jazzy Giraffe

Women's fashions from an array of international designers, fine shoes, and accessories are offered in this fun shop. 757-903-4884

J. Fenton Gallery

This gallery carries jewelry in sterling, glass, bronze, and mixed media; women's clothing, handbags, and hats; Radko glass ornaments; and Steinbach nutcrackers. 757-221-8200

The Kimball Theatre

This beautifully restored theater offers live performances, concerts, plays, and films. 757-565-8588

Ocean Palm

This specialty shop carries Palm Beach–style clothing, including Lilly Pulitzer apparel and accessories, Vineyard Vines, and Eliza B. 757-229-3961

The Peanut Shop of Williamsburg

Hand-cooked Virginia peanuts, specialty nuts, confections, old-fashioned bulk candy jars, regional specialty foods, and giftware are available in this local favorite. 757-229-3908

The Precious Gem

This is a jewelry store like no other with custom jewelry by designer Reggie Akdogan, featuring diamonds and colored stones, including emeralds, rubies, and sapphires. 757-220-1115

Quilts Unlimited

This shop carries women's clothing, including flax linen clothing and tie-dyed pieces from Nepal, artisan jewelry, hats, scarves, and fun socks as well as colonial clothing for the entire family. 757-253-8700

R. Bryant Ltd.

A Merchants Square fixture, this classic men's store has been serving discerning gentlemen looking for quality traditional menswear, imported and domestic, for thirty-four years. 757-253-0055

R. P. Wallace & Sons General Store

Williamsburg T-shirts, souvenirs, jewelry, toys and gifts, nostalgic tin signs, bulk candy, Coke products, and medicines are all for sale in this old-fashioned general store. 757-229-2082

Scotland House Ltd.

Gifts and apparel from Scotland, Ireland, and England, from cashmere sweaters to fine English pottery are available in this shop. 757-229-7800

Shoesters

Shoes sold here are designed to fit the shape of the foot. 757-229-6999

The Silver Vault Ltd.

This shop carries sterling jewelry, silver hollowware and frames, sterling and silver-plated gifts for babies, tabletop accessories, and exquisite Christmas ornaments. 757-220-3777

Talbots

Talbots is a favorite with women everywhere, offering versatile separates, sportswear, dresses, and fashion accessories. 757-253-6532

Williams-Sonoma

The leading destination for home cooks in America offers cookware, utensils, linens, cookbooks, dishes, glassware, specialty foods, and ingredients. 757-220-0450

WILLIAMSBURG At Home

This beautiful flagship store of WILLIAMSBURG-brand home furnishings and accessories carries furniture, bedding, rugs, light fixtures, prints, fabrics, decorative accessories, dinnerware, and flatware—all inspired by the items in Colonial Williamsburg's collections of furniture, antiques, textiles, folk art, and decorative arts. 757-220-7749

WILLIAMSBURG Celebrations

Shoppers enjoy the selection of Byers' Choice, Department 56, Jim Shore, and other classic WILLIAMSBURG collectibles along with seasonal floral arrangements, holiday decorations, and garden accessories. 757-565-8642

WILLIAMSBURG Craft House

The Craft House tradition continues, complete with the full line of WILLIAMSBURG fine ceramic giftware, folk art, tavern products, seasonal specialties, flatware, and jewelry. Engraving is available. 757-220-7747

Wythe Candy & Gourmet Shop

A favorite of locals and visitors alike, Wythe carries freshly dipped caramel apples and chocolates, handmade fudge, and the region's largest selection of candy. 757-229-4406

Jane VOBE

Jane Vobe (by 1733–1786) was one of several female tavern keepers in Williamsburg. In 1765 a French traveler recorded in his diary that hers was "where all the best people resorted." Both locals and visitors frequented her business including George Washington and Thomas Jefferson as well as burgesses, councillors, and governors. Her tavern was a communications hub and the site of many political meetings.

Extant records tell little about Vobe's early life. She may have learned to run a tavern from Thomas Vobe, who operated an ordinary in Williamsburg and who may have been her husband. In 1751 an enslaved man broke into her house and stole five gallons of rum, an amount suggesting that she was by then keeping a tavern. By 1769 she had expanded her workforce to thirteen and acquired a riding chair to better serve more genteel customers.

Vobe's workers included enslaved men, women, and children. She allowed them to receive religious instruction and sent two slave children to the Bray School, where they studied reading, writing, and etiquette as well as religion. One of her slaves, Gowan Pamphlet, became a Baptist preacher and met, mostly in secret, with a congregation of other blacks, although historians suspect Vobe knew something about Pamphlet's activities. She also placed an ad in the *Virginia Gazette* offering a reward for the return of a runaway slave.

Vobe's tavern was originally on Waller Street east of the Capitol; in 1771 Christina Campbell opened a tavern in the house Vobe had left. In 1772

Vobe announced in the *Virginia Gazette* that she has opened a tavern "at the Sign of *The King's Arms*" and advertised for a cook. She operated the King's Arms during the Revolution, hosting several Continental officers, including General Thomas Nelson Jr. and Baron von Steuben in the weeks before the siege of Yorktown.

After the Virginia government moved to Richmond and after the Revolution, business declined at Vobe's tavern. In 1785 she announced her intention to move to Chesterfield County, where she opened another tavern.

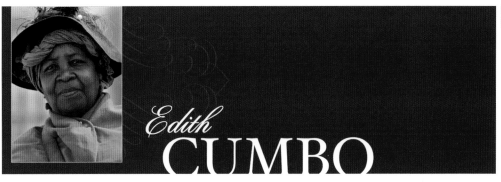

Edith CUMBO

One of only a handful of free women of color living within the city limits was Edith Cumbo (ca. 1757–?). The daughter of Richard and Fortune Cumbo, she was likely born in Charles City County, Virginia, several miles from Williamsburg. Fortune Cumbo was a free woman when Edith was born, and eighteenth-century Virginia law provided that a child born in the colony inherited the free or enslaved status of the mother.

From Charles City, Edith Cumbo moved to Halifax County, perhaps because one of her brothers was there. Her son was probably born there. In August 1769, the churchwardens of Antrim Parish in Halifax presented her to the county court for having a child out of wedlock. The judges found her not guilty.

By the late 1770s, Cumbo was a resident of Williamsburg. Her mother, father, and four of her brothers were also living in the area. As a free black woman in the slave society of eighteenth-century Virginia, Cumbo had to be resourceful. Although there is no evidence of her occupation, she likely earned a living as a domestic servant, laundress, or seamstress. In 1778 she took steps to protect her property and household by suing Adam White for trespass, assault, and battery.

Cumbo may have attended Bruton Parish Church. She probably read from the Bible and the Book of Common Prayer, and she might have been familiar with black Baptist preachers such as Moses and Gowan Pamphlet.

THE REVOLUTIONARY COMMUNITY

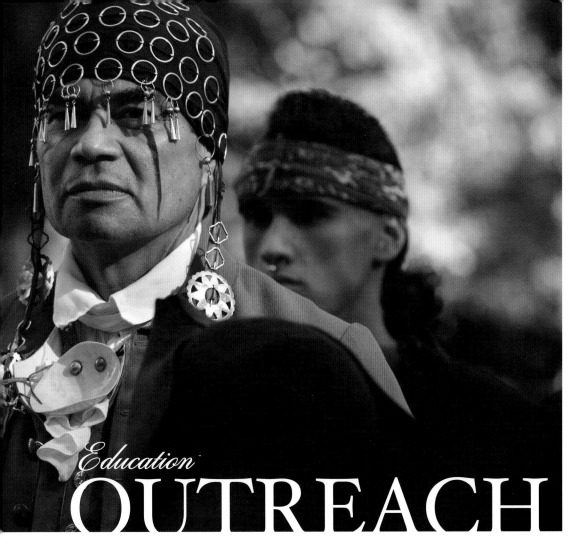

Education
OUTREACH

T he Colonial Williamsburg Foundation actively supports history and citizenship education through a wide variety of multilevel programs that reach beyond the geographical limits of the Historic Area to engage students, teachers, and lifelong learners throughout the world.

THE IDEA OF AMERICA

The Idea of America is an innovative way to learn about all of American history, from our origins to the present, and to understand the meaning of American citizenship. The program examines history through the lens of shared American values that exist in tension with each other: freedom and equality, unity and diversity,

common wealth and private wealth, law and ethics. Sixty-five case studies explore how each generation of citizens throughout the nation's history has engaged in an enduring debate about these values and thus shaped the Republic.

Unlike a traditional textbook, the Idea of America is a fully digital program. It features video interviews with historians, eyewitness testimonies, historical audio and video footage, primary source documents and images, audio support for the narratives, and interactive games, projects, and activities.

A companion website, the Virtual Republic, provides students with the opportunity to discuss and debate current events in the context of historical events.

To learn more about the Idea of America, visit history.org/idea.

HERO—History Education Resources Online

HERO is a searchable, expanding multimedia history library and electronic learning environment featuring a wide range of educational content for teachers and students. Materials such as dramatic video segments, student activities and games, classroom lesson plans, and teacher guides are available on demand.

To learn more about how to be a history hero in the classroom, visit history.org/HERO.

Electronic Field Trips

Colonial Williamsburg's electronic field trips convey the story of our nation to students and educators across the country. These live, one-hour, award-winning programs are available on broadcast television channels or via online streaming. The programs feature documentary and dramatic video in combination with live discussions with historians, experts, and characters from the past and interactive opportunities for viewers.

To learn more about electronic field trips, visit history.org/trips.

Teacher Professional Development

Colonial Williamsburg's teacher professional development workshops expand teachers' knowledge of our nation's founding principles and help teachers use those principles to develop the citizenship skills of their students. The programs infuse educational technology with historical content, use a broad range of materials from primary sources to multimedia, model differentiated instructional strategies, and provide lesson plans that promote literacy and historical analysis skills and explore American history from multiple perspectives.

Colonial Williamsburg offers programs in Williamsburg and other historical sites as well as in teachers' home districts that immerse teachers in American history. Distance learning options include webinars, tutorials, and online courses, all designed to help teachers bring history to life in the classroom.

To learn more about teacher professional development, visit history.org/history /teaching/teacherdevelopment.

COLONIALWILLIAMSBURG.ORG

Colonial Williamsburg's educational website provides a wealth of information about American history and citizenship, the American Revolution, and life in colonial and Revolutionary

Virginia. The site offers resources for teachers, students, and researchers; information on Colonial Williamsburg's collections; and games and activities for kids.

To learn more, go to colonialwilliamsburg.org. For information on visiting the Revolutionary City, go to colonialwilliamsburg.com.

SCHOOL AND GROUP TOURS

The Revolutionary City offers a variety of ways for groups of all sizes, interests, and ages—from kindergarteners to senior citizens, from scouts to families—to learn about American history and citizenship.

For more information on tours for school and youth, adult, or homeschool groups, go to history.org/history/teaching/grouptours.

JOHN D. ROCKEFELLER, JR. LIBRARY

Through its specialized collections of books, manuscripts, images, and databases, together with its fellowship program, the library supports and encourages research in the political and economic life of the thirteen colonies and the new Republic, African American studies, the decorative arts and material culture, archaeology, architectural history, and historical preservation.

George WYTHE

George Wythe (ca. 1726–1806) was born on a modest plantation near Hampton, Virginia. Wythe's family was not wealthy, so he received no formal education. What he learned from his mother, whose Quaker grandfather wrote one of the first antislavery tracts in American history, was enough to provide him a solid foundation in Greek and Latin. In the 1740s, he began to study law under his uncle. When he was twenty, he became a lawyer and married Ann Lewis, who died a year later. Wythe then plunged into learning about the philosophy of law and its place in society. By the time he married again, about 1754, he was well on his way to becoming one of America's greatest legal and classical scholars (Wythe was known during legal arguments to quote passages from Homer's *Iliad* and other classical works). His second wife, Elizabeth Taliaferro, was the daughter of a wealthy architect and planter who built them a home in Williamsburg, where they lived for the next thirty years.

During the 1760s, as the constitutional dispute with Great Britain heated up, Wythe took on the role that would define him: that of a teacher. His students included Thomas Jefferson (who called him "my second father"), John Marshall, and Henry Clay—three of the most influential men in American history.

Wythe employed his Enlightenment framework—influenced primarily by Francis Bacon, Isaac Newton, and John Locke—in arguing for independence as a delegate to the Second Continental Congress in 1776 and as a signer of the Declaration. Wythe championed Enlightenment philosophy also by his method of teaching. He questioned his students on points of history, biography, and grammar, and he encouraged their own methods of induction. He demanded that his students put their thoughts to use, either to gain greater insight or to arrive at new ideas.

By examining the natural laws that governed the world, Wythe and his students recognized human rights that could neither be granted nor taken away by any government, such as a king or a parliament, which were artificial institutions created by men for their own ends. Such beliefs demanded that patriots break with their British past. Wythe and his followers had an almost intoxicating idealism; they believed in the perhaps endless capacity of men, properly educated, to continue to improve their world. Wythe and Jefferson attempted to apply those principles in what was their most ambitious joint project: revising all of Virginia's laws in 1779. In 126 separate pieces of legislation, they tried to reshape the core of Virginia's society by introducing proposals to ensure religious freedom, establish

public education, make property ownership more equitable, abolish slavery, and establish fairness in criminal justice. Many, if not most, of their laws would not be enacted for decades, or even generations, but they made an important start.

Wythe was appointed the professor of law at the College of William and Mary in 1779 and remained there until 1791. He was also appointed a senior judge of one of Virginia's highest courts. His wife died in 1787, after which he freed several of his slaves and then left Williamsburg for Richmond. He stayed on the bench, and continued teaching, until his death, which may have been a murder at the hands of a relative, in 1806. He is buried at St. John's Church in Richmond.

Although admission tickets purchased by guests provide one major source of funds needed to support Colonial Williamsburg's educational and museum programs, the Foundation needs and encourages gifts and bequests from all who believe in our mission "that the future may learn from the past." Friends interested in discussing gifts to Colonial Williamsburg are encouraged to write to the Director of Development, The Colonial Williamsburg Foundation, PO Box 1776, Williamsburg, VA 23187-1776 or to send an e-mail to gifts@cwf.org. Additional information may be found online at donate.history.org.

The Colonial Williamsburg Foundation Board of Trustees expresses its deepest thanks to *all* our donors. Since 1926, Colonial Williamsburg's honor roll of donors has grown from its original benefactors to more than 113,000 a year. Listed are Colonial Williamsburg's most generous benefactors: individuals, foundations, and corporations that have made gifts and grants of $1 million or more.

COLONIAL WILLIAMSBURG'S FOUNDERS

John D. Rockefeller Jr. and Abby Aldrich Rockefeller

GIFTS AND GRANTS OF $20 MILLION OR MORE

Lila and DeWitt Wallace

DeWitt Wallace Endowment Fund

The Annenberg Foundation

June S. and Joseph H. Hennage

William R. and Gretchen B. Kimball

City of Williamsburg

Abby and George O'Neill

GIFTS AND GRANTS OF $10 MILLION OR MORE

Ann Lee S. and Charles L. Brown

Ruth P. and Joseph R. Lasser

Forrest E. Mars Jr.

GIFTS AND GRANTS OF $5 MILLION OR MORE

Martha Baird Rockefeller

John D. Rockefeller 3rd Fund

The Winthrop Rockefeller Charitable Trust

Henry H. and "Jimmy" deH. Weldon

Royce R. and Kathryn McCormick Baker

Bob and Marion Wilson

David and Peggy Rockefeller

Joan Jarrett and Robert J. Woods

The Grainger Foundation

National Endowment for the Humanities

Barbara W. and Amos B. Hostetter Jr.

GIFTS AND GRANTS OF $1 MILLION OR MORE

Blanchette and John D. Rockefeller 3rd

Elizabeth and Miodrag Blagojevich

Rockefeller Brothers Fund

The Kresge Foundation

The Pew Charitable Trusts

Dr. Lowry Kirby

Frances M. McDermott

Institute of Museum and Library Services

Mary Lou and George B. Beitzel

Jane and Marshall Steel Jr.

The Marshall Steel, Sr. Foundation

Ambassador Bill and Jean Lane

Pauline and Samuel M. Clarke

Louise Coon

Inez R. and C.O. Middlekauf

Letitia and Edward C. Joullian III

Mrs. T. Richard Crocker

Ambassador Randall L. and Marianne W. Tobias

Gladys M. Whitehead

Estelle and Harold Tanner

Pat and Jerry B. Epstein

Frances B. Crandol

Virginia S. and Robert L. deCourcy

Marcia and John R. Donnell Jr.

John A. Hyman and Betty C. Leviner

Marilyn L. Brown and Douglas N. Morton

Carolyn W. and James R. Millar

Shirley H. and Richard D. Roberts

Joshua P. and Elizabeth D. Darden

Leslie Anne Miller and Richard B. Worley

AT&T Foundation

IBM Corporation

Maureen M. and James W. Gorman Sr.

Virginialee and Edward Lynch

Image Credits

28–29 Detail of *Washington and His Generals at Yorktown*, attributed to James Peale, 1782–1791, Museum Purchase, 1958-1. **29** *Portrait of William, Duke of Gloucester*, attributed to Edmund Lilly, 1696–1700, Museum Purchase, Mr. and Mrs. Thomas W. Wood and Mr. and Mrs. William H. Murdoch, 1974-133. **30** Detail of Bodleian Plate, attributed to artist William Byrd II and engraver John Carwitham or Eleazar Albin, ca. 1740, gift of the Bodleian Library, 1938-196. **31** Detail of *A Map of the Most Inhabited Part of Virginia . . .* , cartographers Joshua Fry and Peter Jefferson, engraver Thomas Jefferys, 1768, first published 1753, Museum Purchase, 1968-11. **32 top** Tarpley, Thompson & Company Broadside, 1760–1763, Museum Purchase, the Friends of Colonial Williamsburg Collections Fund, 2007-113. **32 bottom** Detail of *Tobacum Latifolium* from *Hortus Eystettensis*, ca. 1640, engraver Basil Besler, Museum Purchase, 1956-121. **33** Teapot, Staffordshire, England, 1766–1770, Museum Purchase, 1953-417. **35** *Portrait of Patrick Henry*, Thomas Sully, 1815, Museum Purchase, 1958-3. **37** Plate, Jingdezhen, China, ca. 1755, excavated from the site of the Governor's Palace, 20AA-01082. **40** *The Alternative of Williams-burg*, attributed to Philip Dawe, 1775, Museum Purchase, 1960-131. **41** *The Three Cherokees, Come Over from the Head of the River Savanna to London, 1762*, publisher George Bickham, ca. 1765, Museum Purchase, 1958-484. **42** *Portrait of Thomas Jefferson*, Gilbert Stuart, 1805, Museum Purchase, John D. Rockefeller Jr., 1945-22. **43** *Enslaved Girl*, Mary Anna Randolph Custis (later Mrs. Robert E. Lee), 1830, Museum Purchase, 2007-34,1. **44** Tobacco Note (1,000 lbs), Virginia, 1780, gift of the Lasser family, 1994-210,926. **45** *Miniature Portrait of Charles, first Marquis Cornwallis*, attributed to John Smart, probably 1792–1795, Museum Purchase, 2006-83. **46** *Miniature Portrait of St. George Tucker*, Pierre Henri, probably 1799, Museum Purchase, the Friends of Colonial Williamsburg Collections Fund, 2007-45,1. **47 left** *Portrait of George Washington*, Gilbert Stuart, 1795–1796, bequest of Mrs. Edward S. Harkness, 1950-337. **47 right** *Washington and Lafayette at the Battle of Yorktown*, Reuben Law Reed, probably 1860–1880, gift of Abby Aldrich Rockefeller, 1931.101.1. **48** *The Surrender of Cornwallis at Yorktown*, ca. 1781, Museum Purchase, 1960-879. **49 bottom** Frenchman's Map, 1782, courtesy of Earl Gregg Swem Library, the College of William and Mary, Williamsburg, Virginia. **50 top** Detail of Bodleian Plate, attributed to artist William Byrd II and engraver John Carwitham or Eleazar Albin, ca. 1740, gift of the Bodleian Library, 1938-196. **59 left** and **63 left** Virtual models created in conjunction with the University of Virginia's Institute for Advanced Technologies in the Humanities (IATH) with funding from the Institute of Museum and Library Services (IMLS), the National Endowment for the Humanities (NEH), and the Andrew W. Mellon Foundation. **63 right** Apollo Room of the Raleigh Tavern, possibly Benson Lossing, ca. 1835, Special Collections, John D. Rockefeller, Jr. Library. **69 right** Marketplace drawing, Erik Goldstein, 2014. **76 right** Plan for the Governor's Palace, Thomas Jefferson, 1779, Collections of the Massachusetts Historical Society. **194–195 top, 196, 197 left** Courtesy of Preservation Virginia (Historic Jamestowne).

INDEX

Boldface page numbers indicate illustrations.

| G |

Y

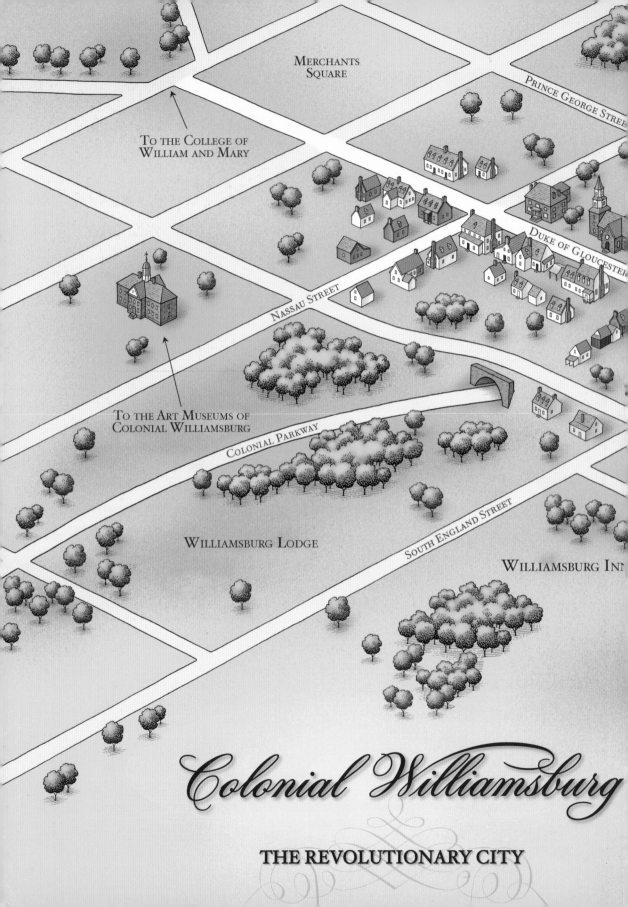

MERCHANTS SQUARE

PRINCE GEORGE STREET

TO THE COLLEGE OF
WILLIAM AND MARY

DUKE OF GLOUCESTER

NASSAU STREET

TO THE ART MUSEUMS OF
COLONIAL WILLIAMSBURG

COLONIAL PARKWAY

WILLIAMSBURG LODGE

SOUTH ENGLAND STREET

WILLIAMSBURG INN

Colonial Williamsburg

THE REVOLUTIONARY CITY